MORNING BY MORNING

Morning

By

Morning

How We Home-Schooled Our

African-American Sons to the Ivy League

PAULA PENN-NABRIT

VILLARD (V) NEW YORK

VILLARD BOOKS and "V" CIRCLED Design are registered
trademarks of Random House, Inc.

Library of Congress Cataloging-in-Publication Data

Penn-Nabrit, Paula.
Morning by morning : how we home-schooled our African-American sons
to the Ivy League / Paula Penn-Nabrit.
p.   cm.
ISBN 0-375-50774-4
1. Home schooling—United States. 2. African American boys—Education.
3. Academic achievement. I. Title.

LC40 .P45 2003
371.04'2—dc21   2002033051

Villard Books website address: www.villard.com

Printed in the United States of America on acid-free paper

24689753

First Edition

Book design by Jo Anne Metsch

To C. Madison, who was there every morning too.
Thank you for being such a great father to our sons.
Peace.

Now faith is the substance of
things hoped for, the evidence
of things not seen.

HEBREWS 11:1

ACKNOWLEDGMENTS

I WANT TO thank my dear friend Lisa Wager for introducing me to Brian DeFiore. I want to thank Brian for being such a good agent and walking me through the complex world of literary publication and especially for introducing me to Melody Guy at Random House. I want to thank Melody for being such a good editor and patiently guiding me through the sometimes frustrating process of actually writing a book. I also want to thank my best friend, Dr. Linda James Myers, for always taking the time to gently say, "Now, let's think about that . . ."; my brother David for his smiles of encouragement; and my mother-in-law, Mrs. Vernice Nabrit, for keeping me supplied with extra reading materials when I needed a break. I especially want to thank my parents, Mr. and Mrs. W. L. Penn, for teaching me my first and most important life lesson: that I can do all things through Christ. And I have to thank my mother, and my sisters, Cheryl, Courtney, and Sonjia, for reading and commenting on this book in its various stages of development and for being excited for me and with me. A great big thank-you goes to C. Madison for listening to me read and reread these chapters aloud and, most of all, for his relentless support and encouragement. And finally I have to thank Charles, Damon, and Evan for trusting their dad and me enough to go through the process of home schooling with us. It was hard, but I'm so thankful for the opportunity of this shared experience. You guys are the best!
    Peace.

CONTENTS

INTRODUCTION

THIS IS A story about several things. First and foremost, it is a story about our home-schooling experience. Home schooling reminds me of that old commercial for the Navy, "It's not just a job—it's an adventure!" When I think of adventure, I think . . . exciting, unusual, bold, and maybe risky—something with an unpredictable outcome. Home schooling was all of that and more. But it's also about the difficult nature of change and transition. As products of African-American, middle-class, college-educated families (arguably some of the most conservative of all Americans), our family's decision to forsake access to and the integration of traditional schooling was a significant change, and it was not well-received by many of our family, friends, and associates. Middle-class black people, like most middle-class people regardless of race or ethnicity, are most comfortable following the rules. Typically, it takes the very poor or the disenfranchised—those who know the rules won't help—or the very rich—for whom the rules really don't apply—to buck the system. Our society says independent private schools or upper-middle-class suburban public schools are "the best," so that's what middle-class African-American parents have sought for our children. Home schooling has not been viewed as an option for middle-class black people. So, this is also a story about exercising different options. Finally, this is a story about faith. Before we began home schooling it was rather easy for me to say, "We walk by faith, not by sight," but it was hard for me to learn actually to take that first step without a definite outcome in sight. We began our home-schooling adventure in the midst of enormous change by stepping out into darkness: without a guide, without a map; stepping out with nothing but faith.

IN 1991, my husband, Charles (known hereafter as C. Madison), and I started home-schooling our sons. When we began, Evan was a fourth-grader, and our twins, Charles and Damon, were big-time sixth-graders. No one else thought this was a viable idea at the time. There was real concern about the boys' future ability to get into college. While home schooling wasn't new then, it certainly wasn't common in the black community. A lot of people thought it was risky, and some people just told us it was "mighty white." During our home-schooling experience, we tried a lot of new things, we had some failures, and we learned a great deal. The ideas were somewhat radical, and initially I was uncomfortable sharing those ideas with others. As we were still in process, I couldn't really substantiate the results, and so I didn't feel I could make any definitive observations.

But all that changed in August 2000, the official end of our home-schooling experience. Charles and Damon were students at Princeton University, and Evan was entering his first year at Amherst College. The 2001 *U.S. News & World Report* again ranked Princeton the number one university in the nation and Amherst the number one college. What's remarkable is that our home-schooling "experiment" was successful enough to launch three African-American males into the most competitive post-secondary institutions in the country. We had three "students" and all have sailed over the hurdle of college admissions with flying colors. I know of no school—public, private, or parochial—that can point to a higher success rate. The Nabrit household has sent 100 percent of our graduates to the designated top schools in the country! Since college admissions statistics are the basis by which secondary educational institutions are most often measured, I guess we did a pretty good job. I know we did a good job in terms of the kind of people Charles, Damon, and Evan have become. Based on that, I have a few things to say about families and education in America. And I have a lot to say about how the experience of choosing to stop being a pawn of the system, and of taking control of our sons' education, changed five lives for the better.

In each chapter, I have tried try to reflect anecdotally and objectively on both sides of the issue of our home-schooling experience. (Of course, total objectivity is impossible, primarily because there are so many issues under review.) On the one hand, we were successful in terms of the narrow perspective of college admissions. On the other hand, the equally limiting perspective of the adjustment to college has been less successful. Ultimately, our principal objective was to help our sons mature into holistically healthy adults—African-American men capable of functioning in and contributing to society with a high level of conscious awareness. That's a big objective, and while we're confident of our success, those are profoundly difficult areas to quantify. In any event, our being right doesn't make everyone else wrong. Many of the criticisms leveled at us challenged us to examine our educational experiment continually and critically. But back to the narrow perspective of college admissions: In that context, you can't argue with success.

PART I

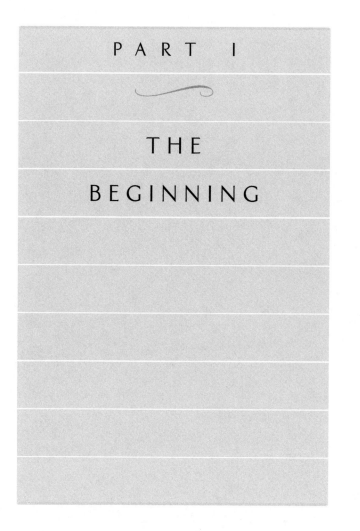

THE

BEGINNING

"OH, JESUS! . . .

WHAT HAPPENED?"

I WISH I could say we began home schooling because we knew it was the best thing for our sons. I wish I could say we took our time, examined our options, and came to the calm and rational decision that home schooling was the preferred educational experience for them. Regrettably, I honestly cannot say those things. We did not begin home schooling because we thought it was the best thing for our sons. We did not take our time and examine our options. We did not reach the calm and rational decision that home schooling was the preferred educational experience for them. Most embarrassing of all, our entry into home schooling was brought about by external factors—something happened, something terrible and traumatic. As much as we work at being free and conscious people of color, independent actors rather than reactors, the truth is we began home schooling as a reaction to something some white people did to us.

When we moved from Jacksonville, Florida, to the Columbus, Ohio, area in 1989, we enrolled our sons in the local country day school for boys. I was elated! It was the school affiliated with the all-girl country day school I had attended as a young girl. The grounds were expansive, with stately brick buildings atop gently rolling hills that gave way to several perfectly framed playing fields. It offered academic programming from pre-K through twelfth grade in three manageable divisions—Lower School, Middle School, and Upper School—with imaginative after-school programs as well. I expelled a huge sigh of relief when we enrolled the boys; I thought there would be no further educational choices to deal with until they were ready to apply to college! As I followed the impressive line of expensive SUVs, vans, and luxury sedans up the long and winding drive, the idyllic scene created an atmosphere of renewed optimism for me every morning. I comforted myself with the belief that an environment so aesthetically appealing had to be good for our sons. And surely, no institution attentive to the soil requirements of each tree, shrub, and rhododendron could be insensitive to the needs of a child— any child. Plus, the school was horrendously expensive, at least by Columbus, Ohio, standards, and like many middle-class parents, we thought anything that costly had to be good. Overall, C. Madison and I felt comfortable with the school, and felt certain our family would be a welcomed and contributing addition to the community. After our combined twelve years in prep school, Wellesley and Dartmouth, everything about the place was familiar: the facilities, the administration, the faculty, the students, and their parents. We recognized this population: There were moderate Democrats and compassionate conservatives, and, of course, a lot of Anglophiles; it was a gentle combination of Protestant Gentiles (mostly Episcopalian and Presbyterian), a few Catholics, a smattering of Reform Jews, and a tiny representation of Buddhist, Islamic, and Hindu families. Many students were the children or nephews of kids with whom my sisters and I had gone to prep school. It was the kind of school where mothers wore jumpers and coordinated turtlenecks with little designs on them, and a mom or a dad could show up for a parent/teacher conference in a cotton crewneck sweater, cords, and boat shoes with no socks, without an eyebrow being raised. There was a definite L.L. Bean look to the place.

It felt like a very "white" place to us; and, in that sense, it didn't feel negatively alien or strange, just different yet familiar. We had absolutely no doubt about the wisdom of enrolling our boys there. We knew it wasn't perfect. We didn't expect it to be perfect. We were making a conscious trade-off: cultural relevance in exchange for academic competitiveness.

During our brief, two-year tenure there, the boys did well. They were well liked, well behaved, and well adjusted. We got along with most of the faculty and the other parents. I sincerely enjoyed my engagements with the other "Mommys"; and although we had different variations on it, our theme issues were the same. We each wanted the best for our sons. We had lots of informal get-togethers and play dates, and the boys' friends and classmates were always welcome at our home.

At the boys' school, I was "Head Homeroom Mother," served on countless and hideously time-consuming committees (book fairs, antiques shows, and patron parties), and was an assistant den mother of Evan's Cub Scout den.

School turned out to be a part-time job for me. Because there were so few black children, and no black faculty or administrators, we felt we needed to be visible for our sons' benefit and for the benefit of the rest of the academic community.

When I was in prep school, I was the only black student in my class. There were no black teachers or administrative staff. The only black adults were the folks on the kitchen and janitorial staff; they were wonderfully supportive and never missed an opportunity to tell me how proud they were of me and how confident they were of my success. But even with the support of my parents at home and the black workers at school, I definitely felt the sense of isolation of being different and somewhat set apart. Often, such physical isolation leads to psychological isolation, alienation, and fragmentation. The absence of black adults and the accompanying isolation of African-American children in predominantly white schools can be unhealthy. Creating the impression that academically talented black children are an anomaly is unhealthy for everybody because it supports the myth of the exceptional Negro. This is the person who looks black, but isn't really like "them." The myth contributes to self-loathing and a desire to disassociate from other black people.

Initially, we were well aware of the challenges facing black kids in white schools, but we were convinced we could make the situation at prep school work for our children. Overall, the private school experience was good. The facilities were excellent, the faculty was good, and the environment seemed adequate. What was our chief complaint? We wanted the school to live up to its commitment to diversity within the community.

The school said it was unable to find any African-American adults, much less male adults, who were qualified to teach at such an outstanding educational institution. The school asked for the help and assistance of the black parents in finding and recruiting such rare and elusive individuals. While I didn't say it, I felt the school was making the issue of black faculty solely the responsibility of the black parents, and I felt this was inappropriate. But I tried to be cooperative. The school had a diversity committee that met in the evenings, ostensibly so parents could attend and participate. The group met for months to discuss the issue facing us, namely, how to find black faculty without lowering the standards of the school. After all, none of us wanted that, did we? What would be the point of our sons' attendance if the school's reputation was tarnished? The unstated and racist assumption here was that it would take some kind of Herculean effort to find any black people, much less black men, who could match the qualifications of the current faculty and administration. In fact, while the faculty and administration were certainly appropriately educated for secondary school employment, there was hardly an abundance of spectacular credentials, e.g., Oxford or Ivy League–level PhDs. Primarily, this was an institution run by state and land grant college graduates. It was hard for me to believe that it was really that difficult to find black people at the same schools. I tried to find nice, nonthreatening ways to say this, ways that were not so provocative that people couldn't hear me. I really tried to be a team player.

At about the same time the diversity committee was meeting, the school decided to become coeducational and hired an older, wealthy, white woman as the diversity coordinator. She was extremely well educated and seemed quite sincere in her commitment to coeducation and diversity. During our evening meetings, several black parents expressed concerns about coeducation and its potential impact on our sons; specifically, C. Madison and I felt that adding girls to the mix was a complication the school was not prepared to handle. The concerns the black parents had about our sons were not adequately addressed in a single-sex environment. Many of us were convinced that adding girls, most of whom would be the sisters of the majority population, would further diminish the school's attention to the issues of race and multiculturalism. We were also concerned about the whole issue of sexual tension in a newly coeducational environment where unexamined and unresolved issues of racism were present. I was having a very difficult time expressing these concerns in a way that could be heard.

Thinking the intersecting issues of race and gender were too complicated to grasp in an evening after dinner, I scheduled a daytime appointment with the diversity coordinator. I expressed my commitment to gender equity, because as Sojourner Truth allegedly asked once, "Ain't I a woman?" But I tried to explain that I was as concerned about how the school saw the balance between issues of race and gender. The diversity coordinator listened attentively and then explained that the issues of gender were more important because people can, with enough money, escape the challenge of racial diversity, thereby making it an elective, while the issue of gender is inescapable, thereby making it mandatory. While I thought the analysis was grossly oversimplified and I vehemently disagreed with it, I felt enlightened by our conversation. As a black woman with black sons, I knew the school would place the needs of white girls ahead of those of black boys. The diversity coordinator knew that too; it's just that that wasn't really a problem for her.

We talked to each other, and that was good—it was progress, it was a beginning—but it was insufficient. We were, as they say, "close, but no dog biscuit." I was beginning to see the school's limitations in dealing with the issue. I was beginning to see that what we wanted—change—was at cross-purposes with what the school wanted—modification. The school year ended where it had begun, with lots of dialogue but no black faculty.

In conversations with other black parents over the summer, I thought we should begin the new academic year with a more focused and collective approach. Previously, we each had addressed our concerns individually, even though many of those concerns were collective. We knew they were connected and collective issues because we were all pretty much dealing with the same themes, just with different variations. We discussed these themes with each other to get ideas on strategies and approaches, and sometimes to just vent. This was, as they say, all good, except that the school didn't have a framework for addressing these issues. I thought the school didn't have a framework because it didn't understand that these were, in fact, connected and collective issues within the institution. Because we, as black parents, had consistently addressed our concerns about our sons individually, the school saw the concerns as individual, isolated "incidents," not institutionalized issues worthy of its collective attention. I thought our individual approaches possibly had made it more difficult for the school to see the breadth of the issues. I thought we would all be better served if we could identify and articulate which of our individual issues and concerns were actually collective concerns within the institution. I thought we needed a gathering, and a picnic seemed perfect.

So I decided to organize an unofficial back-to-school picnic for the school's black families. I went through the school directory and created a listing of all the black families, and sent each one a postcard invitation. It was a basic, run-of-the-mill, prep-school-type postcard invitation: heavy, white card stock; hunter green borders with navy blue print (handwritten, of course). It was neither militant nor threatening; there were no kente cloth insignias and no red, black, and green maps of "Afrika." A new school year had begun; it was late September, the weather was still great, and the picnic was a chance for some black families to connect. We didn't live in the same neighborhoods and we didn't belong to the same private clubs, but we did share a common desire to provide the best possible education for our sons with the least amount of psychological damage.

At the picnic, I passed out copies of the invitation list with addresses and phone numbers. We talked about the importance of increasing our visibility in the school. I encouraged more of the mothers to consider becoming room mothers. We talked about the importance of increased financial support of the school, beyond the astronomical tuition. We talked about encouraging black teachers, administrators, and graduate students interested in teaching to apply to the school. We talked about the impact the older boys could have on the younger ones, and how to increase their interaction. (C. Madison and I had used a couple of the older black guys at the school as baby-sitters for our sons, and it had been great. It created another link at the school for our sons, another connection, another opportunity to learn the traditions and unwritten rules that form the bonds that help make a private school education so special.) While there were only a few boys in each grade, there was no reason they couldn't support one another outside the artificial boundaries of grade. Further, there was no reason why we as parents couldn't network and help create a more supportive environment for all our sons.

We all ate; the boys played; and we talked and discussed our concerns from about two in the afternoon until almost eight that night. By the end of the evening, lots of new connections had been formed and old ones were strengthened. We had a great time; the parents felt energized; and the kids were knocked out. I went to bed feeling like we were well on our way to addressing the issues of race and diversity at school constructively and collectively.

The very next week, I was called into the headmaster's office. He was clutching one of my invitations, and he was furious! He could not believe I had had the "audacity" to host such an event without the school's knowledge or his permission. It had never occurred to me ask permission to host a social gathering. After all, this was a picnic, not a coup. I explained to him that this was a social gathering and no more sinister than the countless cocktail parties he had probably attended over the summer with various families from school. He was unable to see the analogy. Further, he was outraged on behalf of some black parents who had been insulted by their inclusion on the invitation list. I sincerely and actively listened both for information and for understanding. Apparently, the insulted black parents felt this was a return to segregation and the headmaster agreed. I asked him if he had been as outraged at any of the segregated events he had attended at private clubs over the summer. Again, he claimed not to see the analogy, an unbelievable allegation for someone so highly educated. In any event, he felt I owed him and the school an apology. I disagreed.

The meeting ended and I went to pick up the boys in the never-ending carpool line. The headmaster and I had had serious disagreements before, so I was not concerned about this latest incident. I was confident of the health of our family's relationship with him and with the school; but, as it turned out, I was very wrong. The conflict occurred late Monday afternoon; on Friday, I was told the boys were expelled.

The school's official reason was tardy tuition. However, the expulsion occurred in early October, and in accordance with our two-year-old oral agreement, our tuition was paid year-round rather than in the school's standard 60 percent in August/40 percent in January formula. As self-employed parents, with three kids and no financial aid, coming up with twenty thousand dollars a year was an ongoing struggle! We were frequently late with tuition payments and the school had encouraged us to apply for financial aid; but, as a matter of principle, C. Madison felt we should shoulder the financial responsibility of our children's education. Our parents had made enormous financial sacrifices to educate us, and C. Madison felt we could do no less for our own children. Further, he felt that financial aid implicitly limits the ability of the recipient to provide, and the donor to hear or accept, constructive criticism. The school commended us on our commitment and pledged to be as flexible as possible on the dates of the payments.

Anyway, despite our agreement, our kids were expelled midway through the first semester. The timing seemed off. If the expulsion was merely a matter of tuition, why were the boys allowed to return at all?—we certainly hadn't paid the customary 60 percent in August. The bursar called on a Friday to warn me that if we sent them back they (the school) would embarrass them! C. Madison was furious. He returned the call with the promise to the bursar and the headmaster that if we received any more threatening calls, embarrassment would be the least of their concerns. In a panic, I spent the weekend calling people on the board of trustees. I explained, I discussed; hey, I even begged for an extension, an exception. Everyone expressed their concern and their sympathy; but, after all, the headmaster had sole responsibility for the day-to-day operation of the school.

Initially, I think, it was difficult for people to believe the facts as I presented them. No one wanted to believe that three kids would be expelled in the middle of the term for any reason other than their own misconduct. And given some of the outrageous behavior engaged in with impunity by some of our sons' classmates, no one could believe expulsion was an option even for misconduct. Yet, there it was: Charles, Damon, and Evan were being expelled because their tuition payment was late.

Within the next two weeks, the headmaster called and offered to reconsider; but, by then, we had begun to examine the situation on a rational rather than reactionary basis. (And C. Madison was still furious!) If the expulsion was a financial decision, then all we had to do was produce a chunk of money—fast. As we worked frantically to raise the money, we began to explore the entirety of the situation. In doing so, it became obvious to us that more than money was at issue. Ultimately, we borrowed the money and paid the amount in arrears, but we did not send the boys back.

That threatening telephone call just could not be ignored. The disrespect, alienation, and real danger reflected in that telephone call raised critical issues that we had to face. Added to that was the fact that the boys' teachers were forbidden to provide their homework assignments so the boys could keep up during the two weeks we thought it would take us to raise the money. The petty, punitive, and seemingly personal nature of this refusal presented another serious issue for consideration. We already knew that the tardy tuition excuse was disingenuous. Was the expulsion in retaliation for our (parental) failure to commend or condone academic policies contrary to our sons' best interests? Was it in retaliation for our presumptuousness in hosting a picnic without permission? Both questions meant we had more than money to raise. We needed to raise our own level of conscious awareness. This was the most serious issue of all.

What did the expulsion mean to the school, to the community, to our kids, and to us? The expulsion helped us realize that we were viewed as "uppity niggers" (and really, is there anything worse?) who had overstepped; we had forgotten our place; and we had not manifested an appropriate attitude of gratitude. Who were we to criticize anything at that school? One should not go to Disney World and complain about the Mouse—if you don't like Mickey, go somewhere else. Likewise, if issues of class, race, and gender bias are a problem, a hundred-year-old independent day school established for the male offspring of the wealthy, white Anglo-Saxon Protestant members of the community probably isn't the wisest education destination.

We had been allowed to be a peripheral part of the community on the condition that we validate (or at least not publicly criticize) the community. The expulsion, coupled with the threat of embarrassment and the refusal to release homework assignments, illuminated the painful realization that we were not truly members of the community. What kind of community doesn't grant its members the freedom to dissent? This realization was a difficult one for us; but, difficult or not, it was a realization we had to accept. We could not send the boys back to that school, and there was no reason to assume our experience would be better anywhere else—it would just be different. We probably would have had a different view of this if we hadn't explored other educational options earlier, or if we felt that we had made a bad or even an uninformed selection previously. The scary part was that we had not made bad choices. Our kids had never attended what I could honestly describe as bad schools. Equally disconcerting was the fact that we had never made a hasty or uninformed choice. In each instance, we had carefully examined every school before the boys attended the first day there. Yet, in spite of our careful observations and analysis and in spite of the excellent reputations enjoyed by each and every school selected, our expectations were never fully realized. As with all kids, Charles, Damon, and Evan were growing up rapidly, and at times it felt too rapid. Childhood has very definite parameters of time, and we were running out of time. We couldn't justify spending any more time with traditional educational institutions when we couldn't harbor any realistic hopes of a better outcome. It was time to consider something different.

We began to explore our options. Throughout the entire ordeal, several scriptures kept running through my mind. One was "Come out from among them and be ye separate." This was hard to get next to, because C. Madison and I come from families that pride themselves on their integration inroads. Our parents had killed themselves paying top dollar for us to attend white private schools and colleges. C. Madison's uncle, James Nabrit, argued *Brown v. Board of Education* with Thurgood Marshall before the United States Supreme Court, for goodness sake. Where did we get off talking about "come out from among them"? The other scripture that kept bubbling up was "all things work together for good." Where was the good in this hideous turn of events? But as C. Madison and I prayed and talked and prayed and talked, we began to realize this was not the end of the world, and we did have some options.

While C. Madison was not overwhelmed with the idea initially, home schooling was a viable option for several reasons.

1) We knew we wanted our sons to experience a holistic education where their spiritual, intellectual, and physical development would be balanced. We knew we were working hard to supplement their current academic experience to make that holistic development happen. Home schooling would allow us to spend our time creating a healthy environment for our kids rather than helping them adjust to a dysfunctional one.

2) Our educational credentials, objectively, were superior to those of any of our kids' teachers. Some people think this is odd for me to bring up, but I don't care. Our academic credentials are a big deal to me. We weren't "legacies." It was hard to get in and hard to get out of college, but we did it and we did it well. Allegedly, the reason people hate affirmative action is its negative impact on merit, standards, and qualifications. So as merit, standards, and qualifications are so highly regarded, regard ours! Wellesley and Dartmouth are two of the top colleges in the United States, and their degrees carry extra privilege for the recipients. That's the reason my parents worked so hard to send my older brother to Carnegie Mellon and me and my two younger sisters to Wellesley.

My father attended The Ohio State University under the G.I. Bill. But although he was a U.S. citizen, a veteran, and a resident of Ohio, he was not allowed to live on campus—because he was a "Negro." He was an honors graduate, but when he was finally hired by a major U.S. multinational firm in the late 1960s, he spent years watching white employees surge past him. The explanation: They had attended "better" colleges. Consequently, my siblings and I were not allowed even to apply to anything but the "best," preferably Ivy League or Seven Sister, colleges.

During the years that our sons attended private school, they never had a teacher with the academic credentials C. Madison and I had. That's probably why I never got over a sense of amazement when teachers, most of whom were not Ivy League graduates themselves, implied that our ambitions for the boys' acceptance at Ivy League institutions were unrealistic.

3) We didn't have the obstacle of being afraid of, or needing to get used to, dealing with black boys, nor did we have any unconscious racism to confront.

Meanwhile, in the midst of all this adult haggling, we had to find a way to explain the situation to three little boys. And while these were very smart little boys, they were still little boys. C. Madison and I felt extremely guilty for allowing such a situation to occur. In a very real sense, our sons were being penalized because of our actions, and we knew it. And while our actions had been taken on their behalf, knowing that didn't make us feel any better. I wasn't sure I could even talk to them about it without crying, but we knew that this was a discussion that we had to have. We agonized about how to explain the situation without transferring all our anger and fear to them in the process.

In an effort to improve the odds of our success and to make sure we didn't omit anything, C. Madison and I sat down and mapped out a strategy for what we knew was going to be one of the most important conversations we would ever have as a family. Primarily, we wanted to tell them our plan for their education. We knew it would be hard to explain the significance of a holistic education to people so young, but we knew we needed to try. It was important that they at least hear us articulate, right at the beginning, that we were equally concerned about their spiritual, intellectual, and physical development.

There were three very specific things we wanted to avoid. First, we absolutely did not want them to doubt their ability to evaluate people just because this situation had occurred with someone they knew and liked, such as their headmaster. Our second objective was to ensure that the situation didn't lead to a negative reaction to all white people. Finally, we didn't want them to enter this new phase of their lives filled with anger or animosity. (While a lot of people think this is just bald-faced rationalization on my part, I really don't believe that every racially motivated act is a premeditated or conscious one; and, to my mind, this was no exception. Frequently, such conduct is a reaction to an unanticipated event that previously seemed unimaginable.)

We really tried to anticipate their questions and prepare ourselves to listen for the unspoken. We knew we had to be very careful in our explanations. So, after much prayer and discussion, we felt our strongest position lay in the truth, the whole truth, and nothing but the truth. And while we knew they probably wouldn't understand all the implications and issues involved in all these dimensions of truth, we felt we had to present them and then be prepared to answer honestly whatever questions the boys had.

With a plan in place, we were as ready as we were ever going to be, but we were very nervous. Tuesday morning, we called a family meeting. This was their second day out of school, and they were curious to know what was going on; so, in that sense, the timing was almost perfect. Fortunately, we had a history of having family meetings, so we already had a framework in place for such a discussion.

We began with the facts. We told them we had not paid their tuition bill and that the school would not allow them to return until we did. We told them how very sorry we were that we had been unable to earn enough money quickly enough to have avoided this situation. We then told them that we believed that their expulsion was about more than the money. We talked about the picnic and the school's feelings about it. (They were already well acquainted with our concerns about the absence of black faculty and staff, and they knew that was the primary purpose of the picnic.) We told them that we were working hard to get the money we owed the school, because we had promised to pay it and it was important to try to keep promises. We talked about how financial promises had been very difficult for us to keep, but that even when it's hard and takes a long time, you should still try to keep promises. We then explained that even when we got the money, we didn't think it would be a good idea for us to send them back. We told them that as bad as it was to break a financial promise, there were some things that were much worse. We explained that we thought breaking promises about personal commitment and community were much worse and that we felt the school's behavior was that kind of a broken promise. Finally, we told them we thought we could do a better job educating them ourselves. And then we asked if they had any questions. And they had about a zillion!

At first they were excited and they wanted us to reiterate that they definitely were not going back to school. Not knowing what home schooling might mean, they were ecstatic—this seemed like summer vacation all year! Then they wanted to know who they'd play with, and what about recess? Slowly, the questions became more focused. How exactly would they learn new "stuff," and who would be teaching it to them? And what about their friends from school—would they ever see them again? What about their teachers—wouldn't they be worried? They wanted to know if we were mad at everybody at school and if everybody at school was mad at them. Finally, they wanted to know why, if we broke our promise about the money and the school broke its promise about commitment, we weren't "even." They didn't understand why we felt we needed to pay the money before we moved on to the next step in the process. They felt we should take the money and go to Disney World first and *then* start home schooling. We really tried to answer each question as honestly as possible in a way that was age appropriate.

So, on the issue of playing, recess, and hanging out, we told them that of course they'd still have recess, it'd just be with fewer kids. We told them that they would definitely continue learning new things and that we would hire teachers to help us teach them. They wanted to know if they could help pick the teachers and we agreed to let them sit in on all the interviews. We reassured them that they could continue to see their friends from school, it just wouldn't be at school. We also let them know that we had explained the whole situation to their teachers and that they weren't worried. (It was intriguing to us that in the midst of this enormous change, our boys were able to articulate their concern about their teachers. We didn't have the heart to tell them that none of their teachers had called out of concern for them.) We told them that nobody at school was mad at them and that everybody knew that this wasn't their fault, and that they had not done anything wrong. And because we were committed to telling them the truth, we told them that, while we were certainly mad at some people, we were not mad at everybody. Finally, we tried to explain that two wrongs don't make a right. So, while we were disappointed at the school for breaking their promise to our family, their broken promise couldn't make it okay for us to continue to break ours. We had to pay the school the money we had promised to pay; so, no, we would not be going to Disney World.

Understandably, they wanted to have someone to blame for what had happened, so we told them to blame us. We didn't realize it at the time, but this was really the beginning of our home-schooling experience.

More than anything else, this was a philosophical discussion about their past and future education, and the ethical challenges presented in the change. We moved rather quickly from a descriptive and normative discussion, where we examined statements of facts and values, to the beginnings of a metaethical analysis of what values and virtues really are. As we explained, we really were the ones who initiated the severance. We were the ones who had not paid the bill on time; we were the ones who were pushing to change the institution that the headmaster loved; and we were the ones who had not adequately acknowledged his position of authority. But while all that was true, it was also true that the school's response to the culmination of these issues was not an ethically sound one. We talked for a long time about how people can be good people and still make bad decisions and behave in ways that are not ethically sound.

As a final complication, we reminded them of our spiritual belief in predestination. The boys, like all children brought up in apostolic, Pentecostal, holiness families, were already well acquainted with the Bible and basic Christian theology. So when I reminded them of the scripture, "And we know that all things work together for good to them that love God, to them who are the called according to His purpose," they knew it was from the Apostle Paul's epistle to the Romans. More important than knowing its source, they knew what it meant. So we were able to move forward collectively, acknowledging that we didn't really know what to expect, but knowing that this, like everything else in our lives, was happening for a very specific purpose and that we would all be better because of it. This allowed us to move actively beyond anger. Once we realized that this would work to our good, there really wasn't any reason to be mad at the headmaster or at anyone else. We concluded the family meeting by telling them that they could come to us anytime to ask more questions after they had had some time to think about it and discuss it together. We weren't kidding ourselves. We knew once the three of them got together, without us, the real discussion would begin!

2

WHY WE DID IT

BUT BEFORE I get too deep into the beginning of our home-schooling experience, let me try to put the decision into a historical perspective. In the early 1980s, C. Madison and I had "real jobs": We worked for American Transtech, AT&T's stock-transfer company and wholly owned subsidiary, during the divestiture process in Jacksonville, Florida. While I loved being close to the beach, as only a kid raised in landlocked Ohio could, we were less than thrilled with our educational options in Jacksonville. During our years there, the boys attended an experimental farm school; an award-winning public school; and a private, coeducational, country day school. Each school had positive attributes, but none was an ideal fit. Racial incidents at the schools, while not physically violent, certainly compounded our sense of discomfort.

When Charles's kindergarten teacher slapped him on the hand for talking, in spite of our explicit, written instructions against any form of corporal punishment, we went to see her. When she told us she would not apologize—because he was the most obnoxious and arrogant person she had ever met—we went to see the principal. And when the principal told us the boys were too competitive, too physical, and that we would be seeing psychotic behavior patterns by the time they reached puberty, I was stunned. C. Madison dismissed these white women and their comments as purely racist, and explained to them that any recurrence of physical discipline would require him to administer physical discipline to the offending adult. I certainly understood his anger, but I just couldn't accept such a simple and straightforward explanation or response. So, I made an appointment for us to see the leading child psychologist in Jacksonville. As I told C. Madison, the kids certainly seemed fine to me, but if we needed to hide the cutlery, I wanted to find out sooner rather than later.

We met with the doctor and explained our concerns and suspicions. He listened attentively and agreed to observe the boys alone, together, and in each of their classrooms, but I could sense that he thought we were deluded. When we met later to discuss his findings, he began with an apology. He had assumed we were exaggerating. He knew the school, the principal, and the teacher by reputation, and our concerns had sounded highly improbable to him. However, his observations not only confirmed C. Madison's assessment; he also urged us to remove the boys as soon as possible. As a white male psychologist, he was "gravely concerned" about the adverse impact of the children's prolonged exposure to such thinly cloaked racial hostility. It was spring by then, so we decided to let the boys finish the year there. We looked forward to the new school year with great optimism and excitement.

The next year, in a brand-new school, new racial incidents awaited us. An eighth-grader called the boys "niggers" while they were waiting with their class to enter the lunchroom. At the kindergarten "Mommy and Me" picnic, none of the other mothers permitted their children to participate in any of the play sessions that included Evan. As the sand-castle component of the picnic was winding down, I was struggling with what to say to Evan. I didn't know if I should pretend that nothing was amiss: Maybe he hadn't noticed that everybody assigned to the play group with us was crowded and doubled-up in the remaining groups. Evan didn't leave me to ponder this for long, however. As we finished what was undoubtedly the most spectacular sand castle ever created—complete with coquina-shell walkways, no less—Evan put the question to me directly. "Mommy, is nobody playing with us because we're black or because you're difficult, like Daddy says?" That certainly gave me pause. I told Evan that Daddy wasn't right about everything, but that, yes, sometimes Mommy can be difficult. But I also told him that no matter how difficult I was, that was no excuse for the other mommys to be mean, stupid, and cowardly. We had a marvelous teachable moment about how sometimes people behave differently in a group than when they're by themselves (cowardly), and how sometimes people will allow others to tell them what to do (stupid), and how sometimes people just like to try to hurt others (mean). I didn't say it didn't matter, because it did matter, but I did say that the people doing it didn't have the power to keep us from having a good time—unless we let them. Evan and I had a great time *and* we won the prize for the best sand castle! But in spite of all my words of wisdom to Evan about the importance of not giving away one's power, I was still furious. I was angry with the other mothers for participating in such hideous behavior, and I was angry with the kindergarten teacher for pretending that she didn't see what was happening and essentially tolerating such behavior by tacit consent.

Now, in these and other situations, the schools were not the instigators of the conflicts and, in fact, often tried to mitigate the damage. Sometimes there was constructive intervention and sometimes it even happened in a timely manner. It was wonderful when the institutions responded appropriately, but it didn't alleviate our primary difficulty. The primary difficulty for any parent is trying to remain rational when it's your child on the receiving end of such conduct. It can be very difficult to see the teachable moment while looking at the crushed and confused look on the face of your five-year-old. When faced with those kind of difficulties, even the most appropriate and timely institutional responses don't help a great deal. How many times can these sorts of things occur before the damage to the child is severe? How many times before you, as the parent, will really be tempted to hurt someone else, severely? And for me, anyway, the challenge of maintaining decorum was complicated by the inevitable, concluding comments from the institution about how, while the whole situation was regrettable, at least "we all learned something." We could never get educators to understand that our children were not there as educational aids.

As I was not prepared to see these issues as national ones (that would have been too depressing and overwhelming), I dismissed them as regional. I really needed to believe these were regional issues: After all, we were in the South. In spite of my own educational experiences with institutionalized racism, I wasn't prepared to view those same issues relative to my children. And I certainly wasn't prepared to consider the fact that these might be ongoing issues that were not subject to resolution. I needed to believe things would be better when we returned to Columbus.

Before the expulsion, we—like many if not most black parents—talked about racism as a dormant variable. We knew it existed and could flare up at any time, but we also believed we could challenge it into remission, especially when dealing with rich white people.

Conventional wisdom in the African-American community says that rich white people always are easier to deal with than poor ones. *"They already got everything—they can afford to be nice."* The problem with that myth lies in the assumption that anyone, white or black, will ever really feel, *"Hey, that's more than enough (money, privilege, opportunity) for me—let somebody else have some!"* The other problem with the myth is that it fails to account for the enormous differences in communication styles and how different people, particularly of different racial backgrounds, can translate the same event in very different ways.

Case in point: As much as the administrators, teachers, and many parents wanted us to move beyond race, the response to the expulsion was very polarized along lines of race and ethnicity. Throughout the boys' tenure at school, everyone seemed puzzled and somewhat alarmed by our references to race. Each time we asked about the impact of the variable of race on any given fact pattern, we were immediately reassured that, in fact, race was "not an issue here." This declaration was almost always followed by what was surely intended as a supporting statement, but one that ultimately illuminated our position that race is always a variable. It was either "But Evan is so adorable, we all love him, we don't even think of him as black," or "Charles is so well behaved, he's outstanding, one of my best students. I never notice that he's black." Of course, I have no such examples about Damon: Apparently, he wasn't adorable, well behaved, or outstanding enough for anyone to overlook his blackness, so we had to be satisfied with the simple blanket denial of the variable's existence. If, in fact, we were moving to a color-blind society, then the range of responses should not have been polarized along racial lines.

When Charles, Damon, and Evan were expelled, many of the black parents called to express their concern for our family and to let us know we were in their prayers. Almost all the black parents of boys in the Lower School called. This was not particularly surprising, because Charles and Damon had just finished Lower School and Evan was still in Lower School, so most of the black parents knew us, if not personally, then at least by sight. What was surprising was the number of black parents of Middle and Upper School boys who called as well. Charles and Damon had just begun the sixth grade, their second year of Middle School, and they were a full two years away from Upper School, so these were calls from families who barely knew us. These were calls from families whose sons had never been in class with any of our sons; yet, despite this, there was a genuine sense of concern and caring. Ironically, the response to our sons' expulsion illuminated the community that already existed within the African-American members of the school.

In sharp contrast to the outpouring of support from the black families, of the dozens of white families we had gotten to know over the years, including the boys' teachers, other homeroom mothers, and parents of former classmates, playmates, and fellow Boy Scouts, not one of them called. We only heard from two white people from school. One woman—someone I had never been especially close to or even served on a committee with—did not

call; instead, she came to our home to tell me how sorry she felt about the unethical actions of the school. I greatly appreciated her kindness and deeply
admired her courage in expressing it.

I'm not at all certain that I would have had the courage to come to someone's home after such a traumatic event. And, in all fairness, I am certain that
that same trepidation was the reason more white people did not call or come
by. I think people felt very uncomfortable with the whole situation and just
didn't know what to say. This woman simply stopped by with a lovely plant
and expressed her sincere regret for the ways things had been handled. We
didn't gossip, run anybody down, or pretend that the situation wasn't sad.
But when she left, I felt better and made a mental note about how meaningful even a small gesture can be. Her actions also showed me how important
it is to make the effort at least to try to stretch across those uncomfortable di-
vides of racial and ethnic differences. This woman and I didn't have the same
almost-immediate rapport that I had shared with many of the black mothers
who called, and I know she was as aware of that absence as I was. But we both
really tried to connect and we succeeded. We didn't go on to become lifelong
friends—in fact, I don't think we've seen each other since that afternoon—
but when it really mattered, we connected outside the boundaries of race.

The only other white person who called was a teacher in the Upper
School. He had not taught any of our sons, yet he wanted us to know how
sorry he felt about this disruption in their education. Once again, we didn't
compare notes about the rationale or the ethical or racial implications behind the school's actions. We talked about the boys and their academic and
educational future. He just wanted us to know that he cared about Charles,
Damon, and Evan as people and as students, even if they had not been his
students. It was what I expected from an educator; I was just surprised that it
turned out to be an isolated incident.

Regardless of the frequency, or lack thereof, or the motives behind them, I
was very moved by these acts of kindness, and the rareness of their occurrences just heightened my sense of their significance. Part of what was so
unique about them was the fact that in each instance there was no explicit
focus on the racial element of what had occurred. Neither person even commented on the racial dimension of the expulsion, nor was there any effort to
pretend that race had not been a variable. It would have been virtually impossible for anyone to estimate accurately the impact of race on the school's
decision-making process, and it would have been ludicrous to try. By the
same token, it would have been ridiculous and insulting for anyone to pretend that race had not been a factor at all. The two people who called just
happened to be Caucasian, but they made the effort to connect with us on

the basis of our shared humanity. As their comments and our conversations were remarkably similar to those I had had with most of the black parents who called, I think we experienced a brief glimpse of what a race-neutral society might feel like.

Before I went to prep school, my dad bought me a copy of Machiavelli's *The Prince*. He told me I could never be successful around white people without understanding the basic concepts of power as explained in that text. While I often disagree with my dad on a lot of issues, C. Madison and I did find his comments about the relevance of Machiavelli to be insightful, and so we gave copies of the book to Charles, Damon, and Evan when each of them was about nine or ten. Understanding Machiavelli is very helpful in understanding power, intrigue, and revenge, no matter what the race, gender, or ethnicity of the parties involved.

The other black families in our community saw the expulsion of our sons as a classic example of Machiavellian technique; and, of course, the expulsion had the anticipated ripple effect. If this could happen to a well-established black middle-class family like ours, what did that mean for the other black families? The school knew that many of the other black families came to us with their concerns about the school. They came for two reasons: 1) I had gone to prep school; and 2) C. Madison and I had both graduated from the kinds of Ivy League/Seven Sister colleges they wanted for their kids.

As we examined our own situation and tried to prepare ourselves for the new task of home schooling, we tried to quantify the amount of time we spent at the boys' school on a somewhat regular basis, and we tried to calculate how much time we spent at school unofficially explaining, training, educating, correcting, and observing the faculty, administration, and staff about racism in its myriad forms. We based these calculations upon a review of each academic year and the corresponding number of racial incidents. For each incident, we estimated the amount of time we spent to address the incident constructively at school and the amount of time spent explaining the incident and its implications to our sons. Our calculations indicated an average of three incidents per kid, per year. A few examples:

When Evan was in the second grade, there was one other black boy in his class. This child was often in trouble. Every day, Evan would come home visibly distressed about what was going on with this other kid. He kept asking me to go to school and ask the teacher to stop "picking" on this child, and I kept trying to explain to Evan that this other boy's mommy needed to do that.

School really highlighted the fact that our kids didn't see any line of demarcation between Christian theology and real life. Every time I suggested we mind our own business, one of them would remind me we were to be our brother's keeper. And every time I allowed myself to be led to do the right thing, the immediate consequences were unpleasant! This proved to be no exception.

I made an appointment with Evan's teacher to share our concerns. Evan readily acknowledged this other boy was "very bad." That wasn't my concern. What concerned me was Evan's insistence that this boy was no worse than several other boys, but that he always got into more trouble. Evan was convinced it was because this other boy was "really black." (Translation: This was not an assimilated, middle-class, suburban black kid.) This was a very physical, very loud, and very sweet little boy. He had been at our house several times, and I didn't have any trouble with him at all. While Evan was too young to articulate why, he saw that this boy was treated differently and he worried that the same thing could happen to him. This was my concern.

It took almost two hours before the teacher grasped the significance of the issues. At first, she could not understand the basis for my visit. After all, Evan was "adorable," and certainly, while not academically focused at the level we would have liked, he was very well behaved. Why the visit? How did the experience of the other black boy have an impact on Evan's experience at school? I finally asked her if she ever had been the only white person at a group function. She had not. I then asked her if she could imagine such an occurrence. She could. I then asked her how she would feel if another white person joined the group, but was castigated continually for behavior regularly accepted when displayed by the majority members of the group. Finally, she began to understand our concerns: As long as he attended that school, Evan was a part of the community, and we would not allow him to be made to feel uncomfortable, not by actions directed at him or by actions directed at others like him.

When Damon was a fourth-grader, several white boys began teasing him about his color. (Damon and Charles are fraternal twins. Of our three sons, Charles has the least melanin, while Damon has the most. Interestingly, the difference in their coloring has always been a topic of conversation and fascination for many people. I am always intrigued by people for whom color is everything. These are the folks who say things like "I can't believe they're even brothers—they don't look anything alike!" Even more amazing are the folks who have announced, "Oh, I like the light one!") For several days at recess, these schoolboys would surround Damon in a circle and tease him, calling him "blacky" and "dukey." Damon and Charles both told the boys to stop and both complained to the teachers on duty. Moreover, they both asked us to let them handle it. We agreed.

On the fourth day of this open and notorious bullying, Damon beat up three of the boys involved. Promptly, he was sent to the office. Charles and Evan went with him and refused to return to their classrooms. We were called. When we arrived, the school's policy against violence was reviewed with our sons and us. While we certainly understood the policy and agreed with it in principle, we felt its application needed to be consistent. Consistency demanded that the school oppose verbal violence with the same degree of aggression with which it opposed physical violence. We felt the school's lack of consistent compliance with its own policy was the reason the situation had escalated.

Initially, our point seemed lost on the school administrators. When we explained the reality of verbal violence, the school asserted that "teasing" was a natural occurrence with which boys must learn to deal. We responded that fighting also is a natural occurrence, and that it appeared that all the boys had learned a valuable lesson. There was no acknowledgment of the racial overtones of the "teasing." There was no acknowledgment of responsibility for not responding when Damon and Charles initially brought the incident to their attention. There was no acknowledgment of natural, familial bonding.

It took over an hour for us to reach an agreement on the racial implications of this incident and its negative impact on all the boys involved. We also spent a great deal of time discussing the school's concern over what they considered the unusual closeness of our boys. The school felt the boys' closeness inhibited their eagerness to develop friendships with the other boys in their respective classes.

This was one of the initial reasons for separating Charles and Damon when they enrolled. While we went along with the classroom separation, we did not think it was necessary. Charles, Damon, and Evan have always been highly social children who engage and interact eagerly with other children. The fact that they do not exclude one another was not a problem, in our opinion. It was also not a problem to us that they sought one another's company during recess and at lunch: This seemed natural and healthy, even if somewhat uncommon. What appeared to be more common at school was for siblings to bicker and avoid one another whenever possible. We concluded our discussion by explaining that in the black community there is no such thing as siblings who are *too close*.

True to form, we did not reach consensus on this issue. The school's position was not only that Damon was wrong for fighting, but that Charles and Evan were wrong for supporting him on the playground, for accompanying him to the office, and for refusing to leave until we arrived. We acknowledged that Charles and Evan were wrong for being disobedient; and should the school wish to impose reasonable sanctions for their disobedience, we would understand that. However, it was important to us that the school understand that the boys were more than siblings, they were close friends, and so supporting one another seemed to them natural and appropriate.

We further felt it was important for the school to explore why Charles and Evan felt they needed to wait with Damon for our arrival. What messages were they picking up about the school that made them feel they needed to sit and wait? Why did they think they needed to protect Damon? Perhaps if the school had responded initially to the teasing directed at Damon, his brothers would have felt comfortable allowing Damon to sit outside the office alone.

We openly congratulated Damon for attempting to work through the process and for handling the situation himself when the school was unable or unwilling to do so. C. Madison expressly commended Damon for kicking butt, and commended Charles and Evan for watching Damon's back. We explained, again, that Charles, Damon, and Evan were at this school to receive an academic education. They were not there to be assimilated, abused, ignored, or reinvented as white boys.

In another instance, Charles turned in a research paper, and it was returned at the end of the week with the comment "Be careful of plagiarism." Charles, who is nothing if not self-confident, was livid, and asked me to come with him to discuss the comment with his teacher first thing Monday morning. I agreed, on the condition that he begin by asking what the teacher meant rather than assuming the worst. He agreed.

On Monday, the three of us—Charles, his teacher, and I—sat down in the Lower School library, and Charles asked for an explanation. She said his use of vocabulary was not typical of a ten-year-old in the fourth grade. Charles explained that he knew every word he used, that he was nine, not ten, and that he was not "typical"; he further stated that he was certain he was "the smartest boy in the fourth grade, except for my brother."

Charles's teacher demonstrated a commendable willingness to allow him to express himself and to defend his work. Her openness prompted me to ask her privately if she would have assumed plagiarism if Charles had been a white child. She admitted she probably would not have been as surprised at the level of the work if Charles had not been black. While I appreciated her candor, it did not make me feel better about my sons' academic future at the school.

When Evan was a third-grader, he was only slightly more focused than he was as a second-grader . . . not a good thing. His teacher, who was convinced that he simply was not trying, used yelling and intimidation as tactics to get better results. I went to school and explained that we expect Evan to do his best, that we expect Evan to complete assignments on time, and that if those things didn't occur he should be disciplined. What was not expected was for Evan to be subject to any form of verbal abuse. Evan's teacher told me he knew Evan was uncomfortable with his teaching style, probably because Evan had "no male role model at home."

Once I recovered from the shock caused by such an ignorant, racist, and insulting comment, I explained the dangers of race-based assumptions and asked what he thought was listed on Evan's birth certificate under "Father": "We the People"? I fantasized about pausing the conversation just long enough to call C. Madison so Evan's teacher could see an ABM (Angry Black Man) in action, and experience Evan's male role model for himself.

As tempting as that thought was, I knew it would have been irresponsible for me to share something guaranteed to incite C. Madison just for the purpose of teaching this guy a lesson, so I let it go. Not aware that his life had been spared, he went on to explain that Evan did not seem capable of doing the challenging level of work required in a private school. He recommended that Evan visit with the school's psychologist for testing.

Knowing how much Evan did not enjoy his classroom experience with this particular teacher, I felt any break would be appreciated—even a trip to the school psychologist. So Evan, as a wise old third-grader, began his second round of sessions with a professional psychologist. While he certainly never described it as fun, he definitely enjoyed it more than being in class.

In late spring, after months of visits, the psychologist met with C. Madison and me, Evan's teacher, and the headmaster to go over his report about and assessment of Evan. In a nutshell, we were told that Evan was gifted, the pedagogy in place in the classroom had been inadequate, a number of mistakes had been made, and that, consequently, the school year had been a complete wash. Everyone from the school apologized, including the classroom teacher.

Although C. Madison did not share my sentiments, I admired the teacher's willingness to admit that he had erred in both his assessment of and his approach with Evan. (I think any time someone acknowledges a mistake and sincerely apologizes, that act should be recognized.) I think it took a lot for this teacher to admit his mistake in front of us, but C. Madison was not nearly as amenable to taking the high road on this one. He felt that the teacher's and the school's apologies were wholly inadequate in the face of the negative behaviors and assumptions directed at Evan all year. Given the enormously high level of respect C. Madison has always afforded our sons, he was outraged that the apologies were being proffered to us instead of to Evan.

Once more, in defense of the teacher and the headmaster, I doubt that either would have considered apologizing to a third-grader about anything. As with many adults I know, the concept of respect tends to be most clearly defined unilaterally; in other words, there is a nonnegotiable requirement for children to engage adults respectfully, but there is no corresponding duty on the part of adults in their dealings with children.

Ultimately, the teacher did apologize to Evan, and Evan, in the way of a third-grader at the end of a long and difficult school year, really couldn't have cared less. I think the final insult to C. Madison was the fact that in spite of the school's own description of the year as a "complete wash," no refund of our six-thousand-dollar-wasted-year's tuition was offered. C. Madison is still annoyed.

In another episode that same year, Charles and Damon's social studies teacher called us to arrange a conference. She was concerned about the boys' self-esteem. She said they had been lying in class.

At the conference, she explained the context of the lies. The students had been creating family trees, and they were to place items that best reflected their families on each tree. Many of the children were from families made wealthy either through professional and corporate earnings, the more genteel process of inheritance, or a combination of the two (the best of all possible worlds!). In any event, the items placed on such children's trees (large houses, fancy cars, office buildings) were deemed to be an accurate reflection of their families.

Charles and Damon had not actively involved us in this project other than with the usual requests of "How do you spell that?" or "What was Mama Hattie's real name?" They decided what aspects of their family history they wanted to share, and when their teacher saw their tree she called us. She was concerned and confused. Why did they say their great-grandfather, Dr. James Nabrit, was one of the first presidents of American Baptist College? Why did they claim their maternal great-great-grandmother, Mrs. Hattie Edwards, was a student at Bluefield State Teacher's College before migrating to Columbus in the 1890s? Why did they say their great-uncle, Dr. Samuel Nabrit, received a PhD from Brown University in 1932 and went on to serve on the Atomic Energy Commission? Why did they claim their other great-uncle, James Nabrit, had been the dean of the Law School at, and later president of, Howard University? She knew we would appreciate and share her concern.

We looked at the boys' work and, of course, validated everything on the tree. We asked the teacher if she had confirmed the facts on the other boys' work; but, as it turned out, none of the other work seemed "false" to her. She did not however see this as "a race thing."

It *was* a "race thing," and it took another hour or so to clarify that reality for her. I doubt that the issue was truly clarified: It felt to us that she conceded her point rather than spend a moment longer in our presence.

THERE were several other incidents like that, and I would bet that most black families have had similar experiences with a fairly similar rate of occurrence. When we send our children to predominantly white schools, we know we are making a severe time commitment to our kids and to the school. In light of our calculations, it didn't seem that home schooling would be that much more time-consuming, and it certainly couldn't be more stressful!

As we explored our future educational options, we couldn't help but reflect on our past experiences with schools that could only be defined as good, solid, academic institutions. Admittedly, very few other people had any idea of the specifics of the challenges we had encountered. However, almost every black person we talked to had some conscious awareness of the nature, if not the specifics, of those challenges. Because those challenges are part of the shared academic experience of the vast majority of black families in predominantly white schools, it was understandable that people were confused by our refusal to consider other educational institutions as options.

In fact, most parents, regardless of their race, gender, or ethnicity, have probably had some challenges about their child's school diligently and consistently working to meet the unique needs of that child. Again, home schooling is not the answer for every family. C. Madison and I were (and continue to be) self-employed when we began home schooling. That doesn't mean we had more time than other parents might, but we certainly had more control over our time. Plus, ours is a home-based business, so while we have clients all over the place, one of us could be at home when necessary. Timing and control aren't the only, or even the most important, factors in home schooling, but they are important ones.

Many of the most negative comments we received seemed to come from a place of fear and anxiety. Can it be done and done well? Can you really teach your own kid? How can home-schooled kids possibly be admitted to college?

Those questions, and underlying comments and the presumed lack of positive answers, may be why some families are reluctant even to consider home schooling as an option, even when they know their child's needs are not being met. But, in fact, there are answers to those questions, and they're not bad answers. Yes, home schooling can be done and done well. Yes, you can really teach your own kid (but it won't always be fun!). And, absolutely, they can get into colleges and universities, even the most competitive ones.

Putting some of those fears and anxieties to rest should make it easier for families to examine home schooling objectively, as one of several educational options. If your kid is in a great school (and no, I don't mean perfect), and if you feel your kid's needs are being met there, spiritually, intellectually, and physically, then you don't need to consider other options. And if your kid is in a school that's not great, and it's not meeting your kid's needs spiritually, intellectually, or physically, that doesn't mean "Go to home schooling! Do not pass 'Go'! Do not collect $200!" It just means that when you explore your list of options, make sure home schooling is on that list.

PART II

THE
ADJUSTMENT(S)—
MINE,
HIS,
THEIRS,
OURS

3

WHAT IT
WAS LIKE FOR US

THIS WAS ONE of the most persistent and recurring questions: "Is that healthy?" And it was a hard question to answer, partly because I didn't really know whose health was under review or exactly what "that" was being questioned. I decided to presume that the inquiry was about our health—meaning us, the parents. That only left the question of defining "that." Did people mean taking the kids out of school in October and interrupting their education so early in the year? Did they mean home schooling in general? Or was this a question about our spending so much time together as a family? Sometimes I could identify the reference point by when in the conversation the question was asked, but not always.

So basically—and I'm guessing here—I think the focus of the health question was around the whole idea of us spending massive amounts of time together as a family—trapped, as it were—in that whole home-schooling "thing." This isn't to say lots of people can't stomach the idea of an extra hour or so with their own kids—quite the contrary. But loving your kids, carving out an extra hour or two a week to hang out with them, does not translate into a burning, irresistible urge to spend all day, every day, together.

Sometimes that revelation is a jolt to kids. Even adolescents frequently assume their parents have no life and, in fact, no existence outside their familial capacity. Hence, it's not surprising that kids are sometimes stunned to know that their parents share their aversion to the idea of tons of extra family time. But, in fact, lots of parents do find even the idea of extra time with their kids intimidating. That's why parents "get" those back-to-school jokes: Most of us have experienced that predictable surge of pleasure that always comes with the approach of Labor Day. Sure, we start out sharing our kids' enthusiasm about the halcyon days of summer. But by August (oh, please—who am I kidding?—by July) lots of parents are fantasizing about September and its promised confinement and control of the little darlings. So, I think the health question was fundamentally about the impact of our time together. And in a society with public service announcements urging a return to family dinners, I guess we may have seemed somewhat off.

One of the most obvious challenges of home schooling is the closeness. Kids, in their own adorable way, are like parasites, and parents are the host bodies. They can't help it—kids just suck life. Yes, they're a gift from God, they're a blessing and a joy, but they're not a free gift. Domestic tranquility, peace of mind, free time—this is the "cost" of kids. Modern parents mitigate the cost by spending a good portion of each day involved in separate activities, in separate places, effectively separated from their kids. Before we began home schooling, our sons were in school, away from us, for a minimum of seven hours each day, Monday through Friday. That was the same basic schedule for virtually everyone we knew. It seemed normal.

When we began to consider home schooling, we realized a drastic change would be required. We had never spent all day, every day, together for any extended period of time, other than family trips and family vacations. We weren't sure how it would work. Plus, when we began home schooling, our kids were just ending the cute phase of childhood and were standing on the cusp of adolescence. When we began our adventure, Charles, Damon, and Evan were eleven- and nine-year-old little boys. When we finished, they were eighteen-year-old young men, off to college.

Now that home schooling is finished, we can more easily answer the "Is that healthy?" question. Yes, in retrospect, I think it was, overall, a very healthy experience for us as a family. But when we began, in 1991, all I could say definitely was "I hope so!" (I mean, I don't think very many parents set out to institute family policies that are patently unhealthy. It's just that sometimes it's hard to tell or predict the outcome until you're done, and then, of course, it's too late.)

For me, the whole health "thing" was a difficult question to ponder. After all, I was already grappling with the far-reaching, mental health implications of living as the sole female in a household with four males. (And no, the fact that three of them were still children didn't make it easier.) To facilitate this additional layer of mental health analysis, I began with a simpler, introductory question to myself: Can you be healthy in an unhealthy place? Quite frankly, I decided to do a comparative analysis, like the one Ann Landers advocates when people are thinking of divorce ("Am I better off with or without this person in my life?").

Whether or not home schooling was healthier than the school we had just been kicked out of became the first level of my comparative analysis. I then looked at the contrasting environmental factors to figure out if our current situation was healthy, or at least healthy in comparison to what we had just left. The second level of analysis focused squarely on what it was we were trying to achieve. Unsurprisingly, it's a lot harder to create something positive than to critique something that already exists—but that was our goal, the achievement of which would ultimately determine whether or not our situation was healthy.

One of the most monumental internal environmental factors for us was change. We began home schooling in the midst of enormous change. There is always resistance to change. (I know that because, besides being a parent, I'm a consultant!) Enormous change results in enormous resistance, which brings high levels of stress in its wake. To a large extent, those environmental factors of change, resistance, and stress continued throughout our home-schooling experience. Every day, something was in some kind of flux on one level or another, with varying degrees of resistance and stress.

A good deal of the stress came from the fact that, at least initially, we were all comparing our situation to the one we had just left. And, of course, we continued to fall short. We couldn't meet the standard established by a ninety-plus-year-old independent day school. So we had continually to remind ourselves of our unique and pioneering circumstances.

But the good news—the healthy thing—was that all of it was out in the open. The five of us knew what our issues were, individually and collectively. And, most important, while we certainly never agreed on everything and we definitely had our "us" and "them" camps, we each had a deep and profound love and respect for one another individually and collectively. We were each committed to the separate entity that was our family, and even when we were hacked off at each other, never did we see that commitment waver. I think we felt that some days more strongly than others, but I think it was always there in our shared atmosphere. And while I don't know that I realized it then, that was probably the best part of the entire experience.

Even though people asked us repeatedly, "Is that healthy?" it was hard to know just how healthy or unhealthy our situation really was at those particular moments. I mean, we were living in it, experiencing it daily, and sometimes the stress was all we could feel. I always read, in shocked amazement, those stories about home-schooled families where everybody *loves* it. Nobody wants out, nobody wants to go back to school/work/normalcy, no one wants to silence their siblings or their parents or their kids. It's wonderful to read about families where everybody's of "one mind and one accord," where all the members of the family "touch and agree." It just wasn't us.

At first, I thought, "Well, we just aren't there yet." In fact, we never got there. There were days when I wanted to scream at my kids and days when I wanted to threaten them with bodily harm. While I know some home-school mothers who really do seem to be all sweetness and light, I was not one of them. Some days I felt like Roseanne when she used to yell at her kids, "Run to your room, lock your door, and live in fear!"

Fortunately, my outbursts were always balanced by C. Madison's more temperate approach. This is not to say that he didn't have his own (and quite severe) mental health issues going on here, because he did. C. Madison likes things done with a certain degree of order, plus he can get quite worked up (in his own extremely quiet and pensive way) about as-yet-unrealized, future events. So when I obsessed about the kids' intellectual and spiritual growth, C. Madison was there to remind me that "fussing" does not stimulate intellectual or spiritual growth. Similarly, when he obsessed about their (apparently life-threatening) grammatical deficiencies—"What kind of a thinking person places punctuation outside the quotation marks?" (?)—I was there to remind him that while our boys were certainly brighter than most, they were still just middle-schoolers.

As it turned out, we were the perfect foils for each other. C. Madison naturally focused on the practical and I was drawn to the esoteric. We used that conflict as a tool in the creation of our home-schooling environment. For C. Madison's comfort, the kids grew up having to write and rewrite everything, all the time. C. Madison was never as interested in the topic, or even their approach to the topic, as he was in the pragmatic issues of grammar, syntax, punctuation, and clarity. Conversely, all I really cared about was their intellectual grasp of the material: I was free to push them further in their thinking about their work; all my questions and comments were open-ended ("This is exciting—tell me more!" or "What a brilliant observation—expound!"). Knowing that C. Madison would catch any dangling participle, split infinitive, or misplaced gerund was freeing for me.

Evan was the singular exception. For a number of years, he refused to use any punctuation or capitalization whatsoever. When I'd sit down to speak with him about it, he would act as if I was crazy. I finally told him that only the truly insane write without either punctuation or capitalization. I mean really, even "e.e. cummings" used punctuation! Evan's position was that he wouldn't stop his flow of writing to add commas just to please us! (And you thought my fantasy about violence was unwarranted, didn't you?) Ultimately, Evan, like each of his brothers, came to the hideous realization that they could not break our will.

The conflicts were part of our process of growth, and we each, individually, in our own way and in our own time, learned to embrace the conflicts we had. But it was all very frustrating at times.

For C. Madison and me, the frustration came from trying to create an environment of substance rather than form. We knew that we wanted our sons' educational environment to be holistic, but we really had to figure out what that would actually look like.

We wanted to have less "rush" in their lives: no more alarm clocks—I woke them up myself. They hated it at the time, but we all have a big laugh now about my "good morning" song. I'm not sure which 1950s-era show I stole this song from, *Captain Kangaroo* or *Lucy's Toy Shop* (a regional favorite), but I just wanted to change the way they reemerged into consciousness.

We wanted less pressure on academic busywork. We had very few traditional tests, or even timed work, other than practice SATs. Quiet time, for reading and meditation and prayer, was built into our daily schedule. Schoolwork had a decidedly intellectual bent, with broad, global emphasis, lots of essay writing, intense discussion, and an openness to radically different points of view.

Initially, this process was frustrating, especially for people like C. Madison and me, raised in traditional academic institutions where definitive, quantitative, and comparative measurements were provided at six-week intervals. But, in retrospect, I can see now that that was really the easy stuff.

We struggled to create an all-encompassing, holistic educational environment for our sons. The struggle wasn't because we had never considered their educational requirements before. It's not as though we just sent them to the nearest available school without a moment's hesitation or consideration: We had considered it plenty. But now we were at the pivotal moment of actually being in charge. We were the ones charged with making it all happen, and that recognition took our struggle to an entirely different level.

I don't think we could have articulated this at the time, but the future health of our family hinged, not on our ability to convince other people that we were doing the right thing, but rather on our ability to convince our sons. Sometimes figuring out what to do—getting a vision, as it were—is the easy part. The hard part is sharing it in such a way that other people can see it too.

Two Old Testament scriptures come to mind on this point. The first,

Proverbs 29:18, says, "Where there is no vision, the people perish." We knew we needed a vision, a new way of seeing, when it came to the educational development of our sons, and, fortunately, God gave us one. But the other problem was conveying it to the people most directly affected by it, the kids. What good is a vision if it isn't articulated? This led me to review another verse, Habakkuk 2:2, "Write the vision, and make it plain." Okay, then: We had the vision of home schooling, and now all we had to do was "make it plain."

We struggled to communicate our plans, dreams, and goals to our sons. We were a bit surprised to find we had a lot of assumptions about them, and one was that they knew and agreed with those plans, dreams, and goals.

C. Madison and I had to struggle to clarify for ourselves, individually and as co-parents, what we really wanted for our sons. Of course, we already knew the general stuff: We wanted them to be "serious about their salvation" (a common phrase from Sunday School); we wanted them to be healthy; we wanted them to go to college; blah, blah, blah. But we needed to step back from the edge and critically examine the totality of what we wanted for them and why. And then we had to tell them.

For me, this was very emotional. There were things I felt so strongly and intensely that it was hard to speak them aloud. They were built on the foundation of generations of our families, and a lot of that foundation—all of it on American soil—was extremely painful and dehumanizing.

How do you talk about slavery, Reconstruction, Jim Crow, and segregation to middle-class black kids born in the 1980s? It was hard to know how to explain the physical, financial, and psychological damage of terrorism meted out by our fellow Americans. It was hard to explain the spiritual strength of Christianity, as fundamentally a theology of liberation, that had sustained our ancestors through generations of oppression. Their great-grandparents' (two of whom are still very much alive and kicking) grandparents were probably all slaves in this country. As we worked to explain the intensity of our feelings to the kids, we had to examine it ourselves. None of this was new to us, but talking about it—not theoretically or academically, but personally—was hard. We just didn't have a lot of experience in discussing the practical, day-to-day struggle of people we know and love, what they went through, and what the people they loved went through. It was very hard to communicate how all that shaped our hopes, dreams, and anxieties.

Talking about why our grandparents never talked about slavery or even mentioned their own grandparents was complicated and time-consuming. Home schooling gave us the time and the requirement to explore all of that in detail. It's not that we wouldn't have discussed this if the kids had stayed in traditional schools, because I know we would have. Most of it we had discussed earlier. But this was different. We had the time to explore and examine our history, and our thoughts and feelings about it. The examination was painful, but healthier than the alternative. (Don't forget: Socrates—or Plato; scholars disagree—said, "The unexamined life is not worth living," and that can't be healthy.)

C. Madison and I knew we needed Charles, Damon, and Evan to accept the dramatic change in their lifestyle home schooling represented, which they saw as our fault. We weren't naïve enough to hope for approval, but we needed their acceptance if we were to have any hope of long-term success. Their acceptance was tied to our ability to explain how we got to this point and what we felt called upon to do next. They knew about the expulsion and they knew how we felt about it. But we wanted them to see that the expulsion, while serious, wasn't really the issue. If the problem was the expulsion, we could have simply enrolled them in our local school system, which had a fine public school conveniently located in our perfectly fine suburban community. But the problem was not the expulsion. The expulsion was a symptom.

We worked very hard to put their current situation in the context of their own ancestry. We tracked the paternal line back five generations: the boys; their dad; their granddad Dr. Henry Clarke Nabrit; their great-granddad Dr. James Madison Nabrit; and their great-great-granddad Henry, the Well Digger, born a slave. For drama's sake we examined our current view of education through the lens of this lineage: Their great-great-granddad Henry, the Well Digger, was born a slave and not formally educated; but, as a free man, he and his wife valued education—sacrificed for it—and their son James received his theology degrees. Their great-granddad James, born during Reconstruction, saw education as the cornerstone of freedom. He and his wife had eight children, all of whom earned advanced degrees in the 1930s and 1940s.

These eight were members of some of the earliest graduating classes at historically black colleges like Morehouse, Spelman, and Fisk. They broke individual educational barriers, like Uncle Sam, the first African-American to earn a PhD from Brown University, in 1932. And they broke institutional ones as well, like Uncle Jim, who helped successfully argue *Brown v. Board of Education.* These eight children, our sons' great-aunts and uncles, grew up to become ministers, college presidents, scientists, lawyers, publishers, and CPAs.

In those first three generations, the family moved from slavery to having held the presidencies of Howard University and Texas Southern University. Their granddad had three children, including their dad—and he had them.

C. Madison explained to the boys that education was the Nabrit family cornerstone, and that each generation had examined and challenged the educational standards of their day. Essentially, he told them that he intended to continue the tradition of challenging the status quo.

Now, Charles and Damon were only eleven, and Evan was only nine; so, in a very real sense, many of the details and implications of what their father said was probably lost on them. But, at an intuitive level, I think they understood what he was asking of them.

C. MADISON has always maintained an extremely high level of engagement with the boys. It is not something about which he has ever been flexible. There is no shouting or screaming in anger in this house, or at the members of this household—by anyone. C. Madison does not raise his voice to the boys and he has never allowed anyone else to do so. In more than twenty-six years of marriage, I have never heard a word of profanity from him. He has always insisted that the members of this family speak to one another respectfully.

This was a big shift for me, inasmuch as I think the expression "Shut up!" is an especially effective form of communication. I was never allowed to use such language in my parents' home, but the enormous levels of vulgarity and profanity added (in my mind, anyway) a delightful dimension to the otherwise sometimes tedious "white-bread" dialogue I heard at prep school and Wellesley. Now, that's not to say that I hadn't heard profanity and vulgarity in public school, because I had. The difference was that the girls I met in prep school who used such language knew it was viewed as a phase and not as an indication that they were uncouth. So I figured if it was a phase for them, it could be a phase for me, too. And as long as my folks weren't in earshot, I verbally indulged myself. I considered this one of the perks of being an adult. C. Madison did not concur, and my colorful vocabulary was severely curtailed.

Unfortunately, the boys have inherited my delight in such impolite language. While we have never stooped to the use of profanity, we have been known to fall out over something as vulgar and childish as "Oooooh, I smell dukey!" or when one of us flashes a "train wreck" when C. Madison isn't looking. (FYI: A "train wreck" is when you chew up a lot of different-colored foods and then stick out your tongue.) But we do that quietly and respectfully, primarily because we each appreciate the level of civility C. Madison has mandated, even when we appear to be mocking it.

.   .   .

C. MADISON'S serious and respectful approach to everything involving the boys has paid enormous dividends, and that first became clear in our efforts to introduce home schooling to them. They never, ever approved of home schooling while they were participants. But because C. Madison always treated them with such deep and abiding respect, they were willing to try to accept this thing from him. They listened to him carefully, and I could see that they genuinely tried to understand the enormousness and the significance of the task as he saw it.

Another aspect of our struggle was trying to encourage critical thinking in our kids—and learning to hear and respect it, even when the criticism was directed at us. Initially, we were so excited about their critical thinking, we plunged right into an examination of ethics, values, morals, and paradox. It felt so great to see their young minds grapple with the effort to expand their aesthetic beyond the typical social constraints. It felt great until they began, with a somewhat irritating level of condescension, to point out the areas where our own aesthetics had stagnated.

We hadn't been home-schooling two years before Charles and Damon decided they wanted "dreads." Now, I like Bob Marley as well as the next person, possibly even more than the next person, but that didn't mean I wanted my babies to stop combing their hair. Plus, we lived in Westerville, a small suburb of Columbus. We weren't in New York, San Francisco, or L.A.; we weren't even in Cleveland. We explained how handsome and neat and clean-cut they looked with their neatly trimmed hair, carefully parted on the side. We explained the regional limitations of our residency. We explained how really ugly we thought dreadlocks looked, especially at the initial growing-out stage.

They listened very attentively to our arguments and then, with the most patronizing looks and gestures (they patted my hand, for God's sake!), they explained how our aesthetic had been stagnated by the Eurocentric impact of our academic experiences. We were stunned, and at first I was annoyed. They went on to explain that talking about a broader and more inclusive (*they* said "inclusive") aesthetic was not nearly as important as accepting one. They told us they understood that we might feel uncomfortable and even embarrassed by their appearance. They told us they were sorry about that, but that we should think about why we felt uncomfortable.

We were shocked. Their arguments were brilliant and they explained them to us clearly. We had been challenged by our kids! The next day, we sat down and admitted that our aesthetic did have a decidedly Eurocentric lean to it. We thanked them for challenging us and we agreed upon a compromise, a type of Senegalese twist. They were able to grow their hair into a style they felt more comfortable with, and I was able to make sure it was adequately washed and groomed. An unexpected pleasure was the time I got to spend chatting while I did their hair.

I was so moved by their arguments that I grew my own hair out into twists for a time. I had consistently kept my hair "natural" during the years of my marriage, but I always wore it very short. Charles and Damon helped me see that the beauty of our hair in its natural state didn't need to be conventional, contained, or confined.

Our kids quickly became acclimated to challenging us and making us think. Becoming comfortable with them challenging me was a struggle. However, at the risk of sounding trite, the struggle made us stronger individually and collectively, and that was good. Before we began home schooling, we were involved parents who spent a great deal of time with our sons. So I'm not going to take the extremist approach and suggest that without home school-ing, parents and kids can't really get to know each other. That's simply not true. Home schooling is *not* the answer for everyone: it's not for every family; it's not even a good idea for all the families currently engaged in it. But for us, home schooling was very healthy. We were able to participate in our sons' development at a level that simply would not have been possible in a less-adventurous educational experience.

Home schooling was more than an educational adventure, it was a family adventure. As we developed and continually reviewed our home-schooling goals and curriculum, we were forced to examine and reexamine our goals for our family. Now, I'm not going to say we would not have done that if our kids had been in regular school, but we wouldn't have been forced to do so. Home schooling forced us to consider seriously and consciously what we wanted as a family. Our desire for a holistic educational experience where their spiritual, intellectual, and physical development would receive equal at-tention was an extension of what we wanted for our family. We weren't just talking to them about what we wanted for them or expected from them: We talked about what we wanted for and expected from ourselves.

We had to move past holding ourselves out as the example, past comments like "I'm not the one taking algebra" and "I already know how to write a term paper." We had to talk about our own feelings of frustration and fatigue with the work. We began home schooling with the express purpose of teaching our sons; but, upon reflection, we were learning as well.

We felt that we were doing the right thing, but this was a faith walk, right from the beginning, and that made it very hard and frustrating at times. But our frustration was always about the work: the work we needed to do with the kids; the work they needed to do (or do over!); and the work we needed to do with clients.

We weren't frustrated about spending our time with our kids. We weren't doing this because we felt we weren't qualified to do anything else. We weren't doing it to get tuition waivers.

We didn't have any teacher's pets in our school. We didn't have low expectations about any of our "students"; we had no fear or curiosity or negative stereotypes to overcome about any of them. There were no discipline problems we felt unable to quell—instantly. There was no administrative "paperwork": no attendance sheets; no permission slips to be collected. We had complete and total control, and I think that allowed us to be magnanimous with our students. I doubt that they would concur—but we were!

ONE thing that was obvious to us as parents, fairly early on, was that while home schooling was certainly stressful, it was surprisingly less stressful than school. But at the beginning—during those first few weeks—we just didn't have any way of knowing what was going to happen or how we would feel about it. The only thing we knew initially was that we were being forced to give up on prep school.

I wish I could say that we defiantly withdrew our sons from prep school without a single backward glance, but that would be a lie. It was very hard for us to give up on prep school and everything prep school represented. Sure, we had plenty of reasons to leave—and God knows we had complained, vociferously, along with lots of other parents—but the embarrassing truth is, if we had not been forced out, I'm not sure we would have done so voluntarily, or, at least, not for a few more years. We, like lots of other black parents at our sons' school, and at other similar institutions, knew the school wasn't perfect. But we really believed it was the best thing available for our sons, and we were convinced we could make it work for them. We were wrong.

The expulsion forced us to a new level of consciousness. Our previous assessments, educational beliefs, and projections had turned out to be, if not inaccurate, incomplete. We weren't ashamed of those past assessments, beliefs, or projections; I mean, I don't think there's any reason to be ashamed when growth happens. I think every new enlightenment has to illuminate some previous shortcoming. Plus, I hate it when people have a change in circumstance, and instead of really looking at the thing just pretend that their current view is the one they held all along. Consequently I had no intention of pretending that we hadn't made a radical, 180-degree turn from where we had been fewer than thirty days before, when we had enrolled the boys for the school year. Those past assessments, beliefs, and projections were an accurate reflection of where we had been. They were the basis for our decisions about what was best for our sons at that moment. They, along with our spiritual beliefs, were what had sustained us in our ongoing struggle to be good parents and make good choices for our kids. As my good friend, clinical psychologist Dr. Linda James Myers, always says, "We're all in process, and everybody's doing the best they can at this particular moment in time." Of course, I'm too judgmental to really believe that, but it's a reassuring thought; and in our case, it was true, at least about our parenting decisions. We were in process, and we had been doing the best we knew at that particular moment in time.

The expulsion just made it clear that we had to come up with a new set of assessments, beliefs, and projections, because the ones we had been using had collapsed. We just couldn't hold on to them any longer once we had been forced to a higher level of consciousness. Sometimes it's hard to acknowledge truth, because it can cast such an unfavorable light on the past. But I have to agree with my tax professor, Morgan Shipman, on this one: "Never complain when wisdom comes late, because sometimes it never comes at all."

There was no reason to pretend that we hadn't felt the way we had about the school just because things didn't work out. There was nothing to be gained by lying about our feelings, past or present. That would have been unhealthy—and confusing to our kids. We had loved the school. We had been proud of the fact that we were able to send our boys there. We were proud that their admissions applications had been accepted. (If you're neither very wealthy nor an alum, the admissions application is subject to—shall we say—an "invigorating" level of academic scrutiny. Happily, our sons had passed through that scrutiny with no complications.) We were also very proud of what a wonderful contribution our sons made to the moral and ethical life of the school. They not only stood up for themselves and for one another, they could also be counted on to stand up for other kids who were picked on, either by other students or, in some instances, by teachers. And, of course, there was an element of financial pride going on too. We were proud of the fact that we were able financially to support three kids in that school. Again, we weren't rich, and our kids didn't have grandparents underwriting their educational expenses. This twenty thousand dollars plus in tuition was money we had to come up with, annually, on top of our regular living expenses—and it wasn't easy! We were struggling: We were trying to get a relatively new business up and running, and both of us had other jobs as well.

It can be hard to stay motivated when you're working all the time but never have any money. We lived in a tiny little house; we never ate out; and only the kids got new clothes. We were consistently scuffling to pay for our sons' education, and while it was tedious, we felt proud of the fact that we had our priorities in order. While we would have loved to be able to have a larger house, cool cars, beautiful clothes, and wonderful vacations, we knew we couldn't afford private school together with those things, and we felt our children's education was more important than anything else.

I think that was healthy. We had been committed to the school, and we had truly believed we were part of the community. But in all fairness to us, we were a part of the community only on the most shallow and superficial levels. We were not, as I had supposed, a vital part of the school community. We didn't see that critical distinction until the end. We allowed ourselves to be seduced by the school's reputation, by its history, and, most important, by its stated promises and implied threats.

The promises surrounded the commitment to the success and development of every student. In retrospect, it was naïve of me to think the institution could readily live up to such a commitment, especially when the development of some students might require a dramatic change in the way the institution operated. (There's a certain level of change that goes right to the core of an institution's existence. It wasn't clear to me then, but I now realize that the issue of self-preservation is as real for institutions as it is for individuals.)

Balanced against the stated promises of commitment were the implied threats that a separation from the institution could only result in negative consequences academically and socially, both immediately and in the future. In other words, this school was the best—which, at least to me, meant that going anywhere else was tantamount to settling for less than the best. Why else would we (and lots of other parents) make the enormous financial sacrifice to ensure our kids' attendance? (I realize this sounds pathetic and trite, but it's true.) I felt very comforted by the fact that my sons were in this school, despite its flaws. And like so many people, I took great comfort in having our sons at "the best" school. (Isn't it interesting how the best is almost always the most exclusive?) Often the goal is to find the best, find a way to get some of it, and then find a way to pay for it. (Why is the best often the most expensive?)

I have learned that terms like "the best," "top of the line," "state of the art," "cutting edge," have a downside, a cost factor frequently not examined until there's a problem, and then it's too late. It's like when my parents built their dream home in the mid-seventies and my dad insisted on using only "the best," "state of the art" appliances. They were beautiful, sleek, and expensive, but when they needed to be repaired, none of the repairmen in Franklin County who were sent to the house had ever *seen* any of those appliances in real life!

Sometimes things that are the "top of the line" cannot maintain high levels of performance over extended periods of high utilization. Just as some very expensive and specialized automobiles are not intended for the daily grind of commuting through city traffic: They're cool, sleek, exciting, and expensive, but you need another car for everyday use. Similarly, some private schools have all the cool stuff—great student-teacher ratios, tremendous facilities, outstanding college admissions rates, and huge endowments—but none of that means it's a healthy educational environment.

I was stunned when I finally realized that fact, and the corresponding fact that "the best" is not only not synonymous with perfection, the designation has no meaning without an understanding of who's giving it and what is being defined. I guess I hadn't realized that because I hadn't stopped to ask myself the source of these designations of distinction, much less what was being measured by them.

The promise, of course, was that this was *the* place to be to get the best and most competitive secondary education, the kind of education necessary for admission to the finest colleges and universities in the land. But when our boys left prep school, we began seriously to examine all of our previously held assumptions, and in doing so we were able to launch our home-schooling adventure. (Ironically, the same issues about "the best" resurfaced when we began the college admissions process.) Of course, the critical difference was that home schooling really wasn't an option at the post-secondary level. But I'll talk more about that later.

There were several questions that we asked ourselves at the beginning of and sporadically throughout the process. Those questions might not be as illuminating for other families, but they really helped us to clarify some essential issues.

1. *Have we truly explored all our options?*
2. *What do we want for our kids' education that has been missing elsewhere?*
3. *Do we think we can do a better job ourselves?*
4. *Do we really want to take on the responsibility of home schooling?*
5. *Can we imagine being with our kids all the time, or at least most of the time?*

6. *Can our kids imagine being with us all the time, or at least most of the time?*
7. *Can our kids imagine being with one another all the time, or at least most of the time?*
8. *Are there resources in our community to help us home-school our kids?*
9. *What will be the biggest challenges to our home schooling?*
10. *How will we know if we've been successful in our home-schooling efforts?*

4

WHAT IT

WAS LIKE FOR

OUR KIDS

WHAT WAS IT like for our kids? They hated it, from the beginning until the end. And no, I'm not exaggerating: They never got over telling us how much they hated being home-schooled. Now, they might have been exaggerating to make a point. They may have appreciated the experience at a deep level never communicated to us. But in terms of what they said to us, they *hated* it.

They said they hated it because they missed school, and there was certainly some truth in that—they did miss school and all the social engagements school provided. But I know some other kids who have been home-schooled exclusively, and they didn't like it either.

I think home schooling is a very complex process that can become fraught with conflict, depending in large part on the personalities of the people involved. There's a certain normalcy in children wanting and, in fact, needing some separation from their parents, physically and psychologically. There's a certain normalcy in kids—especially as they approach and enter adolescence—preferring the company of their chronological peers. While some kids love being home-schooled, not all kids do. Consequently, I doubt that Charles, Damon, and Evan's response to this educational option would have been significantly different even if they had been home-schooled exclusively. They had a great deal of nostalgia about school, and that certainly contributed to their frustration about being home-schooled. But the dominant source of conflict was the fact that our kids are highly social, and home schooling does change the nature of the social lives of the participants. That's what they didn't like.

Fortunately, we expected a great deal of discomfort, so at least it wasn't a surprise. We didn't try to dismiss or minimize their feelings about the change, because they were legitimate feelings. Our focus was on continually explaining our rationale for the change. It wasn't essential for us that they agree with our reasoning, and we didn't really expect them to agree or even fully to understand. I don't think it's realistic to expect kids to see the world the same way that adults view it. Although our kids were certainly present during their past educational experiences, their assessments of those events couldn't match up precisely with ours, given the differences in our ages and life experiences, and that was okay.

It wouldn't have been appropriate for us to assume that they could fully appreciate our reasons for making such a drastic decision. And the fact that we didn't consult them before making the decision didn't make them like the decision any better. We expected a lot of resistance and, quite frankly, I think I would have been concerned if they hadn't been resistant.

Someone once said, "Every seed bursts its container." Part of the growth and development of kids should be about bursting their container and pushing forward into their own independent existence, and that's something we definitely wanted to see happen with our own kids. But the fact is that we were approaching them and their development as seeds of immeasurable worth, so we weren't willing to turn their cultivation over to gardeners with questionable track records. Weeds can grow and flourish beautifully under almost any kind of condition, but we just didn't see Charles, Damon, and Evan as dandelions.

Because C. Madison has always maintained some sort of garden, and because he always had the boys work with him on it, they had a clear frame of reference on how different kinds of seeds are nourished and then flourish. Those conversations didn't move them closer to an agreement with us, but the analogy did give us another context in which to discuss the decision.

Ultimately, however, the boys were determined to be miserable, and so, of course, they wanted us to be miserable, too. Now, that probably sounds unhealthy, but the fact of the matter is, I'm not sure kids have to be pleased with every decision their parents make. Truthfully, I don't think perpetual pleasure is healthy, but, of course, *that* wasn't a problem for us.

What *was* a problem was helping our kids recognize that they were experiencing a healthy and happy childhood. This is far more difficult than it sounds. Remember how Dorothy had to go all the way to Oz before she learned that her heart's desire was right there, in her own backyard, all the time? I always think of Dorothy's concluding monologue as Hollywood's variation on the epistle of Paul the Apostle to the Philippians. Admittedly, as a reference point, Philippians is probably not as familiar as *The Wizard of Oz*, but chapter 4, verses 11 and 12, are still relevant: "Not that I speak in respect of want: for I have learned, in whatsoever state I am, *therewith* to be content. I know both how to be abased, and I know how to abound: every where and in all things I am instructed both to be full and to be hungry, both to abound and to suffer need." Charles, Damon, and Evan had to learn that, too, and eventually they did. They finally came to the realization that joy and happiness are experienced, not as a result of the places we go or the things we have, but as the result of spiritual decisions we make. In other words, we either choose to be conscious, thankful, and contented or we choose to be unconscious, ungrateful, and discontented.

Being content comes from being thankful, and being thankful—literally *full* of thanks—comes through genuine conscious awareness. At the risk of overworking the references, neither Dorothy nor Paul was able to be content until they had a revelation of consciousness. Both revelations required a significant fall, one off a horse on the road to Damascus and the other out of a house caught in a tornado in Kansas. Once Dorothy became fully conscious, she was full of thanks for Auntie Em and the guys on the farm, and once she was full of thanks, she was able to be content—even in Kansas.

ONE of our goals was to help Charles, Damon, and Evan each see himself both in his own magnificent and individual splendor, and as a wonderful and critical member of this family. I think that is an amazing and challenging dual revelation for anyone. Home schooling can facilitate the consciousness of each child. Unlike traditional institutional educational environments, home schooling can allow the child to exist singularly, as an independent agent, within a natural unit, rather than as part of an artificial group designed by social architects.

Looking back on my kids' institutional educational experiences, I can see that the collective quality of their classroom environments—clusters cordoned off by grade and ability—was reminiscent of the Borg, from *Star Trek*. In many respects, institutionalized education acts as the structure and essentially becomes the Borg. And as any self-respecting Trekkie will tell you, when one encounters the Borg, resistance is futile.

As ugly as it is to say, groups of children are not always a pretty thing: Remember *Lord of the Flies* and *Children of the Corn*? Anyone who's ever seen a group of kids get nasty on the playground knows exactly what I mean. Mob rule is not a singularly adult phenomenon. Conformity is the price for acceptance, and nowhere is this truer than in school.

Conformity is not always a bad thing: Society needs rules. But conformity imposed at an early age sometimes can produce bad results. The effect of those negative results is amplified when those clusters of children are seeking conformity designed by teachers and administrators who themselves might not be the healthiest or happiest people on the planet.

Home schooling gave us the freedom and flexibility to help Charles, Damon, and Evan create and maintain some space between themselves and their cluster—even when they didn't want or know that they needed the space. Granted, it's a lot harder and scarier to see oneself as an independent agent rather than as a part of the Borg, but we had to believe that, ultimately, the rewards for our children would be worth it. In the end Charles, Damon, and Evan, each in his own way, chose to strive for consciousness. And while they never *admitted* it, we could sense their genuine thankfulness. Ultimately, they became content: They learned to choose joy, peace, and happiness in the midst of a situation they did not select or approve. The strength, grace, and maturity they developed through this process of conflict might very well be the most healthy and positive outcome of our home-schooling experience. Of course, I'm saying all of this now, a decade after the beginning.

IN the beginning—way back in 1991—there were many times when I didn't think we would make it. This was a hard thing to do and to continue doing, especially when Charles, Damon, and Evan appeared to be so unhappy.

As most parents know, it is incredibly difficult to deny one's child anything. No one, at least no one in her right mind, wants to see her child upset or unhappy. That's why it's so difficult to say "No." It's part of our nature as parents. We want to indulge our children. We don't need the incentive of whining, pouting, and crying: We naturally want to satisfy our children's whims. (Actually, the whining, pouting, and crying really helped toughen me up for the definitive "No!" Good thing kids don't know that!)

C. Madison and I are no exception. We knew our kids wanted to go back to school. How could we not know? Everybody knew! It was not fun for us to watch them struggle to adjust to home schooling. We knew they were uncomfortable and we knew that the transition was difficult. But we also knew that discomfort and difficulty are part of the human experience, and they need not result in unhappiness.

We understood that on the surface, Charles, Damon, and Evan were struggling to understand what was happening and why. But on a deeper level, I think they were struggling to understand the difference between the fleeting happiness that comes from conformity and the genuine joy that comes from a life well lived. Many adults would struggle with the concepts of joy and happiness as the subjects for a "compare and contrast" essay, so it's not surprising that children would find it hard. And at the time we were introducing this topic for discussion, Charles and Damon were only eleven and Evan was just nine! They were little boys.

Certainly we know home schooling is not the exclusive pathway to a life well lived. And after years of observation and participation in the home-school community, we definitely know that every child being home-schooled is not experiencing a life well lived. But in our instance, the freedom to form a holistic educational environment helped to create a life that was well lived. Our sons thought they were happy in school, in spite of the difficulties, and they thought they would be unhappy being home-schooled. While they appeared to be happy, we felt they were merely showing the signs of resiliency adults so often point to in children when they want to minimize negative circumstances.

I understand the temptation to rely on the resiliency of childhood. I have relied upon it many times myself. But I really think that my responsibility as a parent is to make sure that I don't use their resiliency as an excuse to let me off the hook. I am very uncomfortable when I see parents use their child's resiliency as a blind. It's so easy not to see the strain we put our children under, especially when they work so hard to adapt to the strain.

So, while they were convinced they were just fine in school, we thought they adapted to the demands of school, and they performed well there. That is not intended to be a minimizing statement, because we, too, as their parents, had adapted and performed well. So we knew firsthand that it was not a trivial accomplishment. But adaptation and performance became irrelevant after the expulsion.

It was painful to admit that we had left them in an environment that we were now telling them was unhealthy! While they didn't actually ask this, we knew they were wondering, "If it was so bad, why were we there this long?" For C. Madison and me, it was one of those classic moments of enlightenment in which you have to admit the painful truth to yourself and to others. We had to tell them the truth they were going to discover eventually anyway— namely, parents really *don't* know everything. We apologized. We admitted we had made a mistake, and then we apologized again. We hated the fact that they were paying for our mistake. But we also told them that once you know something is wrong, you have to stop doing it. It wasn't planned, but that discussion allowed us to transmit a critically important life lesson: It's okay to make a change when you realize you've been wrong. In fact, once you know you're wrong, you have to change. I think it's a terrible sign of weakness to continue on the same path, just because changing course means admitting you were wrong in the first place. One of the unexpected pleasures of home schooling is the frequency of opportunities to work through such issues collectively.

WE weren't surprised or disappointed that our kids couldn't grasp the contradictory notion that people can expect you to act as an individual while they evaluate you as part of a group. It was tough to articulate the paradox of the double consciousness W.E.B. Du Bois talked about: the idea of seeing oneself through the lens of being an American and, simultaneously, seeing oneself as black.

Part of the essential nature of the view of oneself as an American hinges on the view of oneself as an individual. Conversely, part of the essential nature of the view of oneself as a black American is tied to the realization that one will always be seen as part of that group. The weight of the contradiction can feel enormous, especially when you forget it exists, the way we did at school. We had to admit that we had forgotten, and that our forgetting had led us to this place.

Critiquing exclusionary institutions is a privilege accorded to individuals, and acknowledgment of individuality is a luxury accorded only to certain sectors of the American populace, none of which included us. When black people choose to act as individuals—what I like to think of as free people of color—that evokes ire and unpleasant consequences.

Charles, Damon, and Evan were well aware of the range of unacceptable yet tolerated behavior that went on at school without *any* serious disciplinary response. Frequently one of them would describe something bad that had happened at school—the usual kid stuff; e.g., using bad words, teasing other kids, disrespectful behavior toward adults—and they'd look to see if I was shocked. When profanity was at issue, they'd try to spare my delicate ears by using just the first letter of the vile utterance. And then they'd check to see if I "got" it: "Mommy, do you know what the 'A' word is?" Sadly, I would confirm that, yes, I was familiar with many bad words, all the while trying not to laugh out loud. But I would always conclude with this casual question: "What do you think *I* would do if I found out you did such a thing? And you know I'd find out, because I'm the mommy and I know these things!" They'd sigh and respond flatly, "You'd spank us." I would happily affirm their assessment with bright enthusiasm.

Discipline is important, so that the child can learn self-control as an avenue to enjoyment. When I see children out of control—you know, the poor souls screaming like banshees because they want ____ (fill in the blank)—I feel so sorry for them. They aren't enjoying themselves, and they aren't enjoying the nasty looks they're getting from their parents and other adult observers. The problem is that they actually do not *know* how to act.

When I was a girl, it was very common for parents to say things like "You *know* you know how to act!" or, even more condemning, "You know better." But the fact is nobody *knows* better; at least, not on any instinctual level. We behave when we're taught to behave. We behave even better when we get all the positive strokes that come from good behavior.

A lot of people thought I was crazy and shallow for saying this when my boys were toddlers, but little kids are judged by two things: (1) how well they behave, and (2) how cute their clothes are. (I hedged my bets by buying my kids the cutest clothes in the universe and making sure they were extremely well behaved.) As they got older, my attention shifted from cute clothes to appropriate clothes. Now that they're young men, I have almost nothing to say about their fashion choices, but I always pay attention to and comment upon their manners, criticizing when necessary.

I don't believe in beating kids. I don't believe parents have the right to abuse their children in any way. I think abuse includes any kind of hitting in anger or frustration, or hitting anywhere other than the behind. Abuse includes ignoring kids, being too busy really to be there with them, fully present in the moment. It includes thinking your work is as important as (or more important than!) they are. I also think abuse includes allowing kids to grow up with no limits, no boundaries, and no discipline. Children who are not loved or respected enough to be disciplined seem to have a very difficult time learning to respect others.

My own years at prep school marked my first encounter with children being openly disrespectful to their parents, especially their mothers. When I would come home and tell my mother the things I had heard some of the girls in my class say to their mothers, she was shocked. To her, such behavior was inconceivable. She repeatedly told me and my sisters, "You are at that school for one reason and one reason only—to get an education. Period! Don't bring that behavior home."

One of the ironies my sisters and I had to navigate was the fact that the general assumption at our prep school was that we were being given a unique and wonderful dual opportunity: This was not just an academic opportunity, it was an opportunity to view what our headmaster described as "the good life." There didn't appear to be any awareness at school that our parents viewed our exposure to "the good life" as a dubious thing at best. I honestly think the school administrators and faculty would have been stunned to hear that, in fact, my parents didn't admire everything about them and their lifestyles, and that they absolutely did not want us to emulate everything we saw there. Our parents were adamantly opposed to us picking up what they regarded as the spiritually unhealthy lifestyle of wealthy white people.

One proof that many of us become our mothers is that I went through the whole "us and them" thing with my own kids. My focal point was respectful behavior and good manners. There are different ways of being in the world, and some of those ways are shaped by a variety of factors, including religion, age, economics, culture, gender, and race. I reminded them that I was not the kind of mother who would respond to every infraction with a time-out or the withholding of privileges. I wanted them to understand that there were different ways of being a parent and that each set of parents had to figure out their way for themselves. It was important to me that they know our traditional, conservative, black, middle-class way. I knew from firsthand experience how difficult it is to move between two worlds that intersect both race and class. And in spite of parental admonishments, it's easy to forget yourself. The forgetting is even easier when adults at school engage in the *verboten* behavior, which makes it seem acceptable.

When Charles and Damon were fifth-graders, they had a fairly young, white, male English teacher. All the boys thought this guy was quite cool. Charles and Damon were very enthusiastic about his class. But they kept mentioning his use of profanity in class, and I could see they were confused by it. Part of their dad's rationale for the prohibition of profanity and colloquial expressions was his opinion that such language was a reflection of a lazy mind and an underdeveloped vocabulary. But this guy was their English teacher—surely *he* couldn't have a lazy mind and an underdeveloped vocabulary.

While I didn't expect school to echo our personal spiritual views, I did expect basic standards of conduct would be adhered to by the faculty, and I fully expected abstinence from profanity to be included in those standards. So, I made an appointment to go see this teacher. Our meeting started off pleasantly enough, but when I expressed my concern about his language, he reminded me that my children were boys who would someday become men, and that this was how men talk. In return, I explained that—surprise, surprise—my husband, their father, was a man! and he never used such language. I further explained that it was inexcusable for an English teacher to use such language in class. If it continued, I would have no choice but to have Mr. Nabrit come in and discuss it with him, "man-to-man." It stopped.

BUT, back to the question at hand. Everyone thought our sons' self-professed suffering because of home schooling had to be unhealthy. How did people know they were suffering? They told everyone who would listen. I always felt their goal was to make us objects of public ridicule and scorn by letting everyone know that we were, without cause or justification, making their lives a living hell! And they never gave up lobbying us directly for a reprieve. For the first year, they told us how unhappy they were each and every day. Eventually, we settled into a once-a-week fit.

For the sake of variety, they would attempt to rotate the role of "emissary," but, ultimately, Charles provided the concluding arguments. The designated emissary would come and present the fit of the week. Sometimes the discussion would begin calmly enough with a detailed listing of why home schooling was a bad idea; most often, it would conclude with crying, table-pounding, scowling, and pouting.

We would listen and respond to any specific questions. When the emissary finished, we would reiterate our position that the decision about their education was ours to make. C. Madison would explain that our family was not modeled after a simple democracy, under the premise of one man, one vote. Our family incorporated a spiritual as well as a political model. Spiritually, C. Madison, as the husband and father, was the head of the house, and while he had a spiritual obligation to listen to me as his helpmeet, and a moral and ethical obligation to listen to his children, the spiritual responsibility for this family rested with him.

Interestingly, the boys had no difficulty whatsoever accepting my position as helpmeet. They didn't care about that—they just wanted to be equal policy-makers with their dad. This was my first indication that they had some gender issues. We continue to work on that with them.

The political model was no less easy for them to understand or accept. Ours was essentially a capitalist democracy. The beauty of a capitalist democracy lies in its simplicity: "If you don't own nothing, you don't run nothing!" As we gently reminded them, we owned the means of production in this small capitalist democracy; therefore, we and we alone were responsible for all policies. When such policies become egregious, they would need to terminate their dependent status.

Again, their youth made the understanding of this concept difficult. But given the staggering numbers of adult Americans who apparently don't understand that the formulation of a capitalist democracy was what the Founding Fathers proposed, we weren't surprised that our kids didn't quite get it on the first or even second go-round.

WE repeated our regrets about their decision to nurture their current state of unhappiness, and acknowledged full responsibility for whatever untold social problems they would have as a result of our decision. We had to point out that happiness is a choice. We had to point out that no amount of complaining would wear us down or make us lose our resolve. We had to point out that their opinions did not count as much as ours. We felt it was essential to their future mental and emotional health that we be as honest and forthcoming as possible.

We had regular family meetings, and we encouraged their input and participation, questions, and comments. However, it was imperative that Charles, Damon, and Evan know and understand that we were the adults, we were their parents, and we were the ones responsible for this family. As gifts from God, they were essentially on loan to us, and we had a fiduciary responsibility to ensure that their assets appreciated and were not squandered under our watch.

Long before the second year, they were somewhat reconciled to the situation and began to actively contribute ideas. They informed us they could not spend all day, every day, in our company. We concurred! COSI—the Center for Science and Industry, our local science museum—provided the perfect outlet. COSI had a student volunteer program. They had recently added a home-school component, and our sons were interviewed, accepted, and promptly signed up for two days a week. Ultimately, they each logged more than two thousand volunteer hours. They leveraged their volunteer positions to meet "women" from all over Franklin County and to get themselves invited to parties all over town.

When I complained that I didn't know their friends, they hastened to remind me I should have factored that loss into the cost/benefit analysis of home schooling; after all, if they had remained in school, I would have known their friends, classmates, and, probably, some of the parents. As their analysis was absolutely on point, I had no choice but to agree. We knew that they needed to have tangible evidence that we were able to be flexible about the methodology of home schooling, even if we weren't flexible about the concept. Once policies are established by the policy-maker(s), everybody affected by the policies can help fashion the means by which the policy will be accomplished.

There were lots of areas for us to practice the fine art of negotiation. The boys concurred with our recommendation about two hours of quiet reading every day on the condition that they be allowed to read wherever they wanted to, including in bed or lying on the sofas. This was hard for their dad. He can be somewhat anal retentive, and would have preferred reading to occur in more traditional postures. He also wanted the school day to begin at seven A.M. The boys wanted flextime. We compromised with seven A.M. on the days they went to COSI and nine on their off days.

Describing them here makes these compromises seem sort of small and insignificant, but they weren't. I think these were the things that illustrated our willingness really to listen to them. It's easy to say that you respect your kids, but respect, like love, must be demonstrated if it is to be believed. Our willingness to be flexible proved we really weren't on a "power trip," as they had first believed.

We were incredibly busy and sometimes felt overwhelmed by the competing demands of the business and home schooling, not to mention the regular cooking, shopping, cleaning, etc., etc., etc. But we made it a point to make time when they wanted to discuss policy-implementation issues. Again, it's easy to say your kids are the most important thing in the world, but if work always comes first how real is that statement? We made a conscious decision to treat our position as parents as a career rather than as a job.

The big difference between a career and a job is commitment. The level of commitment is greater in a career than in a job because the expectations and rewards are greater. We saw our role as parents as a career with long-range, strategic expectations and benefits. Granted, a successful and rewarding career is usually comprised of a series of jobs well done, but you never forget that the job is part of something bigger, something more important. Home schooling was just one job, albeit a big one, in the long-term career of parenting. Home schooling gave us the flexibility to illustrate our commitment to our career as parents, and that was very healthy for our kids.

ANOTHER healthy aspect of home schooling was our kids' friendship with one another. Charles, Damon, and Evan deepened their bond as brothers by becoming colleagues, fellow adventurers, and sometimes co-conspirators against us. We were blessed from the very beginning of our family with very little sibling rivalry. But home schooling ensured each boy more parental attention than he could ever want. They really didn't have to compete with one another for our time or attention. We spent so much time together, even when we were each working on different things, that I don't think anyone ever felt significantly rushed, overlooked, or ignored.

Absent sibling rivalry, the boys' friendship was able to grow naturally. Not being separated for eight hours a day in separate classrooms, separate grades, or separate schools or school divisions, they were able to get to know one another better. Their lives were shared.

Lots of people adamantly disagree with us about this, but we think it's very healthy for siblings to find out that they really like each other before they're in their early twenties. Friendships are a critical part of a life well lived, but I don't think those friendships have to or should be focused outside the family. I don't believe families are created by biological accidents: There is a design and a purpose in their creation. There are things we are supposed to learn from our family members that we might not learn from other friends. Often we wouldn't choose our siblings as friends, because they are too challenging, but I think that's the point: I think family relationships, be they healthy or dysfunctional, set the tone for all other relationships in a person's life.

I felt it was important for Charles, Damon, and Evan to develop close, loving relationships with one another so that their later, adult relationships would have that history of love and loyalty as a solid foundation. Psalms 133:1 says, "Behold, how good and how pleasant *it is* for brethren to dwell together in unity!" By the conclusion of our home-schooling experience, I could see that our sons had grown to that point in their relationship.

PROBABLY the healthiest aspect of our home-schooling adventure was our sons' early understanding of the need to take holistic responsibility for their own joy, their own happiness, their own education, and their own lives. By the time they left home there were certain critical life skills they knew. They weren't fully accomplished or perfected in each of them, but they at least had the foundation for a life of self-examination and fulfillment. They knew that joy comes from knowing God, happiness comes from getting things right in relationships with family and friends, intellectual growth is a choice, and a life well lived is a process of committed work. Most important, they knew that they were individually responsible for all of it.

Individual responsibility is a difficult thing to grasp, no matter what age you are. Part of the ongoing challenge C. Madison and I faced with home schooling was recognizing and remembering that we were the ones responsible for the spiritual, intellectual, and physical development of our sons. Sure, we wanted and appreciated the help and support of our families and our community, but ultimately we were responsible, with or without that support.

Quite frankly, sometimes that support was not forthcoming in a timely way. Hearing that you did a good job at the conclusion of a project is wonderful, but it's not nearly as helpful as hearing the vote of confidence before all the results are in. But the hard truth is, individual responsibility is just that: individual.

Once, before grades were passed out for a Latin exam, my headmaster recounted the story of Samson and Delilah. He recounted how Samson had been duped, but he reminded us Samson was responsible for his own actions. He went on to say that no matter what we thought of our Latin teacher or her teaching style, each of us was responsible for our own academic performance. He ended this little talk by making us stand up and collectively say, "I alone am to blame."

At the time, pathetic Latin scholar that I was, I was not amused. But that comment has stuck with me over the years, and it's applicable to the education and development of our children. It's about individual responsibility.

5

WHAT IT WAS

LIKE FOR OUR FAMILIES

HOME-SCHOOLING OUR sons was a grave and serious situation for our extended families, and their concern added to our overall consternation. Our families were very worried about the boys and their futures.

We knew that they loved our kids and wanted only the best for them, and it's not as though we didn't understand and, in fact, share some of their concerns. We just had different views of how to define and achieve the best. We weren't satisfied with the educational choices available, and we were convinced we could do a better job. Most significant, we were willing to take the risk and try.

Conversely, our families are composed of fundamentally very traditional, socially conservative, middle-class, black people. Educational risk-taking was definitely not part of their formula for success. Providing one's children with the very best possible education has never been an option within our families' worldview—it's an obligation. For generations, our families, like many other African-American families, endured enormous sacrifices and hardships in order to meet that obligation.

While it apparently wasn't obvious at the time, C. Madison and I shared their commitment to that educational obligation. We just had a different vision of how that obligation should be met for our children. Our families were convinced that this was probably a mistake, a big mistake, the kind of mistake with long-term and seriously negative consequences.

In that respect, the view of our families mirrored that of most people. The key difference for me was that, while I really couldn't have cared less about the opinions of other people, I cared immensely about what my family thought. Knowing that I was disappointing them yet again (I didn't pass the bar exam, I didn't practice law, and I quit my job at American Transtech!) didn't make me especially happy. I hated for them to think that I didn't respect their opinions and judgments, because I did. The fact that I frequently didn't follow their advice (or even ask for it that often) really wasn't an indicator of a lack of respect. So, throughout the process, I tried to keep our extended family informed of what we were doing.

In general, our parents were not amused. My mother, as always, was the most direct and most vocal in her disapproval.

My mother does not consider anyone to be beyond reproach. And if she thinks you're wrong or "out of order," she will come and tell you to your face, no matter who you are. Typically she has four or five favorite phrases she uses to convey her concern or displeasure with me. If I have not called her recently (read that as within the last twenty-four hours!), she'll call and inquire, "Have you lost your mind?" If I have done something she feels is inappropriate, but she knows it's none of her business, she'll say, "I don't care how old you get—I'm still your mother!" If she thinks I have on too much makeup or jewelry, she'll say, "You look awfully worldly—are you still saved?" If I've done something she thinks is foolish, she'll say, "I may not have gone to Columbus School for Girls or Wellesley, but I know this!" But her most scathing rebuke comes if I have done something she deems unnecessarily risky. Then she'll say, as she did when she heard about home schooling, "You're not white, you know."

When I was a girl in prep school, she used to remind me that rich white people have the luxury to take risks and mess up. From her perspective, they had plenty of money, plenty of chances, and plenty of time eventually to get it right. I, on the other hand, was neither rich nor white, and she wanted me to remember that. Whenever she thought I forgot, she reminded me. When I got married right after college instead of going straight to law school, had the twins while in law school, didn't take the bar exam a second time, quit my job to start my own business—each time she reminded me, "You're not white, you know!"

In this instance, my mother's concerns were focused securely on the welfare of our sons. She was very worried that our decision to home-school, while possibly logical, failed to factor in the unstable variable of race. She was absolutely certain that the successes achieved by white home-schooled families would be foreclosed to us because we were black. She felt our insistence on continuing with our home-schooling plans was naïve, at best. To ignore the variable of race—something my mother sees as a constant to be factored into every equation of life in these United States, especially with regard to something as life-altering as our children's education—was irresponsible. My mother very succinctly expressed the view of many, if not most, in our families' positions on this point.

While our relatives can sometimes be nerve-racking, they are not stupid people. They are, in many respects, the epitome of that old axiom, "You don't get to be old and black being a fool." Our families grew up with the knowledge that success for black Americans required doing more and doing it better than white people. As a child, I can remember my dad commenting upon the rapid success and upward mobility of white men at the company for which he worked. His assessment and rationale for the difference in levels of achievement was quite simple: All they had to do was "be white and show up." Conversely, for black people, merely showing up or even being competent would never be enough: There had to be evidence of superlative excellence. So it's easy to see how our efforts to home-school our kids would never be adequate in terms of supplying the necessary quantitative evidence of superlative excellence essential for admission to the best colleges.

In this instance, our parents' views were distinctly different from those of many of our professional, middle-class black friends. Many of our friends and associates felt strongly that the very absence of white people would invalidate our efforts. Several of our white professional and middle-class friends, and some of my old prep-school classmates, expressed the same concern in less direct terms.

I really think there has been a broad-based misunderstanding of the controlling argument in the historic *Brown* case. That case didn't turn on the argument that in order for black children to receive a good education they had to be educated by and in the presence of white people. The argument was that it was not possible to support the premise of separate-but-equal in the absence of unequal funding and facilities. Further, there is an inherent inequity in requiring the universal tax support of institutions that are restricted to certain segments of the citizenry. But because many people think that case is about integration for integration's sake, the very idea of black children being educated by and in the company of other black people, exclusively, raises grave concerns across racial lines. Many of our friends and acquaintances expressed the view that unless white people were present as teachers and fellow students, something critical would be missing. Conversely, our parents' views had nothing to do with the perceived need for white participation per se. Their concerns centered squarely on their belief that the absence of white participation at this secondary level would render the boys' later efforts at college admissions futile. Our families didn't have any issues about the presence of white people and the impact of their absence on the quality of education the boys would receive. They were concerned about how that education would or could be substantiated in the eyes of college admissions officers, most of whom would be white.

Our parents never expressed any serious doubts about our ability to provide an excellent education for the boys. They knew we were well educated: They had paid good money to have us educated, and they had no doubts about the value received. They merely doubted that any white colleges would accept our assessment of the quality of education transmitted to our kids in the absence of supporting documentation from a recognized and accredited institution. The fact that the quality of education received by white home-schooled students was accepted by colleges in no way made our parents believe the same consideration would be extended to black home-schooled students.

We didn't really disagree with their assessment. How could we? We weren't stupid, either! Our position was not in opposition to theirs; we just looked at it differently. Given everything that had already happened to our sons in traditional educational institutions, it seemed highly improbable that those institutions would provide the kind of quantitative validation of the kids' academic work necessary for competitive college admissions. Charles and Damon made good grades in prep school, but their grades were far from excellent. And if a kid is only making A-minuses and B-pluses in the fourth and fifth grades, there's really no rational reason to assume there's going to be some huge grade improvement in high school. And there were rarely any definitive answers about Charles's and Damon's academic evaluations. Far too often, when we questioned their grades, we got the vague answer, "It just wasn't 'A' work."

Notice I haven't mentioned Evan's academic performance. That's because Evan, unlike his brothers, was not a serious student, and—more important—I never felt the need to pretend that he was. Evan never learned his math facts; Evan frequently did not complete his homework and/or lost it somewhere between the kitchen, the car, and his classroom (along with one of his shoes). While I wasn't pleased by his difficulties, I certainly didn't feel they were important enough issues to lie about them.

I've always believed my sons were closer to perfection than most other humans, but I was never so crazy as to believe they were without spot or wrinkle! Legitimate imperfections and areas of improvement were issues I was always interested in hearing about and discussing with their teachers. However, I was also conscious enough to recognize bias when I saw it. Charles and Damon were serious and excellent students. Their work was done well, consistently. They cared deeply about their academic performance. I was at home with them to assist and review their homework, daily. I was well aware of the level of their potential and actual performance, and their grades were not reflective of either. I was increasingly concerned about the long-term impact of their performance not being adequately acknowledged. How long can a student be expected to do A work and receive B's? And what are the chances of admission to competitive colleges with a B-plus grade point average?

So, along with the high risk of psychological and emotional damage from traditional schooling, there really wasn't any assurance that the quantitative validation—namely, excellent grades; purportedly the reason for taking the risks in the first place—would even be forthcoming. Not only did we feel that we could do a better job educating our boys holistically, with minimal-to-zero psychological and emotional damage, the risk to college admissions, in our minds at least, was no greater than that incurred by leaving them in school.

I ABSOLUTELY believed that home schooling was something God wanted us to do and, consequently, I believed that our faith in pursuing it would be more than adequately rewarded in the final analysis. Plus, I really thought the whole faith argument would win everybody over, or at least shut them up. And, of course, I was right. C. Madison and I both come from families that have "come this far by faith." It has been a dual faith: faith in God, and faith in education.

Historically, our families' access to educational opportunities was seen as a validation of that enormous faith. On both sides of their family, our sons were to be the fourth generation to receive a college education. We have had members of our families attending colleges and universities and earning PhDs since the late 1890s. Long before *Brown v. Board of Education*, the Civil Rights Act of 1964, or even the G.I. Bill made post-secondary education possible for the largest numbers of Americans ever, white or black, our families were attending college.

Our generation—C. Madison's and mine—was the first in our families to have access to private secondary education. And that was a big deal. Our parents, grandparents, and great-grandparents did not have access to the kinds of secondary educational opportunities we were now turning our backs on, and that was understandably difficult for them to accept.

It was really hard for us to link up their awareness of God's past grace with our belief in His ability to reward us in this endeavor. As is so often the case, when past faith has proven successful, there is a tendency to believe it can't happen again. But faith must be an ongoing endeavor. It requires a constant and consistent effort to fight the temptation to begin relying on the educated and successful self, and the institutions that contributed to those successes.

The decision to home-school placed us right back in a position of total dependence on faith. We couldn't, in good conscience, state definitively what the outcome would be. We just knew the outcome would be positive.

Our families were concerned about the practical consequences. No one wanted to see the family go backward. And since their ancestors had been attending the most prestigious colleges and universities since the 1930s, for our sons to do any less would be unacceptable and a sign of undisguised failure.

Talk about pressure! The admissions process at competitive, exclusive Ivy League–type colleges is never guaranteed. Even if our kids had remained at their prep school, there was no guarantee they'd be admitted to those colleges. All it takes is a cursory examination of the rates of admission from the top college preparatory schools in this country to verify that.

But if Charles, Damon, and Evan had remained in prep school and then been denied admission to the best colleges, it wouldn't have been seen by our families as a reflection of our dereliction of duty. Even though we fully grasped the fact that we were taking on an enormous responsibility, our families made it clear that if our sons were not admitted to the best colleges, it would be totally our fault and we would never be forgiven. Now, of course, nobody used such sinister terms, but, when you're family, you know the meaning of each and every unspoken word, arched eyebrow, and pregnant pause.

NEITHER faith nor institutionalized racism was an alien concept for our families. They had a deep and profound understanding of both. To hear them tell it, they understood them far better than we did, inasmuch as they had experienced both far longer. But they felt faith was best acted out within the parameters of available opportunities. We concurred that "faith without works is dead"; it's just that they felt those educational works should occur within the parameters of established educational institutions and we felt those works could best be achieved outside of them. They felt institutionalized racism was something to be dealt with, something to be faced, something to be defeated—and the sooner the better. Conversely, we felt the changing face of institutionalized racism—the subtleties, the nuances, the vagaries of polite society—made the psychological damage of racism on our children too severe. Our parents attended school when institutionalized racism was state sanctioned and supported with their parents' tax dollars: The battle lines were clearly drawn, and even a child could identify them. While I would never romanticize those eras the way lots of people do (so no, I don't think the 1940s and '50s were a great time!), I do think it might have been easier then for youngsters to understand what was happening.

My generation and my children's generation face a different set of challenges, and while things are certainly easier in terms of access, the potential for damage is still profound. When racism is overt and it adversely affects academic evaluations, the victim, even as a child, knows and can identify the problem.

Dr. Robert Coles, the famous Harvard child psychologist, interviewed a young black girl targeted by white racists as she integrated an elementary school. Her ability to pray for those attempting to torment her illustrates the ability of even a five-year-old to recognize that such behavior is indicative of a problem on the part of the tormenters. She knew she didn't have a problem; presumably, that's why she wasn't praying for herself. And while I certainly would never want my sons to experience anything like the trauma that child endured, there was no indication in her interview that she had internalized those hideous events.

On the other hand, when racism is covert, when it's subtle and insidious, how does a child process that? There's no yelling, no screaming, no name-calling. Everybody's being very "nice," but there's always some problem— and the problem seems to be you. There's nothing really wrong with your work—it's good, in fact—it's just not quite good enough. No one can tell you why it's not good enough, or how it can be improved; but really, what's wrong with a B? How can a child (or even an adult, for that matter) fail to internalize such behavior?

As the boys' parents, we felt there had to be another option between overt or covert racism. We weren't advocating home schooling as that option for all black kids. We just wanted to explore it for our own.

WE were and continue to be grateful for the inroads of access to education exemplified by *Brown v. Board of Education*. We applaud that decision (and not just because one of our relatives helped argue it, either). That decision was a victory for America. It moved us closer to closing the gap between our stated values and our conduct, and that's always a good thing, for individuals and for nations. But we believe it's possible to applaud *Brown* and its arguments and still make different choices for our own children.

While it may have appeared so on the surface, we weren't criticizing *Brown v. Board of Education* any more than we were criticizing our parents' decision to educate us in predominantly white schools. Every generation has an inherent obligation to determine, independently, what is best for its children. It's so easy to rest on the laurels of the past generation, to put forth that old, tired argument, "That's how my parents raised me, and I'm okay!" But have you ever noticed how often the people making that argument really *aren't* okay? Sometimes the legitimate desire to honor and respect one's parents can blind us to the necessity for change.

Changing educational direction for our sons was not a reflection of a lack of respect for our parents or the educational choices they made for us; quite the contrary. In fact, we were merely continuing their tradition of change, and following their example of responsibility, by seeking the best for our children. I gently reminded our parents how they had moved beyond their childhood education by seeking different choices for their own children. Both my parents attended public schools, but even in the face of opposition from family, friends, and neighbors, they opted for private school for their kids. My dad attended The Ohio State University, but he wanted different choices for his kids. C. Madison's parents attended historically black colleges, but C. Madison and his sister attended Dartmouth and Harvard. Those decisions weren't about a lack of respect for the choices of preceding generations: They were about making choices, even in the face of enormous costs, obstacles, and no guarantees. Similarly, C. Madison and I weren't criticizing integration or romanticizing segregation, and we certainly were not advocating home schooling for all black families. We just wanted the option to choose what we considered to be the best educational experience for our children, just as our forebears had had that option for theirs.

Here's the bottom line about external support from family and friends: It's great if you can get it, but I don't think the presence or absence of such support should be the determining factor in the decision to home-school. Ultimately, the responsibility for the holistic development of children rests with the parents; but, while I absolutely believe that to be true, I also know that the process of home schooling will be affected by a lack of support. Home schooling is a very difficult, complex, and time-consuming process, and, as with any other long-term process, the presence of support can be exceedingly helpful. Conversely, the absence of such support can make the process even more difficult—if you let it.

I think it's important to involve family, especially in decisions about children. There is much to recommend a longitudinal, multigenerational involve-

ment in the rearing of children, and the abysmal state of many families today highlights the impact of the absence of that involvement. So I think that even though we didn't do this, it's probably better to discuss the idea of home schooling before beginning, rather than presenting it as a done deal after the fact. Generally, people always respond most favorably if they are asked about something major before implementation.

But regardless of how or when the idea is presented, be prepared for some resistance; and the more involved and committed people are, the greater the resistance might be. After all, if people really care about your kids, they're going to have fairly strong feelings about everything that touches those kids' lives. Expect that and welcome it. Try to listen critically, not defensively, to all the issues—they can be very informative. But, ultimately, you have to make the decision and you have to make the decision work, even if nobody supports you and everybody thinks you're wrong.

There's an interesting story in 1 Samuel 30:3–6, in which David and his men return and discover that their city had been burned and their wives, sons, and daughters had been taken hostage. David's soldiers were very angry and upset, and wanted to stone him. I'm sure David would have appreciated a show of support just then—after all, his two wives had been captured too—but no support was forthcoming. But instead of becoming depressed or discouraged, we're told, "David encouraged himself."

Sometimes, with or without the challenge of home schooling, parenting can become quite daunting, and sometimes parents crave a word of support from family and friends. But what I've learned is that sometimes—and it's usually in the roughest of times—there won't be any support. Sometimes you need to encourage yourself.

6

WHAT ABOUT

THEIR SOCIALIZATION?

SOCIALIZATION WAS A prevailing concern of ours even before we began home schooling. We tried to be aware of the ongoing nature of socialization, and we looked for opportunities to model the standards we advocated. For us, socialization was the manifestation of the ethical and moral values we had actually transferred to our kids. In that sense, socialization is more than artic-ulating values and having the kids parrot them back.

I once heard Dr. Robert Coles speak on the moral development of chil-dren and adolescents. One of the most intriguing points he made was the fact that there is a world of difference between the ability to engage academically in moral reasoning and the ability to live a moral life. We desperately wanted our sons to be able to do both! What good is it to be able to engage in the aca-demic acrobatics of ethics, utilitarianism, existentialism, and ethical rela-tivism if one is unable to incorporate the challenge into the process of one's daily life? We felt that was the critical goal of socialization for our sons.

We incorporated our goals for their ongoing socialization into our design of a holistic educational environment. Spiritually, we focused our attention on assisting in their individual and personal relationship with Jesus: Fundamen-tally, we believe that effective socialization—positive and constructive en-gagement with other life forms, human and otherwise—is inextricably tied to a positive and constructive engagement with the Creator. We connected this ongoing spiritual development with the intellectual exploration of religion, philosophy, morals, and ethics. We worked at moving the issue of socialization from an assumption to a responsibility. We looked for opportunities to examine and discuss healthy versus unhealthy socialization patterns within the context of differing and sometimes conflicting belief systems.

The pragmatic elements of their socialization came through their immersion in diverse social, cultural, racial, and economic environments. Athletics and team sports, through Columbus Parks and Recreation centers, provided a great laboratory in which to observe their socialization process. Work at COSI provided a completely different exercise and observation opportunity. We added church activities, academic enrichment/residential camp programs, and NAACP academic competitions for further "exercise." Their world was far expanded beyond the norm of a private school education. We thought we were covering our bases.

Who knew others thought home schooling would relegate our kids to the pathetic arena inhabited by—and this is a quote—"crazy loser freaks"? We certainly never made that connection, but apparently we were the only ones laboring in darkness on this point. Tons of extraneous people felt a compelling urge to assure us that, in fact, that's what we were doing.

I hate to admit it, but in spite of all my best efforts in anticipating questions and developing witty responses, I was totally unprepared for the deluge of questions about socialization. The endless questions about the effectiveness of socialization in a home-schooling environment were amazing. More than questions of time management, objective measurements of academic achievement, and the presumed impossibility of any positive outcomes for college admissions, the socialization questions were relentless.

I was surprised that questions about socialization dominated the field of inquiry about our decision to home-school for a couple of reasons. For one thing, I have always viewed socialization as continuous and unavoidable. I never thought that when our kids stopped going to school they would stop being socialized. Socialization begins at birth and hopefully continues throughout one's entire life span: It's not as much an achievement or accomplishment as it is a process. As is so often the case with my myopic perspective on life, I thought because this view was so apparent to me it must be equally so to others. So it seemed kind of stupid and silly for people to keep asking about it, like it might be missed. Socialization isn't like comparative world religion, AP physics, or the opportunity to participate on a competitive equestrian team. Admittedly, everybody doesn't get stuff like that, but socialization? Everybody gets socialized; it's just that some people are more adequately socialized. Perhaps that's what the questions were really about: the adequacy of their socialization.

It can be difficult to determine the underlying motives that drive questions.

For one thing, what is being asked is frequently colored by underlying assumptions that haven't been critically examined even by the questioner. I couldn't tell if the questions were about the adequacy of the boys' socialization in the absence of school or about the adequacy of their socialization before they left school. When I asked what the real question was, I got the blank stare of hostility for an answer, as if the question was obvious on its face. Initially, I tried to respond lightly by pointing out that we were a family, and don't all families have some sort of social dynamic that impacts and influences socialization and the development of social skills? But my attempts at providing information tinged with levity did not address the issues sufficiently for our detractors. The socialization question just kept coming up. Lots of folks seemed reasonably certain we could perform the academic function, but almost no one thought we could handle the socialization function. Maybe the underlying issue or concern was a reflection of the perceived inadequacy of C. Madison's and my socialization. We have never been the most popular couple, the couple "no party can do without," or anything like that. So maybe the concern was that we might transfer our presumably inadequate socialization to our sons.

The other weird thing about this particular question was the rather obvious negative assumption that, in fact, the kids could not be socialized outside of school. Unlike other questions, which in comparison seemed somewhat neutral, the socialization question seemed completely negative. "What about their socialization?!!" The question always sounded as if it had double exclamation points following the question mark.

Have you ever had someone ask you a question for which they seem certain you have no correct or even appropriate answer or response? These are the kind of questions that have an implied-but-unstated "Gotcha!" at the end. This felt like that.

It's pretty difficult to validate or prove the effectiveness of the socialization process during adolescence. Let's face it, this is just not the most pleasant phase of human development. So, while our kids were sulking, pouting, and generally grousing and being ungrateful, we had the added joy of knowing that people thought all of it was tied to their inadequate socialization—as if teenagers in school are pleasant!

The emotional energy tied up in the question was off-putting. I wasn't seeing a similar intensity of inquiry about the socialization of children in schools, so it was hard to determine the cause of the massive level of interest in Charles, Damon, and Evan's socialization. It is clear to me now that a lot of people honestly could not imagine how the boys could be adequately or appropriately socialized outside of school.

Of course, it's easier to examine the issue objectively now that I'm no longer home-schooling. But while I was in the moment, experiencing a challenging home-schooling environment on a day-to-day basis, I was defensive — way too defensive to see any sincerity and genuine concern on the part of the questioners. It was also hard to decode the underlying race and class elements in the socialization question.

Across the board, the questions started out focused on the stuff you presumably miss when you don't go to school: band, team sports, plays, field trips, etc. But as we talked about other ways to participate in music, sports, and travel, the racial issue would inevitably emerge, and within the race issues lurked the class issues.

The racial issue of socialization tended to have one of two distinct focal points, depending on the race of the person doing the questioning. When black people asked, the focal point centered on preparation. No one black disputed the reality of institutionalized racism; however, there was a definite class divide about the most effective ways to deal with it. For low- and lower-middle-income black people, there seemed to be a greater realization of the severe limitations of the educational options available to their kids, and in an environment of limited and presumably inadequate choices, there is a logical willingness to consider what might be viewed as extreme measures if more choices were available. Pretty much across the board, poorer black people applauded our willingness to try unconventional methods in an effort to do the best for our kids. There was a sense within that sector of the community that strengthening kids before forcing them to confront institutionalized racism was the right thing to do. This realization wasn't that surprising as the direct, overt nature of institutionalized racism directed at black people without economic resources is hard to ignore. Those parents knew their kids were being inadequately educated and psychologically damaged, probably both as a result of their race and their socioeconomic status. So those parents were willing to consider some pretty extreme measures, including home schooling. (In all honesty, I should also point out that I don't know how much of the approval of our decision was tied to the perception of us as separating ourselves from the ranks of bourgeois Negroes by forsaking coveted private and public/suburban educational opportunities.)

Middle- and upper-middle-class black people had a somewhat different take on the whole issue of preparation. This really wasn't surprising, because one of the benefits of economic success, across racial lines, is the availability of options. If the issue was preparing the child to deal with institutionalized racism, then many affluent black parents felt strongly that the best and most effective option would be early exposure to the people who design and run those institutions. Such an option leads to the selection of "the best." It's not that they thought economic security could actually buy a race "pass," it's just that they seemed to think the impact of race would be less severe in exclusive institutions. This was seen as the lesser evil. As we all agreed institutionalized racism existed, there was real concern about the long-term impact of delaying our kids' exposure to it. The assumption on the part of many middle- and upper-middle-class black people was that by delaying the boys' experience with institutionalized racism, we were ensuring that they would be unable to cope with it when they ultimately had to confront it as young adults.

A rebuttal position was difficult, primarily because we could not definitely state that that dire prediction would not come true. We kept reminding people that this was an experiment; that's why we weren't trying it on anybody else's kids. An experiment implies that there is a foundational hypothesis, with supporting premises, leading to a presumptive conclusion. In other words, there is no guaranteed outcome.

We hoped that our outcome would be positive, but we were acting on faith. We had no data definitively to support the conclusion. Our foundational hypothesis in terms of socialization was that delaying the boys' exposure to institutionalized racism would positively affect their overall socialization process. The supporting premises were that: (1) a holistic environment is superior to a fragmented one in creating healthy, well-adjusted, adequately socialized young men; and (2) working toward excellence in any process, including socialization, is easier in a custom-designed environment than in one that is a forced fit. But we did feel that the empirical evidence of the range of quantitative successes by foreign nationals of African ancestry was something that supported our conclusion.

Of all foreign nationals, Africans consistently achieve the highest level of postgraduate education in the United States and Great Britain. C. Madison and I felt that was something to question critically. What impact does educational instruction by an adult image of the child have on that child's sense of self and his potential accomplishment? What impact does such an educational experience have on a child's overall socialization?

I think for a lot of black people this was just too painful a question to explore. After all, realistically speaking, home schooling just is not a viable option for every family or even every child. Most parents, regardless of race, ethnicity, or socioeconomic status, have to rely on traditional educational institutions. If those institutions have inherent biases and we know it and acknowledge it, the burden of guilt we feel as black parents would be almost overwhelming. I think that's why we are often reluctant to examine this issue critically.

. . .

WHEN I absolutely know what I'm doing—which is more than just knowing I'm right—I don't mind being questioned. As a general policy, I try to avoid situations where I'm doing something I don't do well. That's why I don't drive, I don't fry food, and I almost never iron.

Ironing is one domestic skill I have not mastered. While I absolutely love doing laundry, I am terrible with an iron: The temperature settings are confusing, the cord always seems to be in the wrong place, and I have burned myself more times than I can count. Similarly, while I am an excellent cook (really, everybody says so!), I cannot fry foods: I cannot get the temperature set properly; and I either burn the chicken on the outside or it's not done on the inside. And I am afraid of hot grease. (After years of trying, I have accepted the fact that frying foods is a deficiency in my culinary skill set, so I no longer try, though there is some merit in that saying, "If at first you don't succeed, try, try again." I tried and tried again, and I do love fried chicken, but I am not willing to devote any more time to the mastery of frying.) By the same token, I no longer drive. I haven't driven in seven years. I was never a good driver: Driving makes me nervous; I was not an especially attentive driver; and I have no sense of direction. I'm just grateful that I had enough sense to recognize my limitations.

I do not like the sensation of doing anything I don't do well. That's why it wasn't hard to give up ironing, frying, and driving: I don't do any of those things well. The problem with home schooling was that I had no way of knowing if I was doing it well or not! When you mess up ironing, you know. When you mess up chicken, you know. And when you mess up driving, you absolutely know. There are swift, immediate, and unmistakable signals of distress in those enterprises. But with home schooling, I just didn't know, so I had all this anxiety, which made it very difficult for me to discuss the issue of socialization objectively with anybody.

I knew I was right in pursuing home schooling. I just didn't know what I was doing. We were crystal clear on the goals and purposes. The confusing part was the methodology, the means of accomplishing the goals—and that was the area where the issue of socialization lived. I just didn't have the level of confidence here that I needed to be able comfortably to explore critical inquiries.

When I have worked at something until I have developed a level of excellence and the confidence that comes with it, I'm pretty impervious to doubts or criticism. When I'm "on my game" I don't really care what other people think. But when I'm not certain, when I'm not confident, when I'm strug-

gling and questioning myself every day, it's very hard to take even constructive criticism. In this instance I was uncertain and not at all confident about
how we were doing. I knew, or rather believed, we were pursuing the right
thing. I just wasn't sure we were going about it the right way.

I was trying to walk by faith through this process, and, of course, now I'm
glad I did. But the hard thing for me was the day-to-day effort required of
faith. The irony is that as we were trying to assure that the boys' socialization
didn't undermine their ability to think and act independently, that kind of independence was proving difficult for me to achieve and maintain for myself.
I wanted social acceptance. I was struggling with peer pressure even as we
were attempting to help the guys recognize and resist it. I had to admit to myself and to them that I really wanted the assurance of walking a path worn
smooth by others. I didn't like the process of making a path.

When the path is already worn smooth, you can look ahead, and even if
there are twists and turns, you know where you're going. You know where
you're going to end up, and you know what markers and landmarks to look for
on the way to measure your progress or signal that you've made a wrong turn.
When confused, you can look at a map created by others who have gone before you.

The faith thing was hard for me because the path wasn't smooth—it wasn't
even cut. Cutting the path was hard, and not always in a good way. We could
only do a small piece at a time, so we had to trust that we were going in the
right direction. We didn't know what was ahead. Sure, we knew where we
were trying to go, but we didn't know anyone who had ever gotten there this
way. Sometimes it felt like we could barely see our hands stretched out in
front of our faces. We didn't even know what milestones to look for with any
degree of certainty. It was exhausting, and it didn't leave me a lot of patience
with other people and their "Gotcha!" questions.

ONE way I handled the repetition of the socialization question was to equate
it with previous experiences I had had with the boys; that helped me put the
inquiries into some kind of focus and perspective. When we first had Charles
and Damon, I was like most first-time mothers: I was a bit daunted by the
thought of a new baby—and in my instance, I had twins! I'm not sure my
own mother thought I had enough sense to be trusted with two babies. And
no, the fact that I was a college graduate and a third-year law student did not
give her a sense of confidence. My mother was the one who taught me that
academic achievement and true intelligence need not intersect! True intelligence, a.k.a. common sense, is what allows people to navigate the life process

successfully: to maintain healthy relationships, build strong marriages, and create functional families. Academic achievement merely allows people to perform well in school and its various permutations. So, with that as a backdrop, I may have been more nervous than some other new mothers.

In any event, there were a lot of things I didn't know, and I got a lot of unsolicited advice that helped illuminate my vast chasm of ignorance. It's hard to say with certainty whether most of those comments were truly negative or if negative comments always make more of an impression. Either way, I got lots of what felt like negative comments, rather than helpful suggestions, about breast-feeding, how to ensure the navel is an "innie" rather than the dreaded "outie," and, of course, potty training.

The ongoing and inherently negative nature of the socialization question reminded me of the persistent questions about toilet training. When Charles and Damon were toddlers, everybody nagged me about potty training. "Aren't they potty trained *yet*?" "Don't tell me those big boys are *still* in diapers?" Now, granted, all of my kids were relatively old—read that as three—before they were toilet trained, but I continually reminded myself and the inquisitors of several things:

1. This is soooooo none of your business;
2. Nobody's asking you to buy or change one diaper (review note 1);
3. When they are toilet trained, they will know the correct terminology for the functions; and
4. I have yet to see a grown, able-bodied man who cannot go to the bathroom unassisted and conclude the process with an efficient wipe.

While it would have been nice if the boys had figured out the whole toilet thing sooner, I knew it wasn't something I was prepared to have a fit about.

Every day we talked about using the toilet. I told them how Mommy and Daddy liked to use the toilet and stay fresh and clean. The boys even went to the bathroom with C. Madison every morning. They never *used* it, of course, but they did watch. Every day he would ask them if they wanted to use the potty chair and every day they very politely declined. We never stopped talking about it, but we never went nuts over it, either. And when we did talk about it, C. Madison and I always used the correct terms for the process or function in question. I didn't want them saying things like "pee-pee" or "wee-wee" or "doo-doo" or "poop."

I knew they would learn to go to the bathroom eventually. Admittedly, I did have moments of fleeting doubt, fueled no doubt by the disapproving glances of others. However, I kept reminding myself that going to the bathroom is a lifetime thing, and I didn't want the process of learning "to go" to become a problem. I didn't want my sons to grow up with toilet training issues. I'm no psychologist, but I've read enough psychology to know that a screwed-up toilet training can lead to a screwed-up person. Apparently, there's a lot more going on there than just being able to recognize the urge to go. And even though nobody I've ever met actually remembers being potty trained, the process allegedly leaves an indelible mark on its participants. With that fact as a backdrop, I figured I could afford the luxury of giving the boys the flexibility of letting me know when they were ready. As everyone is eventually toilet trained, the question isn't "if?" but "how?" By the same token, as everyone is eventually socialized, it seems the question really isn't "Will they be?" but rather "How will they be?"

Charles and Damon eventually learned because they wanted to do everything their dad did—they were slow, *very slow*, but easy. Now Evan, as always, was another story altogether. For some reason still unknown to me, he just decided he wasn't going to use the toilet, ever. He would come and tell me he was going to "ur-nate," but then he wouldn't go to the bathroom with me. He refused to be impressed by the fact that that was the place everybody else went to "ur-nate." His rebelliousness, his obstinate refusal to comply, his taunting me—all of it was deeply annoying. The way he would come to me, smile so sweetly, and then refuse to do what he *knew* I wanted him to do— oh, it was too much! A murder seemed imminent, but fortunately, for both of us, Charles and Damon intervened. Even though they were only five, they were able to toilet train Evan in one, admittedly long, afternoon. I have no idea what transpired among the three of them in that bathroom, but by the time they emerged hours later, Evan was in underpants. He never wore another diaper and he never had an accident.

While I didn't know it at the time, that was just a preview of how the boys would be able to assist one another with various challenges in life. Probably the most important thing I learned from this was that my kids could teach me a lot. I almost let Evan suck me into a massive (and probably bloody) battle of wills, when what I really needed to do was to look for alternative approaches. The other critical lesson for me was the realization that sometimes the means are every bit as important as the ends. I carried those lessons into our efforts at home schooling.

By the time we began home schooling, I had those lessons to build upon. Once more I had to remind myself that some things are inevitable. Most important, I had to remember not to be so defensive. It's easy for me to forget that just because someone doesn't agree with me, that doesn't mean the person is against me. Something as radical as home schooling is guaranteed to generate a lot of questions and comments because education itself is such a hot topic. I had to try to remember that while everybody is pretty much united behind the ends—namely, education—the means were very much in dispute. And the socialization element of those means turned out to be a trigger point.

All through our home-schooling adventure, Charles, Damon, and Evan kept warning us of the terrible mistake we were making. They were convinced absolutely that, because of us, they were destined to be "queers," "lames," "losers," and general social outcasts. After all, how could anyone denied the opportunity of a traditional, educational experience become anything but a "freak"? Over the years, our sons encountered many adults who openly supported that flawed line of reasoning. (As an aside, let me just say how much I despise adults who sadistically make the job of parenting harder than it has to be by openly supporting adolescent anarchy! And then when your child comes close to destroying Western civilization as we know it, these same "buttinskis" shake their heads and mutter, "Kids today, tsk, tsk.")

I constantly pointed out to Charles, Damon, and Evan the painful and frightening truth that some people have strong social skills and other people just don't. "Geekiness," its origins, and its causes remain a deep mystery. Where does it come from? What triggers it? Why does it go into "remission" for some people when they reach adulthood? Is it like allergies? Who really understands why some children just know how to engage, how to play, and how to make friends, while other kids continually struggle, always saying, wearing, or doing the wrong thing at the wrong time?

At my fifteenth high school reunion (the boys were seven and five then), I was talking to another mom. Most of us in the class didn't have kids yet, so it was a small and general-overview conversation. As we watched our little ones, this other woman turned to me and blurted out, "God, aren't you glad your kids aren't geeks?!" Of course, I wanted to take the mature, sensitive, adult approach and act as if I didn't know what she meant, as if I didn't understand the word "geek." But I figured, why bother? This woman has known me since 1968. She knows I know what a geek is! I looked at her and said, "Girl, you know it!" It was one of those rare moments in my thirty-plus years of engagement in the company of white women when I felt we really understood one another.

Every mother, regardless of her ethnicity, race, or socioeconomic status, wants her child to be able to get along in the world. While I had never said it before that moment, I really was glad none of my sons were geeks. Geekiness has subtle signs and symptoms, and it's something a parent wonders about early on in those preschool play groups—that's where you look for the first signs. By the conclusion of kindergarten, I could see my kids had missed that bullet, and I was on to worrying about other things.

Based on my own admittedly nonscientific conclusions, I knew home schooling would not arrest, retard, or damage my kids' social skills. As we explained to the boys, all the geeks we've ever known, as well as the vast majority of the people in the burgeoning prison population, are products of school and its socialization process. (If you think it was hard explaining the broad scope of socialization to adults, try explaining it to three teenagers! In their defense, they didn't have any frame of reference for such a discussion.)

There is a socialization process that occurs in school, but it was not one we wanted for our sons. Schools alone cannot accept the full responsibility for the breakdown of society, but they clearly play a pivotal role. The socialization process that occurs in traditional educational institutions is flawed. And the flaws touch all racial, ethnic, and socioeconomic sectors of society. The tragic school shootings across the country are a frightening testament to the shortcomings of the socialization process of schools.

Based upon statistical analysis of the end product, the socialization of African-American male children in schools is particularly flawed. While the educational community offers many suggestions as to the causes of disproportionate failure within that segment of the elementary and secondary population, we had some ideas of our own. At least 80 percent of teachers in elementary and secondary schools—public, private, or parochial—are Caucasian-white women.* I know that diversity situation is challenging, be-

---

* Historically, we in the United States have used "Caucasian" and "white" interchangeably. This has not been the case globally. The definitions of "Caucasian" and "white" are conflicting, which has created a lack of clarity in the United States as immigration trends have changed. In *Webster's Ninth New Collegiate Dictionary*, "Caucasian" is defined as "of or relating to the white race as defined by law, specifically as composed of persons of European, North African or southwest Asian ancestry." In sharp contrast, "white" is defined in that same dictionary as "a group or race characterized by reduced pigmentation and usually *specifically distinguished from persons belonging to groups marked by black, brown, yellow or red skin coloration*" (emphasis mine). When the bulk of voluntary immigration to the United States was from Europe, these conflicting definitions were largely insignificant. However, with increased immigration from North Africa and Asia over the past decades, there are many native-born and naturalized U.S. citizens who fit the definition of Caucasian but not the definition of white; and in the United States these are critical distinctions. Generally, everyone who says he is white (and looks white) is also Caucasian, but everyone who says he is Caucasian is not white.

cause I was challenged by the gender diversity all by itself—and I'm the boys' mother! I wasn't even aware that I had any gender biases!

When African-American male children attend school, they are in an environment designed by Caucasian-white men and controlled by Caucasian-white women. The combination of race and gender diversity may explain, at least partially, why so many African-American male children end up in detention, suspended, and expelled.

When academic experts debate the relative merits of single-sex education for girls, the impact of gender is explored openly. Regrettably, it is much more difficult to engage educational experts in objective analyses of the impact of gender and race relative to black boys in schools.

ULTIMATELY, the challenge of socialization has some universal dimensions that apply to all kids, in any and every educational environment. I think all kids need to be exposed to other environments.

If your kids' dominant environment is economically defined as middle or upper-middle class, you probably need to look for enrichment experiences that expose them to a broader socioeconomic reality. One good way to do that is to look for your metropolitan community's arts activities or parks and recreation programs. Arts and athletics are great ways to expand your kids' environment.

Conversely, if your child's dominant environment is economically defined as poor or disadvantaged, you can look at some of those same arts and athletics options, but a broader approach probably makes sense, too. Look for opportunities to involve your children in activities outside their comfort zone. Look for free or cheap activities at local art museums or at the symphony, ballet, or opera.

If your kids' entire social and extracurricular life is tied up at their school, help them find similar interest-based activities in different environments. Similarly, if your kids' social and extracurricular life is tied up in church, to the exclusion of everything else, help them to seek out some broader environments for exploration.

All these issues of expansion apply to home schooling. At its best, home schooling (in my opinion) is about expanding a child's environment in every dimension. Home schooling provides a unique opportunity to expose kids (and allow them to expose themselves!) to varied spiritual, intellectual, and physical environments. Home schooling is not about staying at home and limiting kids' environment to their parents and other home-schoolers.

Contrary to conventional wisdom, very few people home-school in a limited environment—most home-schoolers spend quite a bit of time away from
their homes. Nevertheless, on a universal level, I think most kids are grossly
undersocialized. Single-environment socialization, whether that single, exclusive environment is created in a school or in a home, is inadequate. When
our children emerge into the broader world, they will be forced to engage
outside their racial, socioeconomic, religious, and academic classifications.

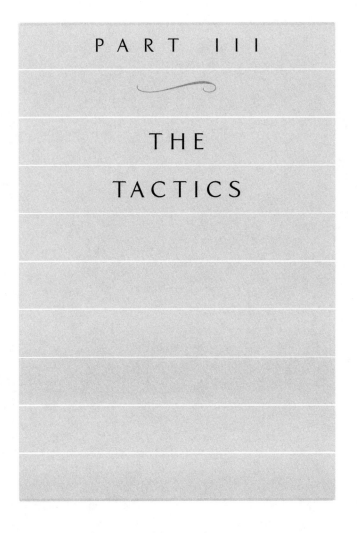

PART III

THE

TACTICS

7

HOW WE KNEW

WHAT THEY NEEDED

FIRST WE DECIDED to home-school; then we looked at the state of Ohio's requirements for home schooling; then we rearranged the basement, bought desks and a blackboard; and then, finally, when we couldn't avoid it any longer, we looked at the issue of curriculum. I know that's backward, and it probably was not the most logical approach, but that's how it was.

I think we may have unconsciously procrastinated on the curriculum issue because it was such a big, fat deal. The curriculum was the bridge between the thinking and the doing of the thing. Initially, we were focused on the theoretical, not the pragmatic, elements. Making the decision to home-school was more of a process of thought than a process of action. Admittedly, there were action points and time frames and all that good stuff, but it was still fundamentally a theoretical concept. Researching the state requirements was purely an academic exercise, something that was almost second nature for us. And while creating an actual, physical space for home schooling was a func-tional, pragmatic process, it wasn't that challenging. But deciding on the cur-riculum? Coming up with a curriculum is how you know you're really home-schooling.

For me, the decision about the curriculum was the most challenging as-pect of the whole thing. The curriculum moved our little educational ex-periment from the realm of the theoretical to the practical. The curriculum felt like the thing that actually made home schooling real, and that was a bit unsettling. Bottom line: I knew that the quality of the curriculum would set the tone for the quality of the education to be delivered.

When C. Madison and I finally sat down to look at the whole curriculum issue, it felt pretty daunting. This turned out to be yet another instance in which creating something original turned out to be a lot more difficult than critiquing something somebody else created. We had spent years identifying and discussing in great detail the shortcomings in the curricula at our kids' school. We had even critiqued the relative worth of the curricula at our alma maters. We were, after all, people who went to college during the seventies. Criticism of the "Establishment," in all of its manifestations and myriad forms, was our undeclared undergraduate major. But while we reluctantly came to the realization that the revolution, indeed, was not going to be tele-vised anytime soon, we never gave up on the concept of revolution alto-gether. As we aged, matured, and added adult responsibilities, we edged ever closer to the Establishment, but we never forgot the purer principles of the revolution. We just became wiser in what we really wanted to accomplish.

We wanted to be "in the world, but not of it." Even as we became success-ful and accomplished participants in and beneficiaries of this capitalist de-mocracy, we knew there were problems, even if they didn't directly affect us. We wanted to continue the effort to create a revolution in our lives and in the lives of our sons, and changing the format of their education seemed as good a place as any to focus those efforts. We reflected on all the aspects of our shared experiences with traditional curricula and tried objectively to identify what worked and what didn't. And, of course, the only way to determine what worked was first to determine our collective educational ideal.

We needed to determine what it was we wanted to accomplish through our kids' education. So we began talking about who, rather than what, we wanted Charles, Damon, and Evan to become as people.

Our examination centered on who Charles, Damon, and Evan "ought" to be. That examination led us to question who would know what they ought to be, because we knew it wasn't us. We felt certain our principal responsibility was far more limited than that: Our job was just to guide them in the process, not to make the determination for them.

As we began thinking about that, it became clear that we also had to try to figure out what it would take to guide them effectively. What would they need to know in order to navigate the process of becoming? These weren't new questions; it's just that we were exploring them on a deeper level. We were now asking ourselves questions about their telos—their highest good; their greatest aim—where before we had been asking normative and descrip-tive questions about academics, race, and culture. This is not to say that we had occupied a place of parental passivity previously, because we hadn't. We had done a lot of questioning of everything (at least on a surface level), and we certainly criticized everything. Educational criticism was our modus operandi, it was one of our raisons d'être, it was our "thing" and we were very, very good at it because—well, practice makes perfect. Home schooling, however, required a paradigm shift. (I know, I know, I detest that overused phrase too, but, in this instance, it is appropriate.) We had to shift from criticizing the educational plans of others to creating an educational plan for ourselves.

The question of what our boys ought to be formed the foundation for our home-schooling plan. The answer to the "ought" question came through much prayer and meditation. We realized that whatever their "ought" entailed, it would require that they first be people in holistic balance. We needed to create an educational environment where their spiritual, intellectual, and physical dimensions would receive equal attention and nourishment, and we needed a curriculum to support that kind of development. Our initial challenge in creating that foundational environment was finding a curriculum to support it. We spent a lot of time talking to educators, including other home-schoolers, and looking for examples of holistically balanced curricula.

Traditional educational institutions didn't seem to be able to provide the answers. Their curriculum suggestions were fine academically, and some of them had some interesting intellectual components, but there was a distinct void in the spiritual arena. Similarly, many of the established home-schooling curricula did not speak to our need for holistic balance either; too often, religious dogma was a substitute for spiritual development. Plus, the intellectual and corresponding cultural elements seemed to get short shrift. So, in keeping with the overall independent nature of the project, we decided to develop our own curriculum. (An added benefit was the fact that developing our own curriculum was a whole lot cheaper than buying one!)

We began the process of developing our curriculum with a commitment to creating one with a holistic balance between spiritual, intellectual, and physical development as the objective. We then examined the components of each of those three critical elements as a way of simplifying our long-term goals. In other words, rather than just looking at the enormous issue of spirituality all by itself, we decided to use the academic component of religion as an initial pathway. Similarly, we decided to use classical academics as a springboard to intellectual development. Finally, we determined that traditional lessons and organized sports would help establish the basis for physical development.

As always, we started with the easiest stuff first. As C. Madison and I had attended two of the best colleges in the country, we felt we knew what should be included in what would be termed a classical education. Now, we knew we probably weren't going to be able to incorporate all those elements—e.g., Latin, Greek, Hebrew, German, and French—we knew we couldn't do that whole foreign language thing. Our version of the classical education would definitely be abbreviated, but we felt certain it would be effective in terms of meeting our twofold intellectual and academic objective.

The objective was both internal and external. Internally, our goal was to create a framework for the kids' intellectual growth and development. Externally, the goal was to make them academically competitive for college admissions.

We felt well equipped to decide what the curriculum should include to achieve that. Practically speaking, the academic element was probably the easiest one for us to clarify and achieve, given our backgrounds. Also, we knew that such a "retrospective" approach would allow us not only to develop, but to maintain a standard of excellence within a narrow curriculum focused on depth rather than breadth. We were absolutely convinced that such a narrow focus would assist us in guiding the boys' intellectual development.

I know intellectual growth and development aren't tied to the number of AP classes taken or the number of fours or fives scored on the AP exams. In fact, I am convinced that a smaller array of course options might actually enhance intellectual growth and development.

Of course, I'm defining "intellectual" in a rather broad and undoubtedly uncommon fashion. Because we define the intellect as the ability to perceive and understand relationships, we could justify our academic focus on a core classical curriculum. Plus, we knew we couldn't offer the spectrum of course selections offered in an elite magnet, alternative, or suburban public high school, much less what was being offered in top-ranked prep schools. Yet, in terms of college admissions, those were the institutions supplying the future competition for our sons, so we had to create an equalizer of sorts. We determined that our curriculum had to be so distinctive and provocative that it would mandate at least a second look when held up in the midst of a potential ten thousand other college applications.

Now, if our focus on their future, quantitative success in the limited context of competitive college admissions seems obsessive and somewhat contradictory, remember, self-preservation is a strong, instinctual motivator: We had to achieve success there or our parents were going to kill us! Plus, it really mattered how our parents felt. (Okay, it really mattered a lot more to me than to C. Madison, but it still mattered.) And, in all honesty, the college admissions "game" really did not contradict or interfere with what we both agreed was our primary focus academically, namely, to facilitate the intellectual development of our sons.

WE were confident we could develop a viable academic curriculum as a springboard for our sons' intellectual development. While we knew they needed the academic component, in all honesty, their intellectual and spiritual development was much more important and interesting to us. Also, we were convinced that if we were successful in assisting and guiding their spiritual and intellectual growth and development, the issue of academic excellence ultimately would take care of itself.

While that assertion might seem a bit far-fetched at first blush, the more we thought about it, the clearer it became. Academic work isn't necessarily self-sustaining. I think that's why it's not that unusual to meet adults who voluntarily stop reading when there are no more exams or quizzes or papers to prepare. Conversely, once the intellect has been stimulated, it really does seem to be self-sustaining. That's where the commitment to lifetime learning begins.

With that assumption as a backdrop, it was easy to see the connection between spiritual development, also a lifetime process, and intellectual development. We decided to gamble on lifetime learning as the ultimate measure of success, rather than academic achievement.

Just as we could see the connection between academic work and intellectual enlightenment, we could also see the connection between intellectual enlightenment and spiritual growth. We did not want Charles, Damon, and Evan to strive to be competitive, to be better than others, or even to compare themselves to others, but rather to strive for excellence, to desire wisdom and understanding.

I think wisdom is the nexus, the connecting tissue, between spiritual growth and intellectual development. "Wisdom is the principal thing, *therefore* get wisdom: and with all thy getting get understanding" (Proverbs 4:7). I really believe that the diligent quest for wisdom and understanding will always result in the attainment of excellence as an inevitable by-product. Based on that belief, our goal each day encompassed the process of striving, not for a grade, not for class standing, not for SAT preparation, but for wisdom, for understanding, for excellence — the process of striving for one's personal best. The effort to know God, to know oneself in relationship with God, to seek the depths of one's potential — we determined *that* as the "ought," the telos: the highest good for ourselves and for our sons.

This was our epiphany. Far too often in school, our sons were compared to others, just as we had always been. And while the comparisons usually were favorable, we did not feel then, nor do we feel now, that comparative analysis—the basis of competition—aids in the quest for wisdom, understanding, or excellence.

So, college admissions formed the quantitative foundation for the development of our curriculum. We knew that, ultimately, our success there would be objectively measured by Charles's, Damon's, and Evan's future admissions (or not!) to highly competitive colleges. It was kind of a one-shot deal: If they were admitted to top colleges and universities, that would mean we had been academically successful, and if they were not admitted, that would mean we had failed academically. And for many observers that single admissions/rejection letter would be the sum total of the academic worthiness of our curriculum and our entire home-schooling adventure. For us, however, college admissions were but one part of our puzzle. Sure, we wanted our sons to get into good schools, but there's nothing unique about that: Most parents want their kids to get into good schools. I mean, nobody ever says, "Gee, come April 1, I hope my kid gets rejected from every school he applied to!"

The difference for us was that we were very consciously aware that college admissions, and even subsequent academic success in college, would not necessarily mean we had succeeded in our home-schooling experiment. The real measure of our success in guiding their quest for their telos would be the quality of their lives in college and beyond. So, while it was tempting to focus on the academic component of the curriculum exclusively, we knew that that element alone would be insufficient to guide them in the process of becoming.

For the sake of consistency, we determined that the curriculum offerings would not change—we simply would plumb each subject at a deeper and deeper level each year. Each year we studied the following subjects:

- Art History and Humanities
- Philosophy and Comparative World Religion
- Current Events, Politics, and Economics
- World History and Geography
- Science (usually Biology)
- Grammar and Writing
- Global Literature, Propaganda, and Paradox
- Mathematics

Originally, we included French, but, regrettably, we had to curtail the size of our "faculty" due to costs.

We examined each subject individually and collectively. We looked for opportunities to highlight the interdependence between the subjects and their relevance for spiritual, physical, and intellectual development. Spiritually, we decided that the consistent study, analysis, and discussion of religion, philosophy, ethics, and morality would be the logical curriculum components. Daily devotion, prayer, and meditation were individual pieces designed to move the boys' spiritual development from the limitations of academic study.

Religion, philosophy, and ethics can help establish a path to spiritual enlightenment. However, true spiritual enlightenment transcends reading and study. We wanted to create an educational environment in which our sons would feel encouraged to seek and treasure personal spiritual experiences. Toward that end, and with an eye toward the necessity of maintaining a narrow curriculum, we further curtailed those subjects. Our work in religion really focused on theology or the study of God. So as we read the Bible, the Qur'an, and the Hindu scriptures, we continually thought about and talked about humanity's quest to know and understand God. Similarly, our study of philosophy really centered on ethics and morality. This allowed us to look at and talk about what different people at different times and in different places thought about concepts like good, just, fair, and duty. The curriculum challenges centered around time management and managing the exploration of conflicting views.

Given our time constraints, it simply was not possible to cover all philosophies, so we went with the path of least resistance and just covered the recognized "biggies," e.g., Aristotle, Plato, Socrates, Kant, Nietzsche, Locke. The conflicting-views challenge was a bit more difficult, but possibly even more important. Here we tried to encompass diunital (both/and) thought. While we wanted the boys to share and even embrace many, if not most, of our spiritual beliefs and values, we didn't think we needed to denigrate the belief systems of others; and we were excited to see their genuine interest in and enthusiasm for religions, philosophies, and values that did not match up like a transparency over ours. I'll admit, sometimes I was a bit nervous, too, but I had to rest in the knowledge that if what one believes to be true is true (with a capital T), there's no reason to be afraid of knowing and understanding the conflicting truths of others.

Physically, we focused our attention on the development of strong bodies and a recognition of the importance of cooperative play. We focused our energies on physical activities and created opportunities for play every day.

Sometimes the boys seemed especially boisterous. (With three boys, that was a daily, and sometimes hourly, occurrence!) One of the great benefits of home schooling was flexibility. On those days when they needed more play-time, we just gave them more playtime. Sometimes C. Madison would take the afternoon off and take them fishing. Sometimes they just needed to be outside. Sometimes we just turned them outside, for unstructured play, to run laps, to work out, or to swim.

We tried to pay attention to their need for physical activity. (They were not penalized because, at the ripe old age of eleven, they couldn't sit still all day.) Part of our professional work involves consulting and training for adult learn-ers. We have learned not to ask adults to remain seated and even pretend to pay attention for more than 90 to 120 minutes at a time. So whenever our kids exceeded that time limitation, we were pleased. Plus, sometimes you need to run and holler, especially after an afternoon of the *Aeneid*!

One definition of "intellect" declares it to be the ability to understand and perceive relationships. Intellectually, we just wanted to escape academic busywork. We wanted to free Charles, Damon, and Evan from an exclusive focus on math facts to a more inclusive understanding of mathematical con-cepts. We wanted them to escape the anxiety of trying to do eight zillion math problems in one-tenth of a minute. We wanted them freed from the drudgery of vocabulary words, out of context and dryly displayed on a page. We wanted the luxury of reading broadly and transcending the boundaries of "age appro-priateness." We wanted the freedom of exploring more than Europe in any course called World History. We wanted the freedom to include writing as-signments across the curriculum. We really wanted the freedom to explore subjects with the kind of intellectual rigor that is rarely achievable within the limits of forty-five-minute classes and six-week grading periods.

School went year-round for us, so we had time to explore, and felt enor-mously free to explore, deeply. For the sake of future college admissions, we knew the boys needed to read all of Shakespeare's plays. But for the sake of their own intellectual development, we knew they needed to read Chinua Achebe, Stephen Biko, and Zora Neale Hurston, too. We used the assigned reading lists from the syllabi of interesting courses at The Ohio State Univer-sity as creative boosts. Long's Bookstore, a longtime staple of the university community, regularly posted the syllabi for most university classes and car-ried the necessary texts. (We began using college texts right from the begin-ning, because intellectual rigor requires intellectual challenge. When the boys' math teacher required an essay on the concept of symmetry along with their regular problem sets, we were delighted!)

C. Madison and I developed a curriculum for home schooling by relying on our past academic experiences. For us, given our appalling lack of advance planning, this was a great approach, but by no means is it the only approach. Here are some other curriculum-development ideas:

If college is something you're looking forward to for your home-schooler, one approach is to contact colleges and ask for an application. When you receive the application, it will provide a very clear idea of what the admissions requirements are. Most of that information can also be found at your local high school guidance counselor's office. And you can find most colleges' admissions requirements on their website: Once you get the link, click on "Admissions" and everything you ever wanted to know about course requirements and standardized test requirements will be outlined. Once you have that information, preferably from several different colleges and universities, you can begin looking for textbooks.

Local college bookstores provide a wealth of information and resources. Once you know what courses you want to include in your curriculum, you can go to the local college bookstore and browse for those subjects. Courses will be listed and displayed by discipline—e.g., History, Literature, Calculus, etc.—and by difficulty—i.e., 100-level courses are usually introductory courses, and the difficulty goes up in accordance with the course numbers. After you select the appropriate beginning point, you can purchase the textbook and then call the publisher and request a teacher's copy of the text. (You'll have to convince them that you're a teacher and not some university student looking for an unfair advantage, but we found most publishing companies to be very helpful.) The teacher's copy will typically come with a fairly detailed sample syllabus. We used and customized those syllabi with great results.

Another option with the college-text approach—if, like us, you decide to use graduate students to supplement your teaching endeavors—is to use their expertise (and sometimes their graduate adviser) to select the texts and the syllabi. If you go that route, make sure you have these advisers give you a hard copy or computer file so you have accurate records of your kid's academic progress from one school year to the next.

If you're reluctant to develop your own curriculum, there are tons of curriculum packages available, complete with detailed daily lesson plans. The Internet is loaded with such sites, and some of them are included in the resource guide at the end of this book. We never used any prepackaged curriculum, so I can't recommend any of them. But be flexible: Start with the smallest purchase possible and see if it works for you and your family. If it does, great—buy the whole thing with confidence. But if it doesn't, you're not out a lot of cash. (Those curriculum packages are not cheap!)

Another good, often-overlooked source of information is the public library. Librarians have got to be some of the most informative people on the planet, and they are so willing to help—and they don't charge. Ask the librarian to help you develop a grade- and age-appropriate curriculum for your child. At the very least, ask for a bibliography of recommended reading, and whether the library hosts reading groups or clubs for your child's age group.

Libraries are also solid locations for general legal information, so they're wonderfully nonthreatening places to examine the legal requirements for home schooling in your state. Home schooling is not federally regulated, which means that each state develops its own requirement. Some states have quite simple requirements, and other states' requirements are more detailed.

Regardless of your views on the viability of your state's laws and requirements, little can be gained by not knowing what those requirements are. Once you explore the requirements, you can determine if noncompliance is something you want to examine as an act of civil disobedience. But ignorance of the law is really inexcusable.

Ohio requires the parent to notify the State Board of Education of the intent to home-school. A notice is also to be sent to the local school district, which is then charged with tracking the child's annual progress, either through standardized testing or review of a portfolio of the child's work, at the end of the year. Ohio also mandates a specific number of instruction hours by an adult with a high school diploma or GED.

Most state regulations can be examined at the local library. Armed with that general information, you'll be prepared to contact your state's Board of Education. It's also a good idea to check the Internet for general legal information on your state's requirements. Lots of other home-schoolers enter chat rooms to discuss their legal experiences and what they've learned.

THERE'S a lot of information out there, and at first it might seem daunting. But I've never met anybody who did a bad job because they had too much information.

8

HOW WE KNEW WHAT

WE COULDN'T TEACH

AT FIRST THIS seemed like one of the hardest issues, because it was kind of tricky. It felt as if there was the definite potential for a conflict of interest in hiring other people to teach in our home-schooling environment. Usually, the term "home schooling" implies education that occurs at home, presumably with the parent—generally the mother—doing the bulk of the teaching. On any number of levels, we didn't match that implied profile of the home-schooling family.

Families undertake the challenge of home schooling for a number of different reasons, and often those reasons are as unique as the families involved. By design, we were embarking on an experiment: We weren't following a pre-designed format. But just as when a customized house is at the design stage and there is some examination of preexisting properties, we were trying to remain original in our design while simultaneously examining the work and ideas of others. We wanted to do the best job we could for our sons. As we weren't trying to prove anything, we could afford to be open and flexible. Most of our educational plan was experimental, meaning most of it was customized. We tried to take a wide-lens view of what was available, but trying to match up our design with some predetermined template wasn't really our first priority. It was just something to think about.

Some other home-schoolers asked us why we were attempting to home-school if we weren't going to go all the way; meaning, I suppose, doing the teaching ourselves. And that was a legitimate, yet ironic, question. The legitimacy of the question was obvious: What was the point of going through all the headaches to home-school if we were going to duplicate certain core elements of educational institutions?

I think some people saw this as a question of our true level of dedication to the concept of home schooling. The irony lay in being asked to justify our educational choices for our children by other home-schoolers, people who presumably left traditional educational institutions to avoid just such requirements. Nevertheless, as with much of the criticism we received, it was beneficial because it kept us from slipping into unquestioned acceptance brought about by semiconscious complacency, the very thing we were trying to escape.

As we struggled to reach what C. Madison referred to as "escape velocity," we were constantly challenged to think about and sometimes to defend every single choice we made, and, in retrospect, I can see that that was a very good thing. In thinking about the possible conflict of interest between home schooling and hiring outsiders as teachers, it became clear that we really were not dedicated to the idea of home schooling as much as we were to the idea of providing our sons with the best possible holistic educational environment. Once we cleared that up, we were able to evaluate the idea of using teachers objectively.

Although we had had our share of differences and issues with teachers, we both knew that when you find a good one, you've found a rare and wonderful thing. The problem for us was that we hadn't had a lot of truly good teachers, and neither had our sons. We began by defining what we meant by a good teacher, because we didn't want to establish unattainable goals. Using high standards as an excuse is tantamount to what Kant calls "the lying promise."

Our standard for a good teacher was defined as follows: A good teacher is a strong communicator, knowledgeable, and full of passion for the art of teaching and compassion for the person being taught. I knew that because I had some good teachers, excellent ones in fact, including Miss Washaball at Highland Elementary School, Mr. Muir and Ms. Johnson at Hilltonia Junior High School, and Mr. Wong, Mr. Fry, and Mrs. Clark at Columbus School for Girls. I also had some good teachers at Wellesley—Ms. Evans, Ms. Putnam— and one at the Ohio State College of Law—Mr. Shipman. But the sad fact is, that's only eight outstanding teachers in the course of eleven years of formal education, during which I was taught by more than fifty-three different teachers.

I considered myself blessed to have had those good teachers, because it made the process of establishing standards and knowing what to look for a lot easier than it would have been if I had never had the opportunity to be taught by them. One thing was certain: Good teachers are not particularly easy teachers. They didn't "give" grades; they helped their students earn them. And, most important, even when my grades were not excellent, a lot of learning, a lot of growth, and a lot of correction occurred. A good teacher sets high standards and encourages students to meet or exceed those expectations.

A good teacher can make all the difference in the world, and sets the tone, actually creating a place for learning to occur. Conversely, a bad teacher can impede the learning process by shifting the student's focus from the subject to how much the student despises the teacher. A good teacher can create that magical moment when time seems to stand still, when you're captivated, mesmerized, wanting to drink it all in—no, not all the time, not every day, but you don't need it every day; occasionally is more than enough. Because even when it's sporadic, it's enough to hook you: keep you open, coming back, hoping, and waiting for more. That's the kind of teacher we wanted to be, and that was the only kind I was going to hire.

C. Madison and I knew there were some things we just were not qualified to teach. Actually, that's not exactly true: There were some things I knew *I* was not qualified to teach; added to that, there were some things I simply had no interest in teaching. C. Madison, on the other hand, was more than qualified to teach everything through middle school, at least, but there was also the issue of time constraints.

Being self-employed meant we had flexibility in our schedule. We could begin work at four-thirty A.M., stop at seven-thirty A.M., resume at eight-thirty A.M., stop at two P.M., resume at eight P.M., and stop at midnight. We could do whatever we wanted; our schedule was negotiable. Travel was the exception. As most of our clients are out of state, we spend a good deal of time on the road. Sometimes we were able to maintain separate schedules, so one of us could be at home, but not always. When necessary, we just planned to travel with the kids—and use the travel as an enhancement to their studies, especially geography. However, we couldn't dispense with a schedule altogether, and because our business was our only source of revenue, we couldn't just stop working and teach full-time.

So, we decided to look at our curriculum and select courses we thought we would love to teach. We figured if we loved a subject, then taking the time to study it, teach it, and discuss it would be a joy—even if we were doing it with our children. We didn't kid ourselves: We knew that the actual work of teaching would not always be fun. Kids have an uncanny ability to suck the joy out of any number of endeavors, and ours were no exception. We knew that they didn't want to be home-schooled and that they would be bringing a lot of angst to the process. That was how we knew we needed to arm ourselves with an abundance of enthusiasm. We were convinced that our love of the subjects we would be teaching would help us overcome their resistance.

Unfortunately, even an abundance of love does not equate to creating extra hours in each day: We still had the original twenty-four to work with, and we weren't sure that would be enough. The presence of love still left the challenge of scheduling, and the schedule had to be broad enough to include time for more than just teaching. The whole process of preparation for teaching—namely, study—meant we really needed to schedule large chunks of time before we could even think about teaching—and that was just for subjects we genuinely loved and cared about passionately. The subjects we didn't love—and in my case, that included subjects I hated, loathed, and was afraid of ("Algebra, Science, and French; oh my!")—we agreed to farm out. That was a big help, but it didn't fully resolve the time/scheduling dilemma. Even the subjects we weren't going to teach required a time commitment from us. There were still the administrative details to cover: The selection of teachers, decisions about the texts, discussions about goals and objectives, reviewing the kids' progress—all of that and more would require time, and we needed to plan for that as well.

Our next step included a series of confirmations and agreements. We reconfirmed our decision to home-school and we reconfirmed our curriculum choices. We agreed we would do the bulk of the teaching ourselves, and we agreed to supplement our efforts by hiring trained professionals. Finally, we agreed we would be very selective in the hiring process and look beyond academic credentials. We were then ready to divvy up the course load. I agreed to teach Art History and Humanities; Philosophy and Comparative World Religions; and Global Literature. C. Madison agreed to teach World History and Geography. We agreed to co-teach Current Events, Politics, and Economics as a joint course, as well as Grammar and Writing. That left Science, Mathematics, and French as courses to be out-sourced.

It wasn't particularly difficult to determine what we couldn't teach. The really hard part was figuring out how to teach the things we thought we could. This was especially challenging in the issue of team-teaching. One example was in our efforts to co-teach Grammar and Writing. This was a battle from start to finish—literally. C. Madison is, in a word, a fanatic about grammar. He really loves grammar, pays close attention to it, and thinks it is critically important. He can actually define a gerund, for God's sake. Who, besides William Safire, even knows what a gerund is, much less cares about its correct usage? Obviously I don't, and so I was concerned about our collective efforts to teach Grammar and Writing. I know grammar is important, both academically and for ease of comprehension. But I also know an obsessive focus on grammar can have a chilling effect on the creative process of writing. Conversely, C. Madison thinks the artistic aspect of writing is much overrated and no creatively crafted sentence can hold a candle to a well-structured one. I wanted to focus our energies on creating an environment in which writing was not seen as a chore or something to be dreaded. I wanted to encourage the free flow of our children's ideas onto paper. I wanted them to learn to be comfortable with writing, and C. Madison wanted them to develop a practiced level of grammatical expertise. Throughout the years we home-schooled, this was a constant struggle. Our compromise, at least theoretically, was that the boys would present an outline, followed by a first and second draft (and sometimes a third one), ending with the final paper. I would review the outlines and first drafts for content, organization, and the clear expression of ideas. C. Madison would review the second draft for grammar, punctuation, spelling, and syntax. We combined our efforts for the review of any subsequent revisions. That way, both our subject-matter objectives were met. We included writing assignments across the curriculum and our teachers helped.

Another challenge presented itself in co-teaching Current Events, Politics, and Economics. We relied on *The New York Times*'s "Week in Review" for current events. Each Monday, everybody had to select one article to read aloud and then lead a discussion on it. We never knew what would capture their attention. Occasionally, it was obvious that articles were selected solely for length. How did we know? When you walk in on kids counting the lines in an article, that's a clue right there. But the point is, we had no way of knowing what would be selected, and often C. Madison and I didn't realize how divergent our views were on certain topics. Politics and economics, while separate disciplines in themselves, were very much a part of everything that happened in the world and were reported in the *Times*. It was a greatly challenging experience for all of us, this process of learning to disagree, intensely, without being disagreeable. Sometimes C. Madison and I had such divergent views from each other and the kids that I wondered if we were even discussing the same event. Even as we were teaching, we were learning that there really are diverse opinions that have elements of truth, and that they are all worthy of consideration, even if you cannot reach consensus. Previously, I had assumed that if we were going to co-teach we would have to be of one mind, but in retrospect I realize that the most critical lesson "taught" was the necessity of actively listening to the contrary views of others. As the boys grew and matured, inevitably their views moved further and further afield from those we set forth, and while it was initially shocking, I came to relish their ability to present contrary, yet rational, arguments.

IF you decide to home-school, try to do an accurate assessment of your academic and intellectual strengths and weaknesses. At the same time, carefully and realistically look at your time constraints. Do you have the time to develop a level of expertise in areas of weakness?

Where you see areas of limitation, don't be discouraged: Nobody knows everything. Start looking for resources to reinforce you in areas where you are weak. A good place to start is with your State Teacher's Association. They may have a listing of retired teachers and their areas of specialization, and while many or even most of those teachers may not be interested in returning to the field, some might be quite intrigued by the prospect of working in the controlled academic environment of home schooling. Other good resources include local colleges and universities, including community colleges. Make a determination of the areas in which you need help and then call those academic departments. This was the route we took, and we were consistently pleased with the results. Simply explain that you're looking for part-time teachers or tutors, and feel free to stipulate what level of academic completion you want in the tutors. (For example, we stipulated master's level or above, but that's not necessary in all instances.)

When we explained what we were looking for, the colleges put a posting up on the job boards in that department, with our names and phone number, and interested graduate students called. We spoke to each person on the phone first and explained what we were trying to do. Most people were curious and interested in exploring the situation further; those were the people we scheduled for interviews. Some people let us know right away that they were very opposed to the whole idea of home schooling and felt it undermined the tradition of free, public education in the United States; obviously, we didn't need to interview them. Issues of our holistic objectives and the individual teacher's academic objectives, along with a determination of textbooks, assessments, scheduling, conduct, and compensation, were discussed during the interviews.

We always ended up with at least three or four people to interview. We tried to schedule the interviews so that Charles, Damon, and Evan could sit in, so we could gauge how we all meshed. If you decide to use outside teachers, it's important to remember that this will become a very collective experience and that the typical boundaries between student, teacher, and parent won't be as clearly delineated as usual. C. Madison and I were consistently involved in the academic process, even when we weren't the designated teacher. Because our business is home-based, one of us was always present during class. Even if we weren't in the same room (and we generally weren't unless the discussion became so interesting we begged to be included!), we could certainly tell from casual listening and observation whether there were difficulties with conduct or comprehension.

Comprehension issues were pretty much left up to the teacher. After all, if I felt I was competent to address those issues, I'd be teaching the subject myself! But the conduct issues, rare though they were, C. Madison dealt with fairly instantly. It was very important to us that the boys view this holistic educational experience with a keen understanding of the critical role of reciprocal respect in the community of student and teacher.

Resources do not have to be limited to academic professionals. Another source of support can be found in the larger community. Whatever your child's interest or your interest on his behalf, someone in your community has expertise in that field. Don't be hesitant to contact people in your community to discuss your home-schooling plans. Don't be afraid to ask for assistance, but also don't be presumptuous. When you ask for something more than a brief telephone conversation, be prepared to offer something in exchange. The exchange need not be purely financial, although money's always an easy thing to quantify. But if money's limited (and isn't it always?), explore some other options. Maybe there's a service or skill you could barter in exchange for that person's time and expertise. Be creative and take advantage of the flexibility that home schooling provides.

Using outside teachers is not an essential element of home schooling or home-schooling success. Tons of people home-school successfully without using outside teachers. Like home schooling itself, the use of outside teachers is an individual choice for each family. Just as you shouldn't allow yourself to be pressured to use outside teachers, you also shouldn't allow yourself to be pressured not to use them. Carefully examine and quantify your situation; specifically, your time, your talents, your resources, and your kid's need for expanded social interactions with other adults. As your kid gets older and academic work becomes more challenging, your preparation time will expand—rapidly. Make sure you factor that into your analysis.

Finally, honestly look at the impact of home schooling on your overall rela-

tionship with your child. If it appears that you are really getting on each other's nerves, intensely, bringing in an outside teacher may make a lot of sense: It gives you and your kid a break from each other, and it relieves some of the time constraints and pressure of preparation for you. And try not to agonize over it. If the decision, whatever it is, turns out not to work, change it and try something else.

9

HOW WE GOT TUTORS

ONCE WE HAD our topic list, we were ready to begin our search for the per-fect teachers/tutors. We are fortunate to live in Westerville, a suburb of Columbus, Ohio, and while it's not Boston, there are a number of colleges and universities nearby, including The Ohio State University, Capital Uni-versity, Otterbein College, Franklin University, and Columbus State Com-munity College. I got my law degree at OSU and I've taught as an adjunct faculty member at Franklin and Columbus State, so I have some familiarity with the demographics of our local academic community.

I was extremely confident as I began the hunt. Regardless of the abun-dance of apocryphal stories to the contrary, I was confident of our ability to track down the ever-elusive qualified black male. And I was right! And it was easy: there were no elaborate traps to be set; no complicated bait was re-quired; we didn't even need any special equipment; and it wasn't even as ex-pensive as I had feared!

As math was the one subject neither of us could even consider teaching, it seemed the most logical teaching position to fill first. I decided to focus my search at OSU because it's so enormous, and I figured that with upward of fifty thousand undergraduate students alone, there had to be some black male graduate students there somewhere. I started in the white pages of the phonebook, flipped through to the business section, looked up "The Ohio State University, Academic-Administrative Offices, Mathematics—Dept. of," copied down the number, and called. I explained to the woman who answered the phone that I was looking for an African or African-American male graduate student to teach/tutor three young boys in mathematics. Imagine my surprise at her lack of surprise. She didn't miss a beat, nor did she seem particularly interested in the implications of my request. She merely took my name and phone number, and while she declined to make a recommendation, she said she would post a notice. Within three days, we had received several calls, met and interviewed Dr. Mulenga, and retained his services to teach the boys math for three days each week. That's right: In less than one week we spoke with three candidates, conducted a final interview, and hired an African male teacher who already had a PhD in mathematics! Dr. Mulenga worked with the boys for the entire first year.

Dr. Mulenga was from Zambia and possessed a uniquely different view of education from the typical U.S. view. While this was not one of our stated objectives, it was a blessing for us to experience such an expanded perspective of education. The view of education as a privilege takes on a different patina when expressed by someone from a nation without access to free public education. Everyone in the United States talks about the importance of education, but what we experienced with African scholars transcended talk: Everything about the learning process was serious and compelling.

Dr. Mulenga approached the teaching of mathematics with the kind of reverence one usually associates with the transmission of religious views. His seriousness and commitment translated into a level of expectation on the part of the kids that was vastly different than anything we had witnessed previously. Granted, there were many complaints, but never addressed to him. Our sons recognized, even as young children, that this was serious to him, and that they and their performance were important to him as well. While his expectations were high (in fact, I often thought they were too high), the boys worked diligently so as not to disappoint Dr. Mulenga.

Frequently, Dr. Mulenga held class for the boys in the mathematics building at OSU. The boys seemed to enjoy going there, and while I wasn't thrilled about them spending a lot of time on a college campus, I felt the overall experience was well worth the risk of potential damage inflicted by premature exposure to all those things that make college fun. The level of mutual respect and consideration forged between this slender young African PhD recipient, far from home, and three young African-American boys, was remarkable, and helped set the stage for the rest of our home-schooling experiment.

At the end of our first year together, Dr. Mulenga was offered a faculty position at a college in the Cleveland area. We were sorry to lose him, but, at the same time, we were very pleased for him.

Our next math teacher was Mr. Francis Cobbina. Almost immediately, we collectively moved to unofficial adopted-family status, and he became Francis, by his request, to us all. Francis was a Ghanaian PhD candidate in physics at OSU, and probably one of the world's great teachers. This isn't to imply that Dr. Mulenga wasn't a superb teacher, because he was. The chief difference was that Francis almost instantly established a rapport with the boys, in particular, that was familial. That familial connection transformed the academic experience into a truly holistic one.

Francis didn't just know how to count. What was remarkable about Francis was his incredible level of involvement and active engagement with the boys. He understood that Charles, Damon, and Evan were still young boys—boys with promise, but still boys—and he seemed more than comfortable with that. Francis really embraced what we were trying to do. His contributions to our efforts were invaluable and truly profound. As an African foreign-national scholar, he, too, had a profound commitment to and appreciation for education, and he worked very hard to communicate that to the boys. What was interesting was more than the concept: It was the way he chose to convey it. Francis did not do a lot of lecturing. He merely conveyed his own intellectual enthusiasm, beginning with mathematics, but quickly and comfortably transcending and including those concepts and principles into broader discussions.

Charles, Damon, and Evan responded marvelously to Francis's academic, intellectual, and spiritual challenges; in fact, we all did. He frequently stayed after class and discussed issues of educational policy and politics in general—domestic, Ghanaian, African, and global.

Once more, an unanticipated benefit emerged: They developed an intellectual and social bond that enhanced the boys' academic experience. The more Francis became a part of their lives, the more work he was able to extract from them. They struggled to please him, and when they couldn't meet his expectations he suffered. His assessment of their shortcomings as a reflection of his own as a teacher was fascinating. The educational process became a collective responsibility that enhanced its effectiveness for the boys.

Francis called the Saturday afternoon of their first SAT test to see how they felt it went. The day the results came back, he took them to lunch and told them he knew they'd do better when they were fourteen.

During the year before their thirteenth birthday, Charles and Damon were preparing for their Rites of Passage, and Francis taught them enough Ashanti that they were able to give an authentic welcome.* Our focus in the Rites of Passage was to give the boys an opportunity to spiritually, intellectually, and physically examine the past, present, and future of African-American men. Francis was there through the entire year's progress, and of course he attended the welcoming ceremony.

Francis taught them holistically, addressing each boy in his entirety as an individual. Even Evan, who regrettably inherited my math-disability gene, was an obvious delight to Francis, who never gave up his belief that one day Evan would grow to love mathematics. It never happened, but that deficiency in no way interfered with Francis's involvement with and influence on the boys.

Ultimately, Francis accepted a position as a physics professor in a local college. As with Dr. Mulenga, once more we were saddened by our loss, but happy about the long-overdue recognition and reward for our brother. I doubt that any of us will ever forget our two years with Francis as a daily part of our lives.

Our last male tutor was an African-American PhD candidate in one of the engineering programs, and he was just a tad too intense. While his political views were provocative, his overall frustration with the institutionalized racism within his department was overwhelming. We had no doubt as to the veracity of his views, but we didn't want his reactions to that racism to be so clearly evident in his encounters with the boys. Part of our rationale for home schooling was to control the timing and temperature setting of their exposure to institutionalized racism. We weren't trying to deny the existence of it or to minimize its impact; we just didn't want them to be caught up in the intensity of reaction. We wanted to be able intellectually to explore the complexity of the issue, in detail, before they experienced it even vicariously. So that relationship was short-lived; in fact, I think it lasted only about eight months.

The other math tutors we hired were also African-American, but they were young women. The first was a master's candidate in the College of Education at OSU, and our last tutor was Ms. Whitaker, a young sister who held a master's in chemical engineering and was pursuing a doctorate also.

We pretty much relied on the same process for each tutor we hired. Virtually all of them were in one of the graduate programs at OSU. All but one worked with us for at least a full calendar year. All of them exceeded our expectations in terms of their involvement with and commitment to the boys

---

* Many ancient cultures used rites of passage to mark the end of childhood. Similarly, some religions use rites of passage to mark spiritual milestones. We incorporated both objectives. For more information, please see www.nabrit.com/boyz.

and their development. And all of them were black. I should point out, however, that in at least two instances we interviewed candidates who were not
black. First, we interviewed a Caucasian-white male as a possible Spanish
tutor. His prior experience as a Jesuit missionary in the Amazon was undoubtedly fascinating, but he didn't feel like a good fit for our home-schooling project.

Our second failed attempt at diversity occurred when Charles the younger
expressed an interest in studying Japanese. When our prospective Japanese
tutor, who was a Japanese foreign-national student at OSU, arrived for the interview, he seemed somewhat surprised by the fact that we were black. In
fact, when I answered the door, he asked for Mrs. Nabrit, repeatedly, and
when I explained, repeatedly, that *I* was Mrs. Nabrit, he was visibly discon-
certed. I had prepared tea, which I frequently do in the afternoon, but when
I offered him a cup he told me he could not drink tea prepared from tea bags.
The tea was prepared from loose tea, but there didn't seem any reason to be-
labor the point. I decided to be magnanimous and view the comment as an
indicator of confusion and discomfort rather than bad manners. While it may
have been a simple cultural difference, I think a universal "Miss Manners"
recommendation would have been a simple "No thank you," rather than a
comment on the preparation of the refreshments. In any event, I didn't really
need to pursue the interview: His discomfort was almost palpable, so I asked
him if he would rather not continue. He seemed greatly relieved as he left.
He didn't even stay long enough to meet the kids.

So while it is true that our all-black environment was not created solely by
coincidence, it is also true that we at least considered other options. As our
project evolved, we found that the use of African and African-American tutors
just enhanced the environmental elements of our efforts to create a holistic
educational experience for the boys. And that was the bridge between the
practical and theoretical elements of the tutor-selection process.

HERE'S how we handled the theoretical elements of the process. Once we
formulated the curriculum and made the decision to use outside resources,
namely, teachers, the next issue was teacher selection. C. Madison and I
clarified our standards for a good teacher, but there were other characteristics
to add if we wanted to test our hypothesis.

It seems unnecessary, but I want to point out that we would not have hired
someone who did not meet our definition of a good teacher just because the
person was male or black, even though we were actively and openly searching for these gender and race characteristics. One of our premises was that

when a child is given the chance to be taught by an adult version of that child, this should be seen as an opportunity, period. It's not racist or sexist, and it only appears to be noteworthy when applied to African-American children. I have known a number of wealthy white Americans whose children have had the occasional black teacher, and the parents were delighted. But I've always wondered how delighted they would be if all of their children's teachers and school administrators were black. I think we know that race and gender matter, and it's always difficult to determine how much; so, sometimes, it's easier simply to ignore the whole thing.

I think that's why there was such confusion expressed over our decision to use African and African-American male teachers. I don't think people actively or consciously believe black kids don't deserve the same qualitative benefits and opportunities as white kids; I just think that, frequently, people are unconscious of the many unearned privileges that are bestowed upon white people. The presumption that most of the educational experiences of white children will be conducted in environments designed and administered by white people is just one of those unearned and unacknowledged privileges. So we tried to construct a parallel universe of privilege for our sons, something that just couldn't have been achieved in school. (According to the U.S. Department of Education, the ranks of the nation's public school teachers have become more female and more white in the last thirty years. In 1972, 88 percent of teachers were white, but by 1991 that percentage rose to almost 91 percent. Similarly, in the early 1960s 31 percent of teachers were male, but by 1996 less than 26 percent of teachers were male. The percentages are better in private schools, but not substantially enough.)

Our overarching objective was to create a holistic environment where our sons' spiritual, intellectual, and physical development would receive equal attention. We had to keep reminding ourselves what the objective was, so we didn't get off track. As business consultants for years, we've seen a number of large, well-established organizations fall prey to the temptation of tangential enterprises. When organizations lose sight of their core business—when growth comes too fast; when new opportunities, while exciting, exceed capacity; when organizations fail to review and remember their fundamental objectives—they encounter disastrous problems. We did not want to lose sight of what it was we were attempting to achieve. Just as the issue was not about our commitment to home schooling, it also wasn't about our commitment to issues of race and gender. The issue was our commitment to Charles, Damon, and Evan. Within that narrow context, hiring African and African-American male teachers seemed a rational and reasonable approach.

Our premise was not based on the assumption that anyone who was not male and of African ancestry was unable to be a good teacher. Principally, this was really not about race or gender or even other people at all; this was exclusively about our sons. We were engaged in the process of trying to determine the best way to achieve our goal for them, the creation of a holistic and healthy educational experience. In that context, it made sense to explore the implications of mirror-image teachers.

Our plan was not based upon exclusion by design, or by default; rather, it was a conscious, intentional plan to structure and limit our sons' educational environment. In developing and working through this process, and in explaining it to others, it became clear to us that all structure is by necessity limiting. For every element included in the structure there is a corresponding element not selected. In some instances—and I definitely believe ours was one of those instances—the potential and pragmatic merits of the limitation outweighed the costs of arbitrary exclusion. After all, there were plenty of statistically verifiable instances of African-American male children being taught by their phenotypic opposites—namely, white women. The evidence of those experiences certainly indicates that the exploration of another educational option was not unwarranted.

While I didn't expect universal agreement, I did not expect such heated disagreement and disapproval. Once again, I learned that what was obvious to me was not so to others. I never got used to the level of amazement generated by the fact that we hired African and African-American graduate students, most of whom were male, to help us in our educational experiment. Apparently, this experimental option was viewed as an arbitrary, discriminatory practice based on an invalid and unethical assumption that only black men could teach black boys.

I know this sounds corny, but I really believe there's a responsibility to share enlightenment when you get some. If you know something to be true, I think there's an affirmative duty to share. Of course Plato's allegory of the cave implies there's a choice. But can there really be a choice? Ethically, can one choose to leave one's brothers and sisters chained in darkness in the cave, even if it's just a cave of tradition or assumption? I don't think so. The myth that there are no qualified black men available to teach was such a cave. We felt obligated to free others from it, and the only way to do that was to expose the statement as false rhetoric. I was amazed constantly by the fact that people were far less interested in the fact that the myth was false than in the fact that we actively and openly sought African and African-American male scholars. Our sons are black males. If we were to start a girls' school or a women's college, I would definitely seek out women for the faculty, staff, and administration: An absence of women in such an environment would be more than contrived, it would be patently unhealthy. Yet, that rational reasoning seemingly did not transfer to the concept of educating black boys.

A lot of people, especially middle-class black people, thought this whole idea was just terrible. There was concern about the impact of this segregated educational experiment on our sons. While no one was quite bold enough actually to articulate this, the implication was clear: "How can they possibly learn anything with no white people there as teachers or classmates?" It reminds me of that sad and twisted joke, "the white man's ice is colder," about the seemingly universal belief in the inherent superiority of anything and everything white. Can one person's ice really be colder? No, and on some level we all know it. Yet, the idea of educating our sons in the total absence of white people seemed like anarchy to a lot of folks, black and white.

In our situation, we were certainly separate but our kids were not deprived. The education they received was more than equal to what was available elsewhere. But in spite of my best efforts to explain the decision of *Brown v. Board of Education,* many people, black and white, thought this was academically irresponsible and patently racist. It isn't. It is decidedly discriminatory, but all that is discriminatory is not illegal, and it certainly isn't racist.

Now this is definitely contrary to conventional wisdom, but I think the suffix "ism" requires the past and present power of the state, either overtly through the historic abuse of police power or covertly through the use of institutionalized norms and traditions. Similarly, if past practices and norms have created a continuing hostile environment that seeks to limit my choices even in the absence of present state action, that's still racist.

What am I talking about? I'm talking about the openly hostile stares and glares many white people give black people who turn up in places they don't belong without a "pass." The pass is given if you're a known quantity: an entertainer, an athlete, or a locally acceptable black person, one of "theirs." If not, expect hostility or at best ridiculous questions: "Is this your first time coming to the opera?"

Another example is the voluntary discriminatory segregation that happens in high school and college cafeterias every day. If given the freedom to do so, students routinely seat themselves in certain groupings, and for the most part no one seems bothered by it. While it might be nice if everyone sat together, or was at least willing to consider it, adults don't do that and it's unrealistic for us to think kids will. (At my prep school, we had assigned seating, so this was a nonissue. But as soon as the meal concluded and we were dismissed, the voluntary groupings reemerged.) Typically, jocks sit with jocks (this is often the most racially integrated group in integrated institutions), popular kids sit nearby (there's frequently much intersection here), and smart kids sit together, as do the druggies. All this voluntary segregation—the process of discriminating about who one eats with—is reflective of the larger society and doesn't generate lots of commentary. But when black kids choose to sit together, somehow the segregation takes on the sinister patina of presumed racism and noninclusion. But racism, like sexism and classism, is about using present or past power to eliminate the choices of others.

Every time someone tried to express concern about our presumed racism, they became increasingly frazzled as I just listened. But enlightenment and truth don't need a majority vote or consensus. You don't have to beat people over the head with truth. It won't become diluted or fade away if it's not recognized immediately. And for healthy people, truth resonates when it is heard. So I just listened, tried to "let my light shine," and waited, knowing that in the fullness of time, even the people in the cave would see the light.

Not seeking white faculty was not racist, just as seeking men (in this instance) was not sexist; this was a case of enlightenment. We knew that when Charles, Damon, and Evan emerged from this educational experiment, whole and intact, the brilliance of their success would be illuminating on a whole lot of levels. By design, this selection process benefited our sons. Hopefully, the news of their success will encourage school administrators to reexamine their reliance on the myth of no qualified black male teachers, and thereby benefit lots of other kids, regardless of their race, ethnicity, or gender.

I THINK one of the biggest challenges we parents have is being honest with ourselves. When we're unconscious and delude ourselves, we unwittingly pass along our anxieties and insecurities to our kids, without giving them the spiritual, intellectual, and physical tools to handle them.

One simple example is my fear of certain things, namely, rats. Actually, it's broader than that: I have always had an irrational fear and loathing for all rodents and quasi-rodents—mice, rats, bats, hamsters, gerbils, chipmunks, squirrels, rabbits; get the idea? I know that's irrational, so when I had the boys I made a conscious effort not to pass that on to them. Now, I wasn't able to have rodents in the house, but I sat through countless Rat Basketball shows (see next chapter) and let the boys handle the rats and mice, et al., when they were very little boys. I didn't cringe or look away, even though my flesh was crawling. It wasn't until they began working at the animal lab at the science museum and wanted to bring the rats home during training that I told them about my fear of rodents. They were untainted by my fear because I knew about it, assessed it, and decided when to share it with them.

Many of our fears and anxieties as parents are just not that simple. We not only have to try to be conscious of the negative societal messages bombarding our kids, we've got to figure out if we're adding to them. This isn't just a challenge for black parents. We've all got issues about race, gender, class, etc.; the critical question is, do we know what our issues are?

It's bad enough if a woman really believes she's less than a man, but what if she unwittingly passes that belief on to her daughters and sons? Or what if I'm so filled with self-loathing and a desire for assimilation as a Jewish person that I stop attending religious services, disassociate myself from other Jews who are *too* Jewish-acting, and ultimately tell people that I'm not Jewish, even though I live in a community where people knew my parents, grandparents, and great-grandparents, all of whom were Jewish, and I act like it's a nonissue? Might my kids have some issues with their identity? What if I'm Indian, Pakistani, or Chinese, but I live in an otherwise all-white community and my kids attend otherwise all-white schools, and I make a conscious decision to shape my and my family's social activities to those things that further our assimilation? Am I helping them by pretending there is no issue, or would it be more helpful to discuss just how complex the issue really is?

Ultimately, I think, as parents, we have to ask ourselves two questions: Does it matter what I am? Isn't who I am what's important? I think the answer to both questions is yes—it matters what I am and it matters who I am, because race, gender, and nationality are more than issues of "what," they help answer the question of "who."

Whatever educational option you select, you still probably need to help your kid work through the dual questions of what and who they are, and how you do that depends on you, your kids, and your community.

10

HOW WE SCHEDULED

OUR LIVES

I BELIEVE HOLISTIC balance is achieved most readily in the midst of joy, and we wanted the boys to experience learning in an environment permeated with joy. As we talked to the boys about our desire for them to experience joy in their home-schooling experience, it became apparent that they thought we were crazy. Part of the challenge was explaining the practical difference between joy and happiness. We tried to explain the difference, but, ultimately, I think the difference has to be demonstrated rather than described. So we tried to manifest the joy we felt in our lives with them on a daily basis. We tried consistently to focus our attention on the joy we felt in having the opportunity to home-school rather than on the hardship the opportunity of home schooling created. Joy is a constant, essentially spiritual state of being. Joy is not affected by events in the external universe. So while we knew there was much challenging and difficult work to be done, philosophically we were determined not to allow the degree of challenge and difficulty to impact our level of joy.

The philosophical part was easy—okay, maybe not easy, but certainly easier than the practical, implementation part. While we knew we wanted to maintain a sense of joy in this process, a schedule was essential if we were to have any hope of achieving our practical goal of college admissions. The challenge was in not allowing the form of the schedule to overshadow the substance of what we were trying to achieve.

We began our schedule development by identifying two core goals to be achieved daily. Every day, we expected everyone in the family to learn some-thing new. We didn't feel the need to attach value to the things that could be learned; we figured it was enough to assert the expectation of daily learning as a lifetime objective. Our second goal was quiet time. Every day, everyone in this family was expected to spend some quiet time, alone. Again, we didn't stipulate how that quiet time was to be spent, whether in prayer, meditation, daydreaming, or just staring off into space: The important thing was the con-scious decision to step away from the abyss of constant, external stimulation.

Our goals were so simple that they apparently appeared to be meaningless when I conveyed them to others. You know the blank stares of disbelief you get when you say something bizarre? Well, I got a lot of those. And, in all fair-ness, I can understand the source of that bewilderment. Typically, when we think of education, we tend to think almost exclusively about the scheduling of classes and subject-matter mastery; e.g., how many forty-five-minute class sessions must be scheduled to teach the history of England from Alfred the Great to Queen Victoria? Within the confines of such scheduling, there probably lies the presumption that something new will be learned every day. And most students in such a scheduled environment probably do learn some-thing new every day, but that doesn't always translate into a quest for lifetime learning.

Making a conscious decision to learn something every day may sound meaningless, but I was convinced that it was a powerful idea. I think there's something to be said for an adage, attributed to Socrates: "The more I know, the more I know I know nothing." Being open to knowledge requires an ac-tive and conscious state of humility, and I think that's an effort for lots of folks, not just me. Consequently, part of our challenge was that we didn't expect just the kids to learn something every day—we were *all* supposed to learn something new every day. That meant that, at a baseline level, C. Madison and I could not pretend that we already knew everything.

Everyone in our house was expected to read for two hours every day, and the boys were required to make a daily journal entry. We included journal writing as a part of our home-schooling experience for several reasons. Pri-marily, we were always on the lookout for writing opportunities. We also felt that writing in a journal is an excellent way privately to articulate and record feelings. Sometimes our feelings can feel too intense for discussion, and writ-ing them out can be very cathartic.

We continually struggled for a happy medium between no schedule and too much scheduling. On the one hand, we didn't want to re-create school in our home-schooling experiment. While the need for a schedule was obvious, we didn't want to lose sight of the fact that the schedule was a means to an end, not an end unto itself. In other words, we didn't want to become so focused on a schedule that we forgot why we were home-schooling in the first place. And while that seems an obvious trap, and therefore easily avoided, it's a trap into which many people fall, home-schoolers and others. Even in traditional educational institutions, it's so easy to get caught up in the schedule that we lose sight of the purpose.

The purpose of education is not to perform a certain number of tasks within a designated time frame; or, at least, I don't think that's what the purpose should be. I think the purpose of education is to stimulate the intellect so that new knowledge can be sought, examined, explored, and embraced. I think that when some of the time constraints are removed, the educational process is enhanced and there's a greater likelihood of retention. It's very easy to become so focused on form that all attention is distracted from substance. So we were actively seeking to avoid the type of scheduling that was more valued than the learning it was supposedly developed to facilitate.

The challenge with most academic scheduling is that it is designed for the middle-of-the-road student; everyone else must struggle with an overabundance or inadequacy of time. The time constraints of scheduling for the mastery of mathematics might seem obvious, but I think they are equally compelling in other disciplines as well. I am convinced that while reading epic poetry aloud is very time-consuming, and might be problematic in traditional classrooms, poetry is meant to be heard and hearing it facilitates understanding. Again, I'm not claiming to be a frustrated classics major who missed my calling because of a denied opportunity to hear the *Iliad* or the *Odyssey* read aloud, but it would have been wonderful to have had that opportunity. And now that I have heard them read aloud, I know for a certainty that hearing adds a dimension of understanding that simply wasn't present from silent reading. We figured that as one of the benefits of home schooling was the fact that we were in charge, we owed it to ourselves and to our kids to keep that in mind when establishing our schedule. And yes, it absolutely took us an incredibly long time to get through the *Aeneid*, the *Iliad*, the *Odyssey*, and the *Peloponnesian Wars*, but it was definitely worth it. To quote my dreaded Latin teacher, Mrs. Valida Vilums, "You learn until you know!"

The challenge of finding the right scheduling mix to maximize the academic achievement of a widely diverse student body is pretty commonly acknowledged. The more obscure challenge in scheduling is making time for reflection. Quiet time is often overlooked when schedules are developed. At an early age, our children find themselves scurrying from one class and ac-

tivity to another. Not only is there inadequate time for quiet thought and reflection, there's often not enough time for adequate rest. I wonder how many
midlife crises, both personal and professional, would be averted if people
were encouraged to spend twenty minutes a day in quiet thought and reflection. I am certain a lot of critical life mistakes would be avoided.

Most dominant world religions admonish us to do as the Buddhists suggest, to be fully present in the moment. The Christian tradition admonishes
in Matthew 6:28–29, "Consider the lilies of the field, how they grow; they toil
not, neither do they spin: and yet I say unto you, that even Solomon in all his
glory was not arrayed like one of these." Being present in the moment eliminates a lot of negative energy. To be angry means we're living in the past, and
to be anxious means we're living in the future. Being present in the moment
eliminates much anger and anxiety about the rewards of our efforts. It doesn't
mean we sit back and do nothing; but, rather we do, we strive, we achieve,
not for a future reward or in response to past hurts, but for the joy of excelling
in the present.

But being present, fully present, in the moment requires quiet time. If I
jump up in the morning, hit the ground running, and continue at that pace
until I collapse into a fitful sleep of exhaustion at night, I cannot possibly be
present in the moment. That's why we see so many people who apparently
haven't been present, not only in the moment, but in the day, the week, the
month, or the year. Sometimes the decision to be conscious or unconscious
is less the result of a decision and more the result of habit and momentum.

We wanted to give our sons the opportunity to have quiet time for thought
and reflection. We wanted to develop a schedule that would essentially create a place for thought, for prayer, for meditation—essentially, a place to be
quiet, even if that meant we had to sacrifice the scheduling of additional academic work. We couldn't talk about holistic balance and then not schedule
for it.

The flip side of the schedule challenge was the fact that we weren't oozing
confidence in the viability of totally unscheduled, interest-led learning, either. Many home-schoolers have great confidence in the concept of interest-
led learning, but I had real reservations about its effectiveness for us. We have
met a number of home-schooling parents who have had tremendous results
by allowing their child complete freedom to explore his or her intellectual interests. Inevitably in the midst of such freedom, the child voluntarily and joy-
fully goes deeper and further than most teachers would ever require in a
traditional classroom setting. It made sense, and I loved the idea of interest-
led learning, but I knew my kids. This is a little embarrassing to admit, but I
had absolutely no confidence in my kids' burning urge to learn anything.

This isn't to say that they were total slugs or anything like that, but they also weren't the kind of kids to beg for more research time at the library. Sure, they liked dinosaurs, and they had a probably higher-than-average level of interest in geography and biology, but I couldn't see that translated into any master's-level, research-based thesis. My kids needed motivation, and in the absence of that I just didn't think a whole lot of learning was going to occur. We were sorely tempted, because interest-led learning would have been a lot less work for us, but, knowing our kids, we knew it just wasn't a viable option.

Sometimes it's hard to acknowledge who your kid really is, especially when you're talking to people who are telling you how they had to drag their ten-year-old to bed after twelve hours of working on an independent science project! But you know what? I had to rely on my own assessment of our boys, and inasmuch as I'm not a psychologist or an expert on child development, my assessment might have been limited, but it's all that I had.

My assessment was that Charles, Damon, and Evan were really quite typical, which is why our ultimate results with them are so remarkable. They were pretty normal kids. They preferred playing, especially group playing, to working. They loved to watch TV, stay up late, eat lots of pizza, sleep late, have their friends over, and ride their bikes. And I was convinced that if left to their own devices, not much more than that would occur. I have no recollection of any of them ever coming downstairs in the morning and asking to review the previous day's discussion of *Richard III* or anything else academic, for that matter. This isn't to say that I didn't recognize how bright, special, and truly unique each one was as an individual; it's just that their specialness didn't require any embellishment from me. I was thrilled with them just the way they were, and I felt they were more than suited to the rigors of spiritual, intellectual, and physical development, even if most of it wasn't based on any of their individual interests. So while we tried to pay attention to their individual areas of interest, we decided to develop a schedule around our curriculum, rather than rely on interest-led learning.

Because we had made some rather difficult decisions about the whole arena of home entertainment years earlier, once we began home schooling, certain standards were already in place. For example, we never had to argue about excessive TV or video games, because we didn't have cable and the kids didn't own a game system. Yes, Virginia, one can live, grow, and prosper without ever owning a Nintendo, Sega, or Sony game system. It is even possible to live without cable—not indefinitely, of course, but we made it for eleven years.

When the boys were big enough to read chapter books—long before our decision to home-school—we had cable removed from our home. There was

much weeping, wailing, and gnashing of teeth, but C. Madison and I promised each other it would be worth it. As much as we enjoyed having access
to cable, we knew that that very access could well become a stumbling block
for our kids. And this was years before cable became chock-full of quasi-
pornographic videos, with obscene lyrics, posing as music.

Now, while I'm not in favor of state-sanctioned censorship, I absolutely am
in favor of parental censorship, and much of what is and has been on cable
definitely should be censored by parents. This is not to say that regular TV is
immune from filth, but I just felt it would be a lot easier to monitor four channels instead of four hundred. Plus, there was the added benefit that so much
of regular television was so boring that, after a while, the kids got tired of even
checking to see if something *good* might be coming on.

I really had no interest in being the TV police, and I just couldn't imagine
that reading would win out over watching almost anything on cable. Now,
again, it might seem that I am underrating my sons and their enormous intellectual gifts and interests, but, really, I'm not. I just didn't see any reason to
believe that my sons were that far removed from the normative behaviors
driving the rest of the population. I look at it like this: I'm an adult and a very
well educated one at that; plus I genuinely love to read and typically read one
novel each week; but television has been known to have an almost hypnotic
effect on me. Why would I expect my children to exercise greater self-control
than I can?

Triumphantly, the week Evan received his acceptance letters from colleges, C. Madison called and had cable reinstalled, and there was rejoicing in
our home! But during our home-schooling odyssey, not having cable or video
games simplified the scheduling issue.

WE scheduled two meals together, as a family, every day. Almost every day for
nine years, we had breakfast and dinner together. During those meals, we discussed our plans for the day and reviewed the day's events. On Monday
mornings, we moved directly from breakfast into Current Events. We used
the "Week in Review" section from the Sunday *New York Times* as our struc-
tural base. Each of the boys selected one article to read aloud and discuss. We
included our local paper, *The Columbus Dispatch*, and sometimes added *The
Wall Street Journal*, *USA Today*, *Newsweek*, *Time*, and a variety of other traditional, mainstream publications. As little guys, the boys' selections were
based exclusively on the length of the articles. As they got older, they grew to
enjoy the exchange. Now, they never matured to the point that they would

admit they enjoyed it, but asking for that admission would have been greedy on my part! More significant, as they got older and more argumentative, they insisted on including commentary from *XXL*, *Vibe*, and *The Source*. *XXL* had a special place in their adolescent hearts, since they were included in an article on home schooling in the inaugural issue—the one with Jay-Z on the cover!

Their additions certainly upped the ante on Current Events for us. The purpose of Current Events was twofold: On the one hand, as citizens, we wanted to stay abreast of events in the world; on the other hand, we wanted the boys to examine the impact of countervailing political positions, propaganda, and paradox in the supposedly objective reporting of news. Such conversations do not lend themselves to scheduling. We always had to break around lunch, because on Monday afternoons the boys had class with their tutors. Notably, those Monday morning discussions sometimes ebbed and flowed all week, with interesting and global input from the boys' tutors!

Tuesdays and Thursdays were COSI days. The kids volunteered at this hands-on science museum twice each week. There, they developed excellent public-speaking skills while learning exhibits and performing shows on diverse science topics: Cryogenics and Combustion, Newton's Playground, The Brain, Rat Basketball, and NASA's Mission to Mars, to name just a few of the exhibits COSI hosted during the boys' tenure. Damon even developed a show, The Physics of Juggling, based on his own prepubescent interest in (read that as short-term obsession with) juggling.

COSI has thousands of visitors annually. Virtually all the public schools in a seven-county radius visit COSI once each year. Our kids routinely gave demonstrations and shows to groups of kids, teachers, parents, donors, and community leaders. Their COSI days were business catch-up days for C. Madison and me.

Wednesdays and Fridays were tutor days, and different classes were scheduled at different times depending on the tutors' schedules. (The schedules with the tutors fluctuated almost every quarter because the tutors were still students themselves.)

In retrospect, it sounds simple, but at the time I felt like Peter Graves's character on *Mission: Impossible*. Everything had to be pretty finely tuned because, as C. Madison likes to say, "Everything depends on everything else." Flexibility was the key to avoiding stress overload. I learned to create a schedule and then plan for the schedule to come apart occasionally. I couldn't afford the luxury of coming apart at the seams every time the schedule did!

Saturdays fluctuated over the years. For a while, we had opera, ballet, and

art on Saturdays. Then we had football, ballet, and art. Then we had Bible
Bowl and art. Ultimately, Saturday became an "all art, all the time" kind of
day.

One of the unexpected issues of scheduling hinged on the reality of time
as a finite resource. It simply became impossible to participate in everything
in which the boys had either an interest or talent. We were adamant about
not allowing Saturday to become the one day of the week in which we put
aside our core-value system; it would be pointless for us to strive for balance
Monday through Friday and then spend Saturday running all over town like
chickens with our heads cut off.

A big part of our responsibility was to help the boys evaluate the enormous
range of options. We tried to help them seek a balance between doing things
they were curious about, doing things they were already interested in, and
doing things for which they had a distinct talent. Inevitably, their activities
varied greatly, just through experience and subsequent elimination. Some
things they were curious about failed to hold their interest beyond a season or
year of participation.

In sharp contrast to Saturday's fluctuations, Sundays never varied. Sunday
is family day. Sunday morning begins with Sunday School.

Everybody in this family goes to Sunday School, because if you don't, my
dad will call and ask if someone's sick, and do you need him to come to pick
you up? Both my mom and dad are superintendents in different Sunday
School departments. We believe in Sunday School as a lifetime commitment, from the cradle to the grave—you will never reach escape velocity.

We worship at the Church of Christ of the Apostolic Faith, and sometimes—
well, we just "have church," and a punctual dismissal is neither expected nor
required. After all, as our pastor says, "We're not going anywhere but heaven!"

My entire family—with the exception of my maternal grandmother, who
sits across the aisle with her friends—sits together in two pews in the center
section every Sunday. You know how people can describe you to someone
else in the congregation by who your parents or grandparents are, and where
you sit during service? Well, we're like that. In our pew, the formation is always the same. It's my dad, my mom, my sisters Courtney and Cheryl, my
kids, me, and C. Madison. My brother David, his wife, Sonjia (who's been
my ace since we were in the ninth grade, so she's really like a real sister), and
their five kids—David, Samuel, Joseph, Benjamin, and Alexandria—sit in
the pew in front of us.

My kids, along with my niece and nephews, are fifth-generation members,
on my mother's side, of this same congregation. Our parents met in this con-

gregation, when my dad came to Columbus to go to OSU on the G.I. Bill. After he graduated, they got married as members of this congregation and raised all their kids there. Today, their kids continue this tradition.

After church dismisses, everybody goes home, changes clothes, snarfs something (remember, we left for Sunday School at ten A.M. and it's now about three!), and heads over to my folks. Everybody is expected at my parents' house for dinner at four o'clock sharp: My mom gets very testy if anyone is late! David brings the rolls, I bring the dessert, the kids set the table, and Cheryl, Courtney, and Sonjia clean up.

My parents shop for all the food on Thursday and my mom does all the cooking. (Okay, she might let one of us stir a pot or something, but that's about it.) It's almost always a great meal (I have to say "almost always" because sometimes we have Swiss steak, and I hate that!) and it's always great fellowship, even when one of us is in a bad mood.

The point is, we all take time out of our lives to really connect with one another, across three generations, and we do it every week! We're there until seven or seven-thirty P.M., which makes for a long day, but it's worth it. It's a lot like that movie *Soul Food*, except our dad's very much alive, our family's male-dominated, my mom won't let anybody else cook in her kitchen, we have no convicted felons in the family, and none of us have ever had sex in any of the bathrooms there!

Overall, the schedule provided the parameters for the implementation of our holistic goals. Each week we worked to achieve balance between the spiritual, intellectual, and physical development of our sons individually and our family collectively. I think we were pretty successful in terms of goal attainment, and I'm convinced that having a schedule made all the difference in the world. It may seem that we were excessively scheduled, and it's not a schedule that would work for everybody. We used a schedule to help us achieve our goals and, as every family's goals are unique, one schedule can't fit every family.

But having said that, I still think every family benefits from having an intentional schedule. One thing I've observed is that if you don't design an intentional schedule for your family, your family will end up responding to the schedule of others. What you want for yourselves as a family should always be the priority, and developing a schedule will help clarify that. If nothing else, your family's schedule will ensure some degree of autonomy and help maintain priorities. Your family's schedule helps prevent overload or the tendency to be-

come overextended, because there's an awareness of time and its value. Again, I'm not advocating a schedule for the sake of having a schedule, but I found that having a schedule really helped us achieve our goals with our kids.

In developing a schedule, the first thing to do is establish your goals. One easy formula to think about is that the greater and more significant the particular goal is, the more time you'll want and need to schedule for it. Another formula I've discovered is that the more quantitative, material, and/or physical something is, the easier it will be to schedule. Conversely, the more qualitative and intangible something is, the more difficult it can seem to schedule time for it.

An equally important consideration is the fact that no matter how important you think something is to you, if it's not scheduled, it probably won't happen. For example, let's say consistent quality time together as a family is a primary goal. Under my first formula, because family time is a significant goal, its achievement will require a lot of scheduled time—so nightly dinner might be something to schedule. The challenge is in the second formula, because the goal of family time is qualitative and the benefits are intangible, so it will be difficult to hold to the scheduled time. The difficulty will increase in the face of quantitative, material demands, like working late or softball practice. But the final point holds true: You still need to schedule for it. Even if it doesn't happen every day, you need to schedule for it, plan for it, and expect it to happen—or it won't.

You can apply those same formulas to scheduling for home schooling itself. Say a primary goal is intellectual stimulation. Because the goal is primary, a great deal of time must be scheduled for its accomplishment. Let's suppose that you select the study of philosophy as the means to accomplish the goal, and you decide to start with Plato's Dialogues. *Now, this is definitely going to take a lot of time, not because they're hard, but because they're the kind of thing one has to read, think about, discuss, and think about some more. This process will definitely lead to the accomplishment of the goal of intellectual stimulation, but it will be time-consuming. Plus, because reading, thinking, and discussing are fundamentally qualitative and intangible, maintaining the necessary and scheduled time commitments will be hard. You can't just work the fifty problems in the workbook and go to the next chapter. It's not that there's no sense of accomplishment, it's just different.*

If one of the essential goals is the development of critical math skills, a different kind of scheduling would be necessary. In the final analysis, you need to figure out what values, ideals, and skills you want to help accomplish and develop in your child's life, and then prioritize them. Once you've completed that, you can determine which educational option makes the most sense. (I think it's a lot easier to develop a schedule within the confines of a specific educational option and specific holistic goals.)

There's one last important detail about schedules: Try to remember the importance of flexibility. Be on guard against the form of the schedule overshadowing the substance of what the schedule is supposed to help you achieve. If you schedule daily family dinner and somebody doesn't make it or doesn't make it on time, don't blow the entire evening by pouting, shouting, or ranting and raving about the loss of quality family time.

11

HOW WE KEPT

THEM FIT

WE USED THE NUMEROUS Columbus Parks and Recreation centers as a means of meeting our kids' need for athletic activity. The boys were able to take lessons in swimming, tennis, golf, tae kwon do, and fencing. Some of those lessons, like swimming and later fencing, evolved into team-sport activities, again through the recreation centers.

We augmented the recreation center activities with community center football and riding lessons at a private hunt club. The equestrian experience turned out to be a pleasant, albeit short-lived surprise. It was short-lived because it was just too expensive to continue, and it was a surprise because Evan actually enjoyed it. Rarely did we find any athletic activity that Evan enjoyed.

Football also turned out to be a surprise, and while not always pleasant, it was informative. Charles and Damon had wanted to play football for years. I didn't want them to play at all, and C. Madison was neutral. I had two issues with football. First of all, football is dangerous, and I don't see how the benefits (for the average child) outweigh the physical risks. Admittedly, many physical activities are dangerous, and, as a general policy, I tried to limit the boys' involvement in those activities. My other issue wasn't physical, but it was just as dangerous: I do not like the way black boys are encouraged to play sports, frequently to the exclusion of everything else. After a young man has spent his high school and college career being defined as an athlete, and receiving tons of benefits and attention because of it, it can be devastatingly difficult to return to a life of relative obscurity, with no education and with minimal marketable skills. I felt the risks of football were too high on too many levels. But flexibility and compromise were vital parts of our home-schooling experience, so I had to compromise and be flexible about football.

When Charles's voice changed and he could no longer sing with the children's chorus of Opera Columbus, he lobbied for football. I was trapped, and so Charles and Damon began playing football with a community center league. The surprise was that Damon didn't like football at all. I don't think he understood how rigorous the training would be, and I don't think he understood how inflexible his dad would be about finishing what you start.

I was at a loss as to how any of the boys could be unclear about C. Madison's obsession about completion, as each of them had experienced it on more than one occasion. I always tried to remind the boys of this fact prior to beginning every new endeavor, but they were always too optimistic initially really to listen. Football proved to be no exception.

After the first week of practice, Damon discovered that excessive exercise, especially running, can cause vomiting. He also discovered that hitting people "for no reason" really didn't appeal to him. This was particularly shocking to him, because Damon had always been willing and able to fight just about anyone. I think what was confusing to him was that while he was happy to fight for an issue of principle, he wasn't a person who could enjoy gratuitous violence. Finally, when his coach explained that stopping to help the people that you knock down was inappropriate, Damon had an epiphany: He didn't really want to play football after all.

After all those revelations, he then had to deal with C. Madison's completion thing. That's right: Damon had to play the entire rest of the season, and he knew he was expected to do his best. Fortunately, Damon enjoyed the other boys on the team, and he liked the coach, and he was happy for Charles, who turned out to be quite the little jock.

Charles—by far the least violent of all my children—turned out absolutely to love football. He ended up playing two seasons and was elected co-captain during his second season. (Damon, of course, played only the one season, and while he got used to the exercise, he never really got used to hitting people for no reason.)

The other thing that we did in terms of fitness was dance. Typically, people think of dance principally as an art form, and while it certainly is art, it is also athletic. Charles and Damon took tap at one of the recreation centers, and Evan ended up dancing with BalletMet for three years. While our sons haven't maintained any interest in dance as participants, I love the fact that they appreciate dance as an art form that demands enormous strength and discipline. Dance also helped illuminate the holistic balance we were con-

tinually striving to create for them. Rather than seeing athletics as some
"manly" thing and dance as some "sissy" thing, they were able to see the illu-
mination of the beauty and strength of the human form in both. So that's how
we did it. Why we did it that way is a bit more complicated.

AT the time we began home schooling, Charles, Damon, and Evan were still
little boys, but they were definitely little boys in transition. Puberty was just
beginning, and we all had to hold out until their change came.

Puberty is hard enough to experience, but what I learned as a parent is that
it's not any easier to observe. Puberty is all about change, and change in any
form is rarely a painless experience. Part of the change Charles, Damon, and
Evan were dealing with was the purely physical development of their bodies
from children into young men. An added dimension was the enormous psychological and emotional changes that went along with that physical development. Here's when we began to see the difference between the idea and
the necessity of physical activity: We knew physical activity was a critical
component of holistic health, but with the advent of puberty we found there
was no better way to burn off all the excess energy released from raging hor-
mones.

Right from the very beginning of our home-schooling experiment we had
discussed our goal of holistic health and balance; now we could see how
critical the implementation of that goal really was. As we anticipated the inevitable changes and challenges, we began to consider how best to assist
them. It didn't require an advanced degree in human physiology to see that,
right off the bat, they needed a lot of physical activity. Initially, we enrolled
them in an array of athletic activities for exposure and participation purposes:
swimming, golf, tennis—those kinds of activities gave them a chance to interact with a lot of different kids at different skill levels. So those athletic activities were regularly scheduled parts of their week. In between time, they
still needed a lot of physical exercise and play. Sometimes we'd go for long
walks, or C. Madison would take them to the track and make them run laps.
Sometimes he'd just take them fishing and let them run around outside for
hours.

We were fortunate that, for most of the years we home-schooled, we lived
in a community with an indoor pool. When the boys seemed distracted or
just plain ornery, we'd take a break, walk over to the pool, and make them
swim laps for twenty to thirty minutes. Swimming is a great way to work off excess energy, and it's good exercise with very little risk of injury. And while our

boys are not competitive swimmers, by any means, they're good, strong swimmers, and swimming is one form of exercise they can continue for their entire lives.

As they got older, their need for physical activity increased along with their interest in organized, team sports. This was much more of a challenge for me than for C. Madison because I had very little experiential knowledge of the benefits of physical activity, much less physical education. Honestly, when I think of sports and physical activity, I immediately think of gym class and, unfortunately, there is no pleasure in those memories. I never had a gym teacher I liked or one that could even pretend to like me. When I think back on good old PE, what I really remember is either not getting picked, being picked last, or being constantly criticized for not showing enough hustle. However, my carefully cultivated disdain and distaste for all things and people athletic—with C. Madison as the notable exception—was one of many bad habits I didn't want to pass on to my kids.

C. Madison had been a gifted athlete and had had a fun and rewarding experience as a student athlete in high school and college. In high school he played varsity football, and in college he was an award-winning member of the track-and-field team. He threw the shot put, and hurled the discus and the hammer competitively, and he not only enjoyed it, but was successful enough to be asked to try out for the 1974 U.S. Olympic team.

Meeting C. Madison forced me to reassess many of my assumptions about athletes and athletics. Remember, I grew up in Columbus, Ohio, home of the Buckeyes, so I was hardly unfamiliar with football or football players. Suffice it to say that the term "academic excellence" would not have been the first phrase out of my mouth in a game of word association if football, much less shot put, had been the trigger. C. Madison was able to show me the defining role of discipline and focus in any successful athletic endeavor, and that including these endeavors in our home-schooling experiment really wasn't about elevating athletics over arts or academics, but about seeing athletic development as another element of holistic health. He also assured me that he would never allow anybody to deceive our sons into thinking that athletic excellence was more important or rewarding than academic or artistic excellence. (We had both seen countless young black athletes lured to college with compelling athletic scholarships only to leave empty-handed five or six years later, after having earned millions for the institution. Statistically, there's a greater likelihood of becoming a brain surgeon than becoming a member of the NFL or the NBA. C. Madison told me that was a fact he would make sure the boys knew.)

That clarifying conversation made it much easier for us jointly to examine the best way to ensure that our sons' physical health and development would keep pace with their spiritual and intellectual development. We were adamant that we would not allow any of our sons to be bullied into athletic participation in any misguided effort to prove their manhood. We were equally convinced of the need to fit athletic activity into the overall fabric of the kids' lives. Given what we wanted to accomplish, we chose physical fitness over competitive sports as our preferred methodology, but the fact that competitive sports were not our preferred methodology didn't mean that we prevented the boys from participating.

CHARLES'S and Damon's football coaches, Packer and Tanksley, really connected with the boys and the parents. For both seasons, C. Madison, my parents, my sisters, and I went to almost every game, even when they were all over town. We did the pre-season and post-season activities, pep rallies, and award banquets. This was an opportunity for me to demonstrate to the boys that even when you don't like something or agree with a decision, once you've expressed your opinion, as part of a family you have an affirmative duty to be as fully supportive as possible.

Charles and Damon were also members of a competitive fencing club. They both enjoyed fencing, and Coach Sherrer, who was an assistant fencing coach at Ohio State, really encouraged them, so much so that they both made the fencing team their first semester at Princeton. (Charles continued with fencing and was on Princeton's 2000 Ivy League championship team.)

While Charles and Damon had their opportunities for successful participation in team sports, that didn't alter our opinion about competitive sports or our preference for a focus on overall physical fitness and health. There were a number of reasons for our preference. Some of those reasons were generic and are probably applicable to lots of other families. But some of our reasons were very specific to us.

In terms of generic reasoning in favor of physical fitness, one obvious issue was the fact that most people are neither able nor willing to pursue competitive athletics as a lifelong endeavor. The combined limitations of time constraints and actual ability unite to curtail competitive sports relatively early in life for most folks. Now, if our sons were athletically gifted, we certainly would have pursued competitive team sports for them. But the fact of the matter is our sons were like most boys their ages: decent athletes, but nothing extraordinary. Looking ahead, it didn't seem reasonable to assume that they'd be playing competitive baseball, football, basketball, soccer, or hockey on a

regular basis well into their forties. And while they seemed to enjoy tennis
and golf—or, at least, Charles and Damon did—there was no great love exhibited for either sport. Charles really loved baseball, but we didn't have the
money to send him to summer baseball camp at the time he was interested in
going.

Beyond the limitations of talent and compelling interest, we knew the
older they got, the more pressing the elements of time constraints would become. I would imagine that it can be quite a challenge to get a game going
on a regular basis when everybody's in their forties, with very full lives.
Against those challenges of a lifetime of participation in competitive team
sports, we balanced the possibility of a commitment to fitness as a lifetime
goal. It just seemed a lot more likely that a habit of regular physical activity
would be one that could be continued for the duration.

Another generic reason for our emphasis on physical health and fitness focused squarely on the issue of talent. Regardless of the number of sports summer camps attended, very few kids are blessed with such athletic giftedness
that they can remain competitive through elementary, middle, and high
school, much less college. If physical activity and fitness are limited to playing and training for competitive sports, it can become difficult to maintain interest when the child is no longer selected to compete. Even more disturbing
is that too often such undue emphasis is placed on competitive sports that the
child chooses to stop participating even while still competitive, simply because it's not fun anymore. We simply weren't confident that the benefits of
participation in team sports would outweigh the potential costs.

Our final generic reason had to do with time. Competitive sports, even for
young kids, can become insanely time-consuming. We were not willing to
allow practice time, game time, and travel time to consume all of our time.
And this wasn't just about us being selfish with our time. We were protective
of our kids' time and our time as a family. We wanted physical health and activity to be a part of our sons' lives, not the sum total of it. We just couldn't see
how building our afternoons and weekends, and summers, falls, winters, and
springs, around sports would fit into our quest for holistic balance. That
much, at least, was very specific, but it wasn't our only specific reason.

At a very early age—long before we ever considered home schooling—
Evan told us "sports are stupid." His revelation came in the middle of a soccer game his dad was coaching. Evan was about four and, as I recall, he was
attempting to stand on his head. Granted, his head was in the right position—
he was a fullback—but he really needed to be standing on his feet rather than
his head. When C. Madison called out to him from the sidelines, "Evan,
stand up!" Evan was quite upset. He walked off the field, came to his dad, and

said, "Please don't ever yell at me—I don't want to play anymore." We were all stunned—for one thing, because there were a bunch of other parents standing around. You know your kids never embarrass you privately—others must be present to see you squirm. But surprisingly, C. Madison didn't seem upset at all. He made Evan finish the play, called a time-out, benched Evan, and then substituted another player for the rest of the game. Afterward, C. Madison and Evan went to McDonald's, alone. When they returned home, C. Madison told me he had explained the importance of being on a team—meaning Evan couldn't just quit in the middle of the season. He also explained that Evan didn't have to play soccer or any other team sport if he didn't want to, but that a lack of personal interest did not mean sports were stupid.

If C. Madison was disappointed in Evan's attitude about sports, there was no evidence of it. I knew then that C. Madison would always make the effort to deal with each of the boys as distinct individuals, not just as "his" sons.

Enlightenment notwithstanding, Evan's view on sports was the antithesis of his father's perspective that athletics and academics go hand in hand. Now, I already knew there was a flaw in C. Madison's reasoning, as I always detested all forms of mandatory athletic activities and I came dangerously close to not graduating from Wellesley because of difficulty in completing my PE requirement, even though the college was kind enough to give me four years to do so. However, when I married C. Madison, I knew he was one of those weird people who somehow managed to graduate in three years, cum laude, with a box of varsity letters. To me, that clearly fits at least one definition of unnatural.

What is remarkable about C. Madison, however, is his willingness to let each of his sons be himself. Unlike lots of parents, C. Madison wasn't trying to relive his own athletic success, or rectify his athletic failures, through his kids. He didn't care if they played team sports. All he cared about was that they be physically fit and active.

ANOTHER benefit of the recreation centers was the opportunity to combine physical fitness with expansive socialization. Our boys excelled in some of the physical activities, and in others they were just average. Some sports were much more demanding than they had anticipated, and some were a lot less interesting. But all contributed to an overall level of health and physical fitness. Socially, the boys ended up playing and hanging out with kids they may never have met had they stayed in private school or attended our local suburban high school.

I have to admit that this was a benefit I had not anticipated. The whole recreation center thing was hard for me to get used to at first, especially when some of the centers began random weapon searches. While I understood and agreed with C. Madison's interest in the boys' consistent engagement with other kids from different neighborhoods, with different life experiences, I found myself feeling a surprising level of anxiety about it in practice.

Let me tell you, broad-based socialization is easier said than done. (I guess that is why, so often, when people leave urban centers with their families they never return.) What I learned about myself was that while I felt perfectly comfortable growing up in a lower-middle-class neighborhood, I wasn't really comfortable with my sons playing in one. Fortunately C. Madison, while sympathetic to my concerns as a mother, was unyielding in his concerns as a father. All of the boys went to various recreation centers, all over town, and did so for years.

Now, when I observe the ease with which our sons, as young men, interact with people outside suburbia and their limited, elite college communities, I feel very pleased that C. Madison was inflexible about the recreation center thing. C. Madison was adamant that his sons grow up comfortable in the company of other black people and confident in their ability to handle themselves in the broadest range of circumstances and environments. It's not that I wanted the boys to grow up to be ignorant, callous, or insensitive to the experiences of other people, and I certainly didn't want them to grow up to be punks or weaklings. I simply didn't realize at the time that physically sheltering them too much—confining their activities to the physical boundaries of suburbia—could increase the likelihood of just such an outcome.

Here's an obvious point that was not always obvious to me when they were little: A healthy black man is the best person to teach a black boy how to become a healthy black man. Left to my own devices, I might have sentenced my sons to spending their formative years lost in suburbia, dressed in polo shirts and boat shoes. The world is so much bigger than suburbia, and there are so many wonderful people who will never live there, people my kids might not have met or gotten to know. Sharing life experiences with people—especially people who look different, speak differently, and have a thoroughly different life experience, even though your lives are lived in the same city—is essential if we have any hope of seeing one another as people. So often, class distinctions lead to the view of other people as just "other." We did not want our sons to grow up viewing poorer people as objects of pity, fear, or disrespect.

In the real world, there are a lot more people who are poor than who are middle class or wealthy. I often muse about prep school parents who ask me about the reality factor of home schooling—as if prep school or suburban schools provide more than a slice of real life. An escape from real life is part of what people pay for when they move to the suburbs or enroll their kids in private school.

C. Madison saw, much sooner than I, that our kids' engagement across a wide socioeconomic population was an effective way to strengthen them spiritually. Part of what he saw they ought to be was compassionate and understanding about the human condition. Additionally, he saw that understanding should begin in their community, their world, before it spread to the third world or anywhere else.

So while we began using the recreation center programs for physical fitness purposes, the end result was extremely holistic. They learned firsthand that there are tremendous intellectual opportunities everywhere, including inner-city recreation centers, and they learned that there are enormous spiritual opportunities created by open engagement, the act of understanding and respecting the lives lived by others.

THE physical conditioning achieved through the various recreation center programs was quite effective. One distinct advantage was that none of the recreation centers had varsity teams or select teams, so there was very little official exclusivity.

The kids who came to the recreation centers came to receive basic instruction in a particular sport and to play it. The benefits to our kids were enormous. First of all, they were exposed to a wide range of physical activities. Some were principally aerobic activities, like swimming. Other activities focused more on strength and overcoming fear—sports like football, for example. Still other activities emphasized strategic thinking, e.g., fencing. And while swimming, football, and fencing gave the boys the opportunity to participate on competitive teams, the nature of each activity was so different that the team experiences were vastly different as well.

Due to the lack of intense competition, they had the fairly unusual opportunity to be on a swim team, a football team, and a fencing team. Had they been in a traditional educational institution, it's doubtful such diverse athletic experiences would have been feasible.

Because our emphasis was on the boys' physical health and development, we didn't feel the need to identify their "best" sport, and instead were free to help them experience a wide range of athletic activities. It really wasn't necessary for them to love all of it or to excel at any of it: They just needed to experience the unique challenges of each. So when they had golf and tennis lessons, they knew we weren't expecting them to follow in the footsteps of Tiger Woods or the Williams sisters. These were athletic experiences, no more and no less than horseback riding or tae kwon do. Each boy had a broad-based athletic experience, and while I can't know for certain, I hope they will have a lifelong commitment to physical health and activity.

What I can say with certainty now is that Charles, Damon, and Evan are fit, strong, healthy, agile, and reasonably fast. Evan still does not deign to participate in any sports, but he is very strong, a very fast runner, and an excellent swimmer. Should he ever choose to participate, his father is convinced he would be a highly competitive member of a good track-and-field team. I, of course, do not care, as long as he and his brothers are healthy and physically fit.

The importance of a commitment to physical fitness as a vital aspect of holistic health cannot be overstated. No matter which educational option you select for your children, it's important to pay attention to the issue of physical fitness. Increasingly, schools are shifting the focus from overall physical fitness and physical education to competitive varsity and junior varsity teams. That shift in focus means a lot of kids are going to be left out, and the level of obesity in America's children is evidence of their exclusion.

A similar difficulty in clarity of focus can arise in home schooling. People home-school for a variety of reasons—religious, political, academic, or some combination of the three—which is fine. But regardless of the reason for home schooling, children need to have physical fitness incorporated into their daily lives. Once you make the commitment to physical fitness, then you can begin to explore different ways of achieving that goal.

A good place to start is by asking your kid what she's interested in, emphasizing interest rather than talent. Next ask her what she's good at, and here you want her to think about her talent rather than her interest, keeping in mind that interest and talent do not always intersect. The two of you now have something to sit down and examine. Look at the two lists, talk about them, incorporate them into one and see what, if anything, is missing in terms of overall health. Try to compile a list of athletic activities that includes aspects of stretching, strengthening, and aerobic conditioning. Make sure the list includes some diversity of approach as well. Mix in solitary activities, like yoga or jogging, with more social activities, like tae kwon do. Also try to blend activities around fitness—e.g., swimming—with activities around teams, like baseball.

Now that you've got a list to work from, start looking for resources. Find out where the activities your kid's interested in are being offered. Be sure to find out when they're offered, and if the times offered don't work with your schedule, ask if other times might be available if enough kids were interested. (This is when it pays to be involved in home-schooling groups: There may be other kids interested in the same class or lesson at the same time.) Another thing to find out is the cost. Almost all recreation centers are underwritten by the city, which means most of their programs are free or almost free, so along with the wide diversity of activities offered, the price is perfect. Local community centers and associations are also good sources to explore for team activities, as they frequently sponsor soccer, baseball, basketball, and football leagues. Finally—though this wasn't an option when we were home-schooling—many public school districts now allow home-schooled students to participate in athletic programs offered in the schools.

Tons of athletic options and opportunities are available. The important thing is to make sure that the same degree of focused attention directed to the intellectual and spiritual development of your kid is directed at her physical health and fitness. There can be no holistic health in the absence of physical health.

12

HOW WE KEPT

THEM CULTURED

I BELIEVE ART has the capacity to inspire the intellect, lift the spirit, en-hance physical activity, and warm the heart. Knowing, believing, and feeling this to be so, we had to incorporate art squarely into the midst of our home-schooling experiment if we had any sincere desire to create an environment of holistic balance for the boys.

There are two tricky things about exposing kids to the arts: timing and tech-nique. In terms of timing, you absolutely must start before they're old enough to have been informed by their peers that the arts aren't cool. At a surprisingly young age, children are incredibly influenced by the assessment and knowl-edge base of their peers. How it is that an otherwise intelligent ten-year-old could really think the opinion of another ten-year-old, or even a twelve-year-old for that matter, could have greater merit than that of a person who's been on the planet twenty-five years longer is beyond me, but it happens. Conse-quently, exposure to the arts needs to begin before kindergarten in order to withstand the inevitable onslaught of uncool commentary that will flow from the mouths of middle-schoolers. Early exposure doesn't mean the kid will brag about participating in or even attending an arts event. But early exposure does seem to reduce the impact of the negative commentary.

The second challenge is technique. This was much trickier. The broader the base of inclusion of what is deemed art into daily life, the easier it is for kids to embrace. Simply stated, I think the arts should be integrated into daily life the same way prayer, worship, reading, and exercise are. These are everyday things, which is not to say that they are ordinary or unimportant things: The universe is full of everyday occurrences rich in significance. My level of consciousness determines my ability to recognize the significance of everyday occurrences. I hate it when I catch myself taking stuff for granted, whether it's a quiet evening of solitude with C. Madison, a breathtaking sunrise over the pond, or watching my sons enjoying their dinner and laughing together. I shouldn't have to wait for a twenty-fifth anniversary, or the view from Mt. Everest, or a graduation gala to get misty-eyed over the blessings in my life. When things that should form the fabric of everyday life become layered in occasion, I think we just miss too much. Similarly, when those things that should be central to a life well lived become layered in the tapestry of exclusivity and status, they become harder to embrace, because they seem artificial.

An example can be seen in church. Church should be a place to gather in fellowship, prayer, and worship; that's why the scriptures teach "not forsaking the assembling of ourselves together." However, if prayer and worship don't happen anywhere else or at any other time in a child's daily life, church becomes a meaningless and empty ritual, and prayer is "as a sounding brass, or a tinkling cymbal." It's like when people talk about how much they love their relatives, yet rarely make any effort to spend time with them except for obligatory appearances at major holidays. We make time and create occasions for the things that matter to us.

Similarly, when the arts are not a part of a child's daily life, attending arts activities can take on a patina of ritualistic falsehood. If the arts are not important enough to be incorporated into daily life, what is the point of going somewhere to see them?

I think this is one example of how issues of status and exclusivity can cloud and restrict our vision of the arts. If the arts are perceived merely as a way of establishing or validating one's socioeconomic dominance or superiority, the importance of the arts wanes in the community. Conversely, when the entire idea of art is expanded beyond the pretense and exclusion that so regrettably accompanies many arts activities, real enjoyment increases across the community—inclusion will occur spontaneously.

In such an environment, the arduous task of outreach would be so much easier. One reason outreach is so difficult is the concern felt by many nontraditional patrons of the arts about being welcomed, both officially and unofficially. Working on outreach in the arts can make one feel like Sisyphus pushing the hideously heavy stone up the hill, only to see it roll back down again. Why does outreach feel like that? Because every year goals are set and sometimes they're met—e.g., we gave away one hundred tickets to an arts event and one hundred first-time children came. But we've been giving away the same hundred tickets for the past twenty years. That first crop of first-timers are now adults. Why haven't they joined the ranks of regular patrons of the arts? And by regular patrons, I don't mean just season-ticket subscribers; I'm talking about folks who may not buy a membership or season series for every arts organization in town—that can be a sizable capital expenditure—but who come out and support various arts events throughout the year. I think we need to explore why so many outreach efforts fail to meet their strategic goals of broadening that critical patron base. My own exploration of this issue evolved from difficulties I encountered in using my technique of taking the boys to arts events early and often.

Naïvely, I thought the total challenge of technique rested squarely on my shoulders. I was convinced that if I created an atmosphere in our home in which art in all its myriad forms was welcomed and celebrated, my work would be finished. I just knew that if art is part of one's home life, going outside the home to enjoy it would seem as natural as exhaling an inhaled breath.

Attending an arts function, whether traditional or contemporary, European, Asian, or African, should be a joyous occasion of excitement and anticipation. I—my race, my ethnicity, my apparel—should not be a source of fascination for other attendees, or at least not obviously so. In other words, what's with the staring? The staring presented the single biggest obstacle to our kids' enthusiasm about attending arts functions. I am at a loss as to why, so often, when African-Americans attend the opera, the symphony, the ballet, or an exhibit at an art museum, they are greeted with stark stares. Granted, not all black people attend such events, but neither do all white people.

Sadly, whatever else our nation took from its European antecedents, a love of the arts was not included. As a consequence, very few Americans, of any race or ethnicity, regularly participate in the traditional arts, even when it's an extraordinary event. For example, several years ago we attended a concert presentation of the complete Brandenburg Concertos at the acoustically perfect Southern Theatre in Columbus. The musicians were all outstanding, but the violinist and the flautist were unbelievable, both in their interpretations and their renditions. Best of all, we had perfect seats—about four rows back—and the tickets cost less than forty dollars each. Unbelievably, the concert was not sold out. In sharp contrast, that same year I attended a Prince concert in Richmond. It, too, was a fabulous concert. Prince was fabulous as both a musician and a performer. Of course that concert was completely sold out, and my ticket cost one hundred dollars. That's where we are with the arts, and with that degree of puzzling inconsistency, how is it that the appearance of a black family generates any notice whatsoever? We received more stares when we took the boys to the Yo-Yo Ma concert in Athens, Ohio, than when we took them on a temple tour in Bangkok, Thailand. While I cannot state this definitely, I'm going to stretch out here and guess that there are a lot more black people in and around Athens, Ohio, than in Bangkok, Thailand.

In other words, I don't believe the staring is as much about surprise as it is about displeasure. It appears as though the inherent value of the experience is lessened if shared by black people. I think this is a clear indication that at least for the starers, being present is less about the art than about the joy of presumed exclusivity. I don't know how else to explain the marked difference in the seemingly sincere and warm welcome we received with the boys in virtually every museum we visited in Paris and the cold, rude, begrudging greeting we have consistently received at the Boston Museum of Fine Arts. I know lots of African-Americans cite Boston as the most racist city in the country, but still, that's just weird. And beyond weird, such nonverbal conduct on the part of adults seemingly in charge—ticket takers, guards, and especially docents ("Attitude" must be the first course in docent training—right before "Intro to Art History" and "Overview of Our Collection"!)—has a chilling effect on impressionable children. The chilling effect forced me to alter my own strategy and technique as I began to see the impact it was having on my kids.

Initially, the behavior of staff, volunteers, and even other patrons at various arts events just wasn't registering on my radar screen. For one thing, I had three little boys to occupy my time and attention, not to mention whatever it was we had come to see or hear. Plus, I had been black for quite some time by then—I think a lot of my sensitivity was dormant. I was shocked into consciousness when the twins were about six and I took them to see an exhibit at the Cummer Museum, a lovely, small museum with beautiful, old gardens, right on the banks of the St. Johns River in Jacksonville, Florida. As we were strolling through the galleries, Charles suddenly turned and asked me why were people looking at us "so mean." I'm not sure I had even noticed, but before I could respond, Damon said, "It's because we're black, isn't it, Mommy?" (It's always so interesting to me how little ones process what they see, which is why I think it's so important to talk with them frequently. In fact, when it comes to talking with kids, I use the old Tammany Hall approach to voting: early and often.) I didn't immediately respond to either boy. I had to sit down first and think for a minute. (As I frequently was caught off guard by their questions and observations, they were used to me needing to take a minute to think.) After a few minutes, I told them I had some things to say, but they weren't completely responsive answers to their specific questions. They said that was okay.

I told Charles that I didn't really know why people behave the way they do; that sometimes I don't even know why I do the things I do. Plus, sometimes people are just sad, or they're having a bad day, or they don't feel well, so they look kind of mean at everybody. No, no, he said, the people who looked mean at us smiled at the other people. Damon very knowingly nodded his head, and patted my hand as if to say, "Poor Mommy, so unaware." So I turned my attention to his question.

It's a hard thing to explain to a black child that while everything isn't about race, so many things are that you have to be conscious of the variable of race and color without becoming overly sensitive to it. As radical, fundamentalist Christians, we believe in predestination as a cornerstone in liberation theology, but, you know, I didn't really want to get into all of that right then. I didn't want to miss the ever-elusive, teachable moment, either. So I told them several things.

First, God gives each of us some knowledge, wisdom, and discernment. Our job here on earth is to learn to respect and use it. If you feel something, examine it critically for yourself. For example, I do not know what is in the minds of other people, so I try not to begin with negative presumptions, including the presumption of racism. However, because God has not given us a spirit of fear, but of peace, of love, and of a strong mind, I can bravely face whatever is really there, and Daddy and I expect you to have that same courage, to face even bad and scary and confusing things.

Racism is real, and pretending it isn't is a sign of fear and cowardice that shames Jesus. He doesn't want us to be victims and use racism as an excuse, but He also doesn't want us to be such weaklings that we cannot face reality. So, if someone looks at you "mean," smile and keep going. You can't know why they are looking mean, but whatever the reason, it's their problem, not yours. Racist or not, they have no power over us unless we give it to them, and we won't.

So I asked them, do you want to sit here and feel bad about the mean looks, or would you rather go on to the park and have our picnic lunch like we planned? Of course they opted for the food, and a serious lesson was covered for them. I was still struggling, of course, and as we left I did notice the mean looks, probably because I was looking for them. But what I also saw was the boys smiling and waving goodbye as they skipped right out the door.

That evening, when I discussed it with C. Madison, we agreed that we'd have to expand our technique by talking to the kids more in advance of these outings. Previously, all we talked about was what they would see or hear—the story line or libretto if we were taking them to an opera, or pictures in Janson's *History of Art* if we were going to a museum. Of course, we talked about good manners and the importance of indoor and outdoor voices, but I hadn't really thought to devote much time to issues of race or racism and how they may be manifest in arts environments. But once it became clear that race was an issue, one they were conscious of, we knew we needed to address it as part of our strategy, or all our plans for a lifetime commitment to the arts would be foiled.

So, while we hadn't planned to go off in that direction, we found we had to introduce the politics and economics of art in order to provide some basis of understanding for the boys. We also realized that we needed to construct some way for them to process and deflect the negative energy being directed to them. So, whenever we went anywhere and people stared, it was my job to initiate the big, warm, friendly smile for our family. If the person didn't smile back, we would look at each other and grin because we knew they were more of the dreaded "starerers." ("Starerers": Yes, it should be "starers," but these were little kids with various weird pronunciations.)

"Starerers" are people who glare and stare with disapproval and confusion at small black children, and won't smile back if you smile at them. It became a game to see when one would appear and which boy would spot the "starerer" first. Sometimes one of the boys would come up and whisper in my ear, "Mommy, I think I see one." That would be my cue to turn and flash my biggest and brightest smile. If I didn't get a smile in return, the boys and I would look at one another very knowingly and with great pity. This game didn't last long, because the boys quickly outgrew it. But for that short period, maybe six months or so, it served its purpose.

Transcending the pull of self-loathing and victimhood doesn't happen through denial of the truth, it comes from facing the truth. A great many political and social theorists decry the influence of victimhood status within the black community, as well they should. My prayer is that eventually those same theorists will have the strength to acknowledge the corresponding need in the white community to cease and desist from racist conduct, both overt and covert. Such conduct negatively impacts the reception one feels in the arts community.

OVER the years, our sons either participated in or patronized various art forms, including ballet, fine art, opera, symphony, jazz, theater, musicals, recitals, and concerts. We were excited about sharing experiences in art with our kids, and it really didn't matter to us what the context or venue was. A Christmas exhibit at the Chicago Art Institute, an African drumming exhibition at the Martin Luther King, Jr., Center for Performing and Cultural Arts in Columbus, a Yo-Yo Ma concert at Ohio University, or a full stage production with the Fugees and Ziggy Marley at the Polaris Amphitheater, were all thrilling experiences. Whether we saw the etchings of Rembrandt at the Taft House in Cincinnati or the murals of Monet in the Tuileries in Paris didn't matter: We were just thrilled at the opportunity to see them. We wanted Charles, Damon, and Evan to comprehend that the opportunity to view and participate in the arts is a gift, something too valuable to the overall quality of their lives as conscious and civilized people to be sloughed off as insignificant or unimportant. What we didn't want was for them to leave our home-schooling experience with the misconception that the arts were limited to what can be viewed at the Louvre or heard at Lincoln Center. Those are wonderful venues, with delightful and provocative art, but they are hardly the sum total of what is included in art. We wanted them to have the same regard for the art expressed in smoky jazz joints, African-American cultural centers, and the music departments of black churches. Art is life and it is everywhere. It is the smallest tangible evidence of God's indwelling, proof that we are, indeed, made in His image. Just as His creation should be observed, viewed, participated in, and, most of all, enjoyed, so should it be with art.

We encouraged the kids to tell us what they liked and what they didn't. Art is personal and has a flexible scale of relative value based upon the age, exposure, and personal taste of the observer. It was perfectly all right with me if they preferred the poetry of Countee Cullen to that of Edgar Allan Poe, and it was fine for them to say they liked Caravaggio more than Mondrian. Over time, our tastes in art may change and mature just as our palate does. Every kid doesn't have to eat peas—there are lots of other green vegetables to be consumed. Similarly, every kid doesn't have to love Dickens—there are a lot of other great writers out there to be enjoyed. All of our sons prefer opera to symphony, and everyone enjoys ballet, except Evan, who swears he has "flashbacks!" Similarly, C. Madison and I are not enthusiastic, or even particularly knowledgeable, hip-hop fans, but we listen to enough of it to be able to recognize and identify major artists. I find OutKast to be quite righteous even though I'm by no means an aficionado, but the point is we each strive to recognize and validate the diversity of art, both extant and emerging, all around us. We do not all enjoy the same art forms or media, and sometimes one of us may not be in the mood to appreciate someone else's artistic preference— that's the making of a conflict, but conflict about art is not a problem. Art is supposed to awaken something in each of us, as viewers, hearers, and participants, and what is awakened is unique to us as individuals. Art is not meant to evoke the same response from everyone. It's highly individualistic—it's art! I don't mind that my kids would rather listen to OutKast than Verdi—I would be concerned if they were unaware of Verdi's work, but they're not. And if I couldn't even be bothered to listen to OutKast, as though no art forms have evolved since the eighteenth century, how ignorant does that make me? Our kids have seen *Rigoletto* and they've heard the major arias from *Aida* and *Otello*. They're familiar with Shakespeare's plays, and the fact that they prefer *Richard III* to *The Merchant of Venice* (my personal favorite) is of no more consequence to me than the fact that they enjoy the urban poetry of Jay-Z more than the works of Tennyson.

The only rigid rule we have ever applied to the arts was participation: That was not negotiable. The boys thought our participation in the sing-along of Handel's *Messiah* was absurd. That was okay. They didn't have to sing with us. They just had to come and be there, to be present in the moment—that's participation. We wanted Charles, Damon, and Evan to be open to just about everything that could fit under the banner of art, without the parameters of peer-group acceptance.

JUST in the context of technique and accessibility, music may be the easiest art form to incorporate into the life of a child. Music, in many forms, was a part of our kids' lives even in utero. They spent their infancy listening to our eclectic collections of tapes, CDs, and albums. (Yes, C. Madison has, and still plays, an enormous album collection!)

Both C. Madison and I had classical-music training as children—piano and violin, respectively. More important (since neither of us plays regularly or well as adults), we grew up in households where classical music was treasured. C. Madison's mother and grandmother both are profoundly talented, and classically trained, pianists and organists. His mother was the accompanist, and his grandmother was the minister of music, at First Baptist Church in Memphis, Tennessee. As a boy, C. Madison spent all of August and the fall listening as his mother and grandmother worked with the full church choir to mount a production of Handel's *Messiah*, to be presented each year on the Sunday before Christmas.

My younger sister, Cheryl, also an extremely gifted pianist, also was classically trained. I can't think of my childhood without hearing her practice, and while I complained about it—vociferously—I cannot hear a recording of Chopin today without comparing the musician's skill to that of my sister.

So, for obvious reasons, C. Madison and I own quite a few traditional, classical recordings. C. Madison is also quite the jazz aficionado. He loves jazz in almost all its forms. While I am not innately attracted to jazz, C. Madison has helped me to develop an ear and a genuine appreciation for it. Because he has always enjoyed listening to the music, Charles, Damon, and Evan grew up hearing great instrumental and vocal jazz.

My musical quirk is country-and-western music—not popular, crossover, urban cowboy stuff, but real country (emphasis on country) works by Patsy Cline, Loretta Lynn, Tennessee Ernie Ford, George Jones, et al. The source? When I was a little girl, Mrs. Effie Brown baby-sat us and kept house while our parents worked. (Effie started working for my parents when I was four years old and stayed until the summer I got married.) Effie taught me that people can be highly intelligent and knowledgeable without any formal education beyond the fourth grade. Effie was from Winston-Salem, North Carolina, and dearly loved true country music, and soap operas, especially *As the World Turns*. While I outgrew any concern about Bob, Nancy, and the rest of the soap "family," I never outgrew my love of country music. I played and sang country recordings so often while housecleaning that when the kids were small, they knew all the words to "There He Goes" and "Turn the Cards Slowly." I knew baby Charles could sing like an angel the first time I heard him sing "I love you honey, I love your money, most of all I love your automobile," the chorus to Patsy Cline's hit "I Love You Honey."

As children in the sixties and college students in the seventies, C. Madison and I both love James Brown, the Philly Sound, and, of course, everything Motown ever recorded. C. Madison has most of this sizable collection in duplicate: original albums and CDs. Our kids grew up hearing the Supremes, the Temptations, the Isley Brothers, and the O'Jays. This was interspersed with music from the "revolution," including Gil-Scott Heron and Nikki Giovanni's poetry, balanced against ballads by Roberta Flack and Donny Hathaway.

There was no modern, popular music played in our home until our boys were old enough to introduce it! Interestingly, as their father and I have been caught in a time warp, musically, and held the kids there with us, they were easily able to identify the background samples so evident in much of hip-hop and rap, which probably enhanced their enjoyment of the music.

And then, of course, there was church music: gospel, hymns, anthems, and all the modern translations and arrangements of all the above. Our church has several choirs, including one sizable pastoral choir. We also have musicians. Nowadays, lots of churches have a pianist and an organist, and so do we, but over the years we also have had trumpet players, guitarists, drummers, and a bass player. On any given Sunday, the music ranges from traditional hymns to very high energy, "jump-jump" praise songs.

By the time Charles and Damon were toddlers, they had received their first tambourine, and music in some form or another was second nature to them—there has never been any status attached to any of it. By the time they were three, it seemed like the most logical thing in the world to begin taking them to the symphony, the opera, and the ballet. They were used to hearing music and seeing it performed in various forums, and they enjoyed all of it. Occasionally, Evan forgot he wasn't at church, where group participation is the norm, so sometimes he'd get up and want to clap his hands or stomp his feet, and I'd have to take him out in the hall. Other than that, we had no problems. And even that wasn't really a problem: C. Madison and I always took the boys to such events together, and we tried to make sure our seats began on the aisle—that way, one of us could whisk Evan out without disturbing other patrons, and still leave a parent inside with Charles and Damon.

By the time they were in grade school, "going out" seemed normal to the boys. When BalletMet, our local ballet company and academy, offered auditions, none of our sons seemed the least bit reluctant to try out—and enthusiastically, at that! Evan received a scholarship for several years and performed in *The Nutcracker* for each of those years. He first performed as a mouse, then the younger prince, and finally the older prince. He was the cutest thing! Simultaneously, Charles sang with the children's chorus of Opera Columbus and performed in *Turandot*. He was also the cutest thing! Meanwhile, Damon was in the Supers' Guild of Opera Columbus and performed as a lion in *The Magic Flute*. And, yes, he too was the cutest thing! (It doesn't seem possible that each of them could have been the cutest thing, but there it is.) Damon also played the violin and took lessons at the Capital University music program.

At about the same time, the boys also were participating in a number of theatrical endeavors. In addition to athletic activities, Columbus Parks and Recreation also runs an arts program at the Davis Center. There, Charles and Damon took tap classes, joined a drama club, and, ultimately, Charles and Evan performed in a surprisingly professional version of *Really Rosie*, starring Ms. Jessica Grove, now an up-and-coming young star on Broadway! Charles was Johnny and Evan played the part of Chicken Soup. They also participated in a production of *Peter Pan*, performed for the Columbus Arts Festival, with Damon in a starring role as Captain Hook and Charles as Smee. For quite a number of years, traditional, classical/Eurocentric art forms consumed a tremendous amount of our time.

When the boys decided they didn't want to continue performing, they had a variety of reasons, almost all of them sound. Charles and Damon wanted to quit opera and join football; and since their voices were changing, continuing with the children's chorus really wasn't an option. Evan didn't have a new activity he wanted to add, he just wanted to get out of ballet. He was, as he told us, "tired of the assumptions." Fortunately, no one said, "I never want to go to the _____ [fill in the arts blank!] ever again," so we continued our involvement with the arts as patrons.

We had no intention of Evan becoming a professional dancer, Charles becoming a famous tenor, or Damon becoming a famous violinist. Dance and music were only two art forms, but they served as a good foundation for the rest of our work in the arts.

I began taking the boys to art museums when they weren't quite two years old. Art museums are an easy outing with little ones because you get to walk around; absolute silence is not a requirement; they have big, clean bathrooms; and there's almost always a place to sit down and enjoy a juice box. Whenever we visit a city, we make it a point to visit at least one art museum or gallery. The boys have been to about fifty or sixty different venues to view art.

At home, I maintained lots of art supplies, finger paints, watercolors, construction paper, glue, crayons, markers, stickers, glitter, etc., and all the attendant junk stuff: shoe boxes, macaroni, old greeting cards, paper towel rolls. It was not unusual for the boys to bring me a "masterpiece," and it was my job to identify the object and find somewhere to hang it. (As I was not the least averse to hanging art work anywhere—living room, dining room, bathrooms, etc.—I was great at the second part. Where I generally failed was in the identification process.)

One day, when Evan was three, he brought me a new piece, and I knew precisely what it was. I looked up and he was holding a watercolor of a swan floating on a lake, with a castle in the background and an astonishingly clear reflection on the lake. I very calmly asked him where he got the painting and he said he had made it. Of course, I didn't believe him, not because he was in the habit of lying, but because it didn't seem possible that he could have done it. I was genuinely curious about where he had found it. I told him that he was so special that he didn't have to lie or pretend to be something that he wasn't. He insisted he had done the painting, so I insisted that he paint another one, right then, with me watching. He did, and I was absolutely shocked. Until that moment I had had no idea he could actually paint—and I mean seriously paint! So, even before we began home schooling in any formal way, we were dealing with the challenge of providing structure for a gifted child. Evan has continued to manifest this giftedness, and when he was seven he won his first of ten annual scholarships to the Columbus College of Art and Design's Saturday school.

Evan continued his studies at CCAD until he left for college, and while there were many challenges at CCAD, in many ways it was an outstanding experience for him. Right off the bat, the validation of competitive scholarships was significant. For a student who is home-schooled, it can be very difficult to have a sense of one's own talent. By design, we hadn't wanted the boys to develop the habit of comparing themselves to their peers: We wanted them to strive for excellence, their personal best. But, pretty quickly, we could see that Evan was establishing his sense of excellence, not in comparison to his chronological peers but to the artists whose work he was viewing in museums. This was clearly a problem, but spending time at CCAD helped Evan put his own work in clearer perspective. Another benefit was the opportunity to interact with art students his own age. He also spent a good bit of time on CCAD's campus over the course of ten years of Saturdays, so he had some sense of the environment of an art school. This proved invaluable when he had to make decisions about college.

While some of the CCAD experience was informative and invaluable, some was difficult and disturbing. As an old CCAD Saturday school alum myself, I basically knew the drill. The early years, ages seven through about ten or eleven, all kinds of kids come to the program, but by middle school it's a bit more focused, and by high school the kids who come have made some definite choices about the role of art in their lives. After all, the fact that Saturday school starts at nine A.M.—such a hideously early start time, on a Saturday no less—is not to be taken lightly. As Evan got older, he found that the environment changed. It became far less diverse; i.e., by the last couple of years there weren't any other African-American males in any of his classes. More disturbing was the increasing level of negative competition masked as disinterest by most of his teachers.

When I'd go in to talk with his teachers about his progress, I was frequently stunned by the negative responses, not only to his work, but to his personality. He wasn't talkative or friendly enough. He was too aloof. He was reluctant to participate in group projects. And the work? He seemed to know a lot about anatomy. He seemed to have had some experience with color. He seemed trapped in representational styles.

Meanwhile, Evan's commentary about the experience was sparse, to say the least. But when pushed, I didn't hear anything positive. In ten years of study, Evan had only three teachers who, in any way, acknowledged his presence in class, much less his talent, at least not directly to him. Each year, a disproportionate number of his pieces were selected for the end-of-the-year show, but it was done so begrudgingly that the encouragement that should have been implicit in such a selection was lost.

The flip side of this was that Evan's personality complicated an already difficult process. To say Evan is intense is a huge understatement. For Evan, art has never been a hobby or an interest—he has approached it with a deep and single-minded focus. It is only due to our constant surveillance, and his brothers' insistence on Evan "acting normal," that Evan hasn't become another obsessed, crazy artist. And because Evan has been focused on the work, rather than on being an artist, he has never been sucked into the tempting vortex of posturing. Evan didn't feel the need to "look like an artist," so there was no tattooing, piercing, or weird dyeing. (Well, once he did dye his hair red, but, fortunately, it didn't last long.) He also didn't feel the need to act like an artist or to fit into the negative stereotypes of artistic behavior, so there wasn't any drinking, drugging, or being dirty. Evan just wasn't a poseur, and he wasn't trying to impress anybody or receive any validation. Evan was there for one reason and one reason only: to work.

Long before he could articulate it, Evan had to work. Evan was always working, from the time he was a little boy—drawing, painting, sculpting—but it was years before he saw it as work. As he got older, he began to realize that he was different, that he had a gift. What is remarkable is his humility. It's not false modesty: Evan knows how enormous his gift is, but he also knows that it is, in fact, a gift, and he knows that it is significant that he was selected to receive this gift. I think that's why he takes his work so seriously. And while it was disappointing that Evan's experience at CCAD was less than it might have been, the negative impact was tempered by an example of divine intervention that occurred at a critical moment in his development.

Although I have a fairly extensive background in studio art, by the time Evan was twelve it was obvious that I had nothing further to teach him—he had far outstripped my abilities. Yet Evan desperately needed instruction, intellectual stimulation, and encouragement, things that he just wasn't receiving with any degree of consistency at CCAD.

I had seen this time approaching, but as the impasse loomed closer, my faith was beginning to falter, and I was talking about the situation to every-body: seeking advice, asking for suggestions. And then, when I least expected it, I got the answer, and it was one I would have never considered on my own. A friend, Linda Willis, came over to talk to me about Space Camp because her son was interested in going. As we talked about general mother stuff, she suddenly asked me about Evan and his art work. I hadn't even remembered discussing it with her, but I immediately told her my concerns about his po-tential stagnation. Linda suggested that Evan work with Dr. Roman Johnson in his studio.

I was stunned. Roman was a well-known, professional artist with paying pa-trons, and this wasn't the 1600s. What possible reason would he have to let Evan come to work in his studio? But Linda insisted that we try, and she agreed to broach the subject with Roman. She called me later in the week and said Roman had initially declined, but she had been so insistent about the quality of Evan's work that Roman had agreed to speak with me.

I anxiously called, and Roman was so short and mean on the phone that I almost hung up, but I knew this might be the chance of a lifetime for Evan. Roman told me he didn't have kids because he didn't like them and he didn't want any in his studio. Before I could respond to that, he went on to tell me that while all artists have a commitment to seek out and encourage younger artists, he doubted my son was one, because "Every old crow thinks her baby's a swan." But since Linda made the recommendation, he was will-ing to look at Evan's sketchbook. I was to bring the sketchbook to Roman's studio, but under no circumstances was I to bring "the boy" with me.

I was thrilled. But Evan would not allow me to take his sketchbook any-where. We weren't even allowed to look in his sketchbook without his express permission. So I had no choice but to take the sketchbook, with Evan, to go meet Roman.

When we arrived, Roman bellowed, "Don't think I'm going to hold my tongue if the work's no good! Give me the book!" Evan stepped forward and handed over his sketchbook without a word. Roman very carefully began with the first sketch and scrutinized every page in complete silence. When he finished, he handed the book back to Evan, turned to me, and said, "This boy is the reincarnation of Albrecht Dürer." He told Evan he would be pleased to have him work with him in his studio, and from that moment on dealt with Evan as a gifted, spiritual being worthy of respect. What is remarkable is that Roman was seventy-nine years old at the time. After he allowed Evan to begin working in his studio, Roman rapidly acquired a unique position in our family, and he has maintained a close relationship with each of our sons.

Because Charles and Damon have always been Evan's biggest fans, they have been quite interested in the pragmatic aspects of the life of the professional artist. We have all listened with rapt attention as Roman has detailed the eighty-plus years of his life. He has shared with us his struggles as an African-American artist painting professionally since the 1940s. As a young man, he studied in Paris and New York; his work has been shown at the Whitney, and the Columbus Museum of Art owns a number of his paintings. He met, worked, and studied with Emerson Burkhart in Columbus and Ernest Fiene and Edwin Dickinson, a student of Charles Hawthorn, at the Art Students League in New York. While I know most of his musings have been in an effort to inform and help prepare Evan, his provocative analysis of art, race, and class in America over the course of forty years has been invaluable to all of the guys.

In a 1999 *Columbus Dispatch* article, Ms. Nannette Maciejunes, senior curator at the Columbus Museum of Art, said this about Roman: "Roman is an important senior figure in this art community. He knows art history. He continues to read and look at the masters. He continues to engage in art dialogue, and that's what artists are supposed to do. . . . We often punish artists for having a wide range of styles and themes. Roman is an experimental painter and interested in a variety of traditions. . . . Johnson has continued with questions and experimentation for 60 years." This is the environment Evan walked into at thirteen, when he began working with Roman.

Evan and Roman worked together every Saturday afternoon, from one to four, until Evan "graduated." Of course, Roman was the commencement speaker! To have had the opportunity to work with someone so talented and so wise was a gift. And the fact that Roman was so delighted to see Evan's talent grow and expand was more than anything we could have ever hoped for at that stage in Evan's life. So while CCAD was a slice of reality, Evan's work with Roman was an indication of God's influence and direction in Evan's development.

In the final analysis, art is a critical component of a well-lived, well-rounded life. Consequently, including and incorporating art in the lives of our children is essential. Having said that, it's also important to remember that the arts are extremely varied and there are many ways to become involved, so each family needs to decide what works for them. Maybe you want to start off by simply expanding your collective recognition of art and how much it is already a part of your lives. Is your child in a reading program at the library? Does your child participate in choir, band, orchestra, or drama? Does your kid enjoy movies, jazz, hip-hop, or dance? Find out where your child's artistic interests lie and then work on expanding them.

More than anything else, help your child recognize that the arts are not about money or social status, race, or gender. As you develop a plan for your child's participation in the arts, try consciously to maintain a balance between traditional or classical forms of art—e.g., opera—with ethnic, folk, and contemporary artistic expressions—e.g., African drumming or jazz.

As your kid matures and begins to develop more distinct and defined areas of interest, try to encourage expansion even within those disciplines. So if your kid loves dance, whether as a participant or patron, try to provide the broadest view of dance: ballet, jazz, Afro-Caribbean, Irish folk dances, etc. If your kid's thing is music, encourage a broad-brush approach, and take her to tons of concerts so she can see a wide range of music performed live. Similarly, theater needn't be limited to Shakespeare: There is a lot of exciting contemporary theater being produced, and an attentive audience is always appreciated.

Finally, try not to let every arts event become some huge, formal, dress-up occasion. Take advantage of informal, outside venues, and enjoy some summer concerts, plays, and art shows. Remember: The more fun the last event was, the easier it will be to get everybody to go to the next event.

13

HOW WE KEPT

THEM CONNECTED THROUGH

COMMUNITY SERVICE

We knew we wanted the boys to leave our home with a clear understanding of the critical importance of community service and volunteerism. And we knew that if we wanted the boys to have the right attitude about community service, we needed to be crystal clear about the purpose. Although we knew we were the parents, it's much easier to get things done with kids when you get their buy-in at the outset. And it's much easier to get buy-in when the ideas are presented in a contextual framework. So we approached the issue of community service and volunteerism in the broadest possible way.

We couldn't afford to have the boys reach adolescence with the misconception that community service is something you do to get into college. We also couldn't afford to have them reach adolescence with the misconception that community service is some noblesse-oblige burden placed on the upper and middle classes. Essentially, we wanted them to understand the vital role of service in any well-lived life, which is a daunting task in a society that doesn't appear to have any real appreciation for service.

Given the obvious challenges, we decided to approach the ideas of community service and volunteerism with the kids first. Once we felt satisfied about our shared understanding and commitment to those ideas, we could figure out the mechanics of what kind of community service or volunteer work they wanted actually to do. As we already had holistic balance as an overarching goal and a framework they were familiar with, we used that to begin our discussion of community service and volunteerism. We started with the spiritual piece.

"And now abideth faith, hope, charity, these three; but the greatest of these *is* charity." In 1 Corinthians 13:1, "charity" is defined as "love." I was brought up with an awareness of love as more of an activity than a theory. My parents are perfectly and evenly "yoked" when it comes to this. Neither of them is a big talker, and public demonstrations of love just don't happen. Once, as a young girl, I asked my dad if he loved Mom, and he looked at me quizzically and said, "I come home every day, don't I?" My mom is equally pragmatic. One of our little jokes with her is that if she's fussing at one of us about some real or perceived shortcoming, we'll try to end it by saying, "I love you, Mom." She'll immediately respond, "Then *act* like it!" While C. Madison and I agree that both my parents are a bit wacky, we both wanted our sons to understand the same thing: Love isn't just about poetry or political rhetoric; love is about passionate and committed action.

When I was a very little girl they used to teach us in Sunday School that holiness is not a religion or a denomination, it is a way of life. Love is like that. It has to be more than a moral, ethical, religious, or theological framework: It has to be a way of being in the world. This was the approach we used with the boys.

If you love God, then you have to love His creation, and love is evidenced by service. Although we were home-schooling, we certainly didn't want our kids viewing their home or their nuclear family as the sum total of God's creation. At the same time, we didn't want to overlook the fact that charity/love begins at home.

I think that learning to think about the needs of others is a skill best taught early. We felt that if we could teach the boys to think about one another and to be open to the joy that comes from that—if they learned that at home, it would be fairly easy to transfer outside.

Part of the inherent difficulty with service is that it usually involves people, and people, sometimes, can be quite annoying. Part of the challenge of service is acknowledging the annoyance and moving beyond it. So when the boys would be angry with us or with one another, I didn't try to make them pretend that they weren't. We allowed them to articulate all the flaws and defects, in detail. But then they had to articulate what was good, wonderful, and important about that person, now and in the future.

Sometimes the hardest thing is looking beyond the moment and your own feelings. The mother of a friend of one of my sons has a bit of sterling advice: "Get off yourself!"

The second spiritual piece to service is that if you love God, keep

His commandments, and remember obedience is better than sacrifice. The biblical references to the good Samaritan, the listing of "the least of these"—commentary about the treatment of widows, orphans, the fatherless, prisoners, the elderly, and the infirm—illustrates what is expected of us. And when you add to that the current needs of all our young, physically healthy sisters and brothers—well, it's obvious that there is a lot to do. And where more is given, more is required.

Charles, Damon, and Evan have been very blessed, and we wanted them to be conscious of it—not burdened by it or guilty because of it, just aware of it. It's not easy to be blessed and not feel guilty, unless you're really conceited and think you deserve it. Obviously, God is free to bless whomever He chooses, but when you are the one being blessed, and you see and know people who are not, it can be difficult to handle.

We wanted our sons to be aware of their blessings and to know that two seemingly contrary truths can be true at the same time: It is true that no one deserves their blessings, and it is also true that no one has the right to question how God picks the recipients of blessings. We also wanted them to be aware of the fact that there are no free lunches, and even God is expecting something from them, namely, some tangible concern and consideration for others.

We knew that with awareness would come a growing sense of responsibility to "pass it on." We really wanted Charles, Damon, and Evan to want to pass on some small part of the grace shown to them. Realistically, we knew it could only be a small part. Nobody can be expected fully to duplicate God's grace; that's impossible. But I don't think it's unreasonable to try to emulate it and, even better, pass it on.

Community service seemed a great way to do that. Once we were clear about the spiritual rationale, we moved on to the intellectual component of the argument.

Intellectually, we presented community service and volunteerism as reasonable requirements for all members of any society. While it appears that community service is something that is done for others, there is a compelling self-interest element. We incorporated two intellectual concepts—diunital thought and the Hegelian dialectic—to explain this idea to the kids.

First, diunital thought—a term coined by a close family friend, Dr. Linda James Myers—deals with the idea of "both/and" rather than "either/or." The idea of diunital thought highlights the mutual dependence shared by all members of this society. When I assist others who live in my community, I am essentially helping myself. How stable is my community if some of us are living in physical comfort while others are struggling for physical survival? History indicates that such imbalance leads to instability, and those previously living in comfort generally have the most to lose in the face of political and social instability. Consequently, I assist others in my community both because I love and care for people and because I benefit spiritually and physically from that love and care. We wanted the boys to understand the inextricable connection we all share with one another. After all, "It's a Small World" is not just a ride at Disney World.

The second intellectual concept we used was the Hegelian dialectic. You begin with the main idea, the thesis, move to its opposite, the antithesis, and then work to achieve a composite of the two, a synthesis. Our thesis was that service as a manifestation of love should begin at home. The antithesis was that volunteerism is most needed in the larger community external to our family. The synthesis was that the spirit that drives love and service within the family should also generate love, service, and volunteerism in the larger community—i.e., the human family. The nuclear family is simply a subset of the community, the human family. The biological, nuclear family need not and should not be exclusive, at least not for us.

Once we clarified our spiritual and intellectual foundation for community service and volunteerism, we were then prepared to work out the physical dimensions of what we wanted to achieve. We began by examining the volunteer and community-service options available to the boys.

Volunteerism is something we wanted them to view as "membership dues" paid as part of the privilege of being part of the community. As with household chores or participation in the arts, volunteer work was not negotiable in our home. Everybody is expected to contribute something consistently. While we were inflexible about participation, we were very flexible about how they chose to participate. All volunteer work or community service didn't have to be through an organization. We wanted our kids to grow up with an eye for service. We wanted them to be conscious enough to look around and see what was needed, and to be willing to assist in supplying that need. Part of our challenge, in the dual role of parent and teacher, was to encourage them to see the enormousness and complexity of need, yet not be overwhelmed by it.

We did not want them to become complacent in their own comfort, but we also didn't want them to become so frustrated that they were blinded to the beauty in life around them. Toward that end, we looked for multiple outlets for service. Some of their volunteer work was extremely organized, e.g., their hours at COSI. Yet within that structured organization, there were many unplanned and unscheduled opportunities for them to be a blessing to others. I know at least five black families whose kids ended up working at COSI because they were so surprised and inspired when they met Charles, Damon, and Evan there. I have had black teachers tell me what an amazing impact the boys had on their students' trips to COSI. Also, a volunteer leader, who attended with a group of students with severe disabilities, thanked me for the extraordinary sincerity, warmth, and consideration shown by the boys. Sometimes, the opportunity exists within the organizational structure to touch and connect—individual to individual—and that is a vital part of community service.

As the boys got older, Damon became concerned about the number of young boys in our congregation without fathers, either in their homes or even in their lives. Damon found out about the opportunity to volunteer at junior church on Sundays, so that he could work with those kids. He recruited his brothers and his cousins so that, within a year, there were five more young African-American men working with the children on Sunday afternoons.

Additionally, during the summers of 1999 and 2000, Charles, Damon, and Evan volunteered as camp counselors at our church's statewide residential camp. Many of the kindergarten-to-middle-school-aged boys assigned to their cabins have no active fathers in their lives. Many of the young girls and their counselors have had limited contact with healthy, respectful, ambitious, self-confident young black men. Many have had extremely limited access to anybody going to college, because, historically, post-secondary education has not been a focal point in Pentecostal or Apostolic congregations.

Our sons are not perfect, and, ironically, I think that's the most perfect part of their involvement. They represent an achievable, realistic example. They're not "Super Saved" or "Junior Jesus," the mocking terms my sister and I used for the "goody-goody" church kids of our adolescence. Charles, Damon, and Evan struggle with the effort of keeping their spiritual, intellectual, and physical selves in balance. That may be part of their greatest community service—the open and honest struggle for balance; the lack of pretense or artifice in their struggle. The best testimonies are the ones where the person testifying doesn't pretend that there weren't desperate and difficult moments. They acknowledge the struggle and they can then stand as a witness to the power to overcome. We wanted the boys to understand that community service is most effective when it involves more than reaching a hand out to the downtrodden. It's most effective when we acknowledge the common experience of needing help.

ALONG with organizational opportunities to help, there were also instances of unofficial, unstructured community service, what I think of as random acts of kindness. Moving their great-grandmother's air conditioner, clearing the walk of an elderly neighbor, inviting some younger kids over for pizza and a swim—these are some of the greatest examples of community service. Such random acts of kindness have also been a qualitative gauge of success for us.

Quantitative measurements of success are relatively easy, but the qualitative ones can be tricky. How does one determine moral and ethical growth and development in a child? How is progress in holistic balance measured, especially the spiritual and intellectual components? Part of our measurement tool was the random act of kindness. We looked for the frequency of occurrence, the ease of attitude in its accomplishment, the satisfaction in completion, and, most important, the lack of need for acknowledgment. We saw the random acts of kindness as a kind of definitive gauge because there was no tangible, quantitative benefit that could flow to the boys. These are not things that can show up on a résumé or in the paper. They're not the kind of things your family will ever even find out about.

Over the years, I learned to pay particular attention to how incredibly comfortable people seemed in asking any of the boys to assist them with anything. That's part of the legacy of random acts of kindness, and organized community service and volunteerism: People can "see" you helping because they see you as a vital, committed member of the community.

When helping your child to become involved in volunteer work, there are a couple of things to keep in mind; specifically, the age of the kid and the constraints of your collective schedules. Age appropriateness is an important consideration, because it will not only shape what kind of work your child can reasonably be expected to perform, it will also impact how your child responds to the work or volunteer environment. If you have elementary-school-aged children and they're interested in helping the homeless, they can collect clothes, toys, books, and blankets, and help you deliver them to a shelter. Or they can go with you and help serve during a meal. An older kid might want to commit to one afternoon a week to read to children in a shelter or to help them with their homework. As your child gets older, he may want to work with Habitat for Humanity or another organization that works to build affordable housing.

Whichever option is selected, try to make sure your kid is able to make a real contribution. One of the difficulties in volunteer work, especially with teenagers, is that it can be difficult for them to maintain focus and commitment when they're not getting paid. Knowing that their contributions are really meaningful is an effective way to offset that.

Another thing to keep in mind is that all community service doesn't have to be structured or occur through an existing organization. Encourage your kid to look for opportunities to help people in their community. If you have elderly neighbors, encourage your kid to shovel the neighbor's walk and driveway when it snows. If you have younger neighbors with toddlers, encourage your kid to offer to sit for a few hours so the parents can have a brief break.

This is community service that works best when it's modeled. When you see people in your community who need some assistance that you can provide with a little effort, do it. Let your kids see you welcome new neighbors, visit folks who are sick or shut-ins, drop off a casserole to a family that's pressed for time because someone's in the hospital. We really need to show our kids that, in a community, we are each responsible for one another.

One of the great things about unstructured community service is that it can fit everybody's schedule. If you see a need today, but your schedule can't accommodate it, there will definitely be another opportunity tomorrow. And there's always time to pray.

14

HOW WE USED

OUR VILLAGE

No, ABSOLUTELY, WE were not the only adults they knew. As evidenced in other chapters, Charles, Damon, and Evan have had close and intimate relationships with the adults within their extended family, but I don't think that's what people meant when they asked about adult involvement with the kids. Maybe because very few families make the effort to develop and sustain meaningful, multigenerational relationships, those relationships are undervalued. In any event, when people asked about the boys' involvement with adults, I don't think they meant relatives. I think the inference was that the adults involved needed to be objective, third-party adults.

I think there were some similar inferences about our involvement as parents. There is a concern that being a parent makes objectivity impossible, thereby making it impossible to do the hard task of education. While I think that's a legitimate concern, home schooling has taught me that this absence of objectivity doesn't often come to fruition.

Now, when my kids were little—very, very little—during that magical season of ages three to five, I had no objectivity whatsoever, and I wasn't trying to get any. My kids were absolutely the most beautiful, angelic, and perfect beings ever to inhale oxygen on planet Earth. Everything about them was dear and darling and adorable to me, and I was absolutely stunned whenever anyone else didn't share my opinion. I wasn't even angry when they didn't. I was just puzzled.

Oh, but then they began to grow up, and my objectivity came with their growth. Home schooling accelerated that objectivity, probably because I got to know them better.

In home schooling, the big difference is not that parents and children get to know each other, it's the *way* they get to know each other that's different. In home schooling, the parent as teacher and the child as student get to *really know* each other in a way that just wouldn't be possible in a more traditional parent/child context. I have no idea (and it's probably still too early to tell) if this home-schooling way of knowing is better than a traditional form of knowing—I just know it's a very different way of knowing. As a home-schooling family, we really came to know one another on levels that transcended our parent/child relationship. We got to know one another on multiple, intersecting levels as teachers and students, lecturers, researchers, presenters, writers, and editors. So while our objectivity was hampered by our biological and familial connections, it was enhanced by our daily involvement, coupled with the fact that we knew we needed to develop and maintain a certain level of objectivity if we wanted to be successful. The need for objectivity was something of which we were intensely aware. Conversely, if the boys had remained at school, I'm not certain they would have been engaged in a similarly conscious level of objectivity.

Our level of parent/teacher objectivity was aided over the years because C. Madison and I were not always the dominant parties or even the parties with the most information. There were lots of occasions on which I felt pretty shaky having to admit I didn't know very much about a topic up for discussion. One Monday morning, I pointed out what I thought was a mistake in the Sunday *New York Times*. There was some article about science and the writer mentioned a "quark." In the midst of my smug mini-lecture on how nobody's beyond the need for editorial review, Evan said, "Mom, don't you know what a quark is?" I was stunned. I had never heard the word before and obviously had no idea what it was. That was just one of many home-schooling experiences in which I learned from my kids. Fortunately, they were almost always gracious about their role as teachers.

As our relationship matured, I think they became aware of the fact that we really weren't engaged in some kind of power play. As they began to understand that our efforts on their behalf were sincere, they became increasingly patient with us. They never stopped saying that they hated home schooling, but they accepted the fact that we were doing what we thought was best. I think that realization helped them be patient and kind when they were in the position of information dominance.

Ultimately, home schooling was a huge growth process for all of us, and let me assure you that while the current outcome seems good, much of that growth process was surprisingly painful. While I'm not certain of the long-term consequences, and I surely hope they'll be positive, I'd be lying if I said I've never had a dark hour or two, in the middle of the night, mulling over that old adage, "Familiarity breeds contempt."

Due to the unique nature of our evolving relationship and the intensity of engagement, we knew it was absolutely critical that the boys interact with as many different people as possible, including adults. It's not that I was more concerned about their adult relationships than their peer relationships. It's just that I knew we'd need to put a lot more effort into creating opportunities for the development of adult relationships. Given the social interests, needs, and demands of most adolescents, or at least my three, it was abundantly clear that they would boldly seek out social opportunities with their peers—with or without my assistance. On the other hand, maybe because they were home-schooled, there didn't appear to be any overt interest or effort in expanding their field of engagement with adults.

We made it our business to ensure that they encountered a number of adults during their home-schooling odyssey. These encounters happened in different places and for different reasons, but the connecting theme was one of interdependence and mutual responsibility, rather than dependence and unilateral responsibility. Just as we worked to create a healthy, holistic environment, we were equally selective in the context of their adult interactions. We openly encouraged their involvement with adults we felt were also committed to the ideal of holistic health. We were convinced that such a commitment would make for mutually respectful and informative relationships.

In school, Charles, Damon, and Evan were wholly dependent upon their teachers to select a path through each discipline presented. The wisdom, integrity, breadth, or depth of any of the paths selected by any of their teachers was not open to analysis or discussion; at least, not with us. As parents, we also had little-to-zero impact or influence on the selection of their teachers and, of course, the boys didn't have any at all. Our sons' responsibility was to follow the path blazed before them by their teachers, regardless of any of the dimensions of the path selected. Any effort on our part to illuminate the path was frequently seen as inappropriate interference. Essentially, the world was divided into distinct subsets: The teachers were the experts, the parents were the parents, and the children were the students. These subsets were not designed to be porous: One couldn't just "flow through" these subsets, because to do so would disrupt the ordered balance.

My problem with such a rigid universe was its artificial reality. Teachers can be both teachers and students, if given the opportunity, and frequently are called upon to act in loco parentis. Conscious parents have been students of their children since conception and are their first teachers. And anyone who has ever spent any time with children knows they can really teach you quite a bit, if you have a willingness to learn. Regrettably, I didn't see a lot of that willingness on the part of the adults occupying our kids' school. Basically, the inflexibility was one of the things I most disliked about school. Added to that was frustration and disappointment about my kids' missed opportunities to engage an interesting range of adults on a broader level than just teacher. Those missed opportunities are part of what construct the box known as school. We wanted the chance to think outside that box.

HOME schooling allowed all of us the opportunity to do more than just think outside the box; we *lived* outside the box. As home-schoolers, Charles, Damon, and Evan were engaged in a series of independent relationships with a range of adults in which objectives for each discipline were discussed and reviewed with them, their teachers, and us. We forged the paths together, and anyone could question the direction. Questioning didn't mean revolt. Often, no change evolved from the analysis and subsequent discussion. What was achieved was critically more important than change, however: We learned both to openly question and to respond to being questioned without defensiveness. We learned to debate an issue and then move on to support, even when the decision was reached in the midst of intense disagreement.

French class was an excellent example of this. There was a great deal of discussion about the selected textbook. The boys thought it was too hard—over their heads. They were eleven and nine at the time, and they knew their teacher was using the same book in the classes he taught at OSU. We were concerned and agreed to set up a time for all of us to discuss the book selection. Their teacher, Dr. Kwaku Geusi (PhD, French), met with all of us and explained his purpose and objective in the selection of that text, and ultimately we agreed and continued. Dr. Geusi, a Ghanaian foreign-national student, explained that American students had notoriously poor grammatical skills. Consequently, while the text in question was used at OSU, he really didn't consider it to be a college-level text. He agreed that the text would be challenging for the boys, but he expressed the belief that education without challenge would be meaningless. He was certain the boys were up to the challenge and he encouraged us all to continue.

Everyone had a chance to be heard, and while there was no change in the textbook, I think the boys felt the respect that comes from being heard. While they weren't consulted over every textbook, they did participate in the inter-view process and selection of almost every teacher we hired, again emphasiz-ing the collaborative nature of the home-schooling project.

Most of their teachers developed an extremely close, personal relationship with our sons—given the size of the class, that was relatively easy to do. But beyond the personal interest in their academic work, there evolved a deep, mutual interest in one another as people. In addition to helping the boys with their Rites of Passage ritual, Francis Cobbina, one of their math teachers, in-vited them to his birthday party to meet his wife and fellow Ghanaian foreign nationals, and he came to Charles's and Damon's graduation. And the boys watched another math teacher, Angela Whitaker, struggle through the aca-demic process of her PhD candidacy.

While it was clear that these adults were the subject-matter experts, their corresponding ability to engage the boys as people worthy of respect was the transforming experience that aided our efforts to create a holistic environ-ment. The boys most certainly would have had teachers who were subject-matter experts had they remained in school, but schools don't always have the flexibility to allow teachers and students and parents to flow together.

ANOTHER source of enlightened engagement with adults occurred at the Center of Science and Industry. Over the course of their volunteer-work ex-perience, the boys each logged more than twenty-five hundred volunteer hours. And while that is certainly amazing and worthy of kudos, what I found to be even more remarkable was the effort COSI made as an institution to en-gage their student volunteers as responsible members of the community. It wasn't a perfect experience—remember it's COSI, not heaven—but the point is that the institution made the effort to move outside the box of tradi-tional, divisive subsets. COSI's interest was in bringing science to the people, and they were open to assistance and ideas from anybody willing to help in that endeavor—regardless of age. The focus at COSI was on mastery of the particular scientific principles demonstrated in each exhibit: The person who mastered the principles demonstrated the exhibit, and it didn't matter if that person was twelve or thirty-five years old. At COSI, the boys rapidly became senior-level volunteers, helping to develop and build exhibits, and by the time Charles and Damon were sixteen, they had both been hired as summer interns—for money!

As volunteers, each of the boys was expected to attend morning staff meet-ings, and they each received quarterly written performance appraisals. Their engagements with the adult staff rapidly moved to a colleague level, in which reciprocal learning and respect occurred as a matter of course. Ms. Jan Morgan, who heads the student-volunteer program, engaged them from the first interview as responsible young people, even though Evan was just a ten-year-old then. By the time they were ready for college recommendations, Jan was able to recommend them both as students and as long-term colleagues.

The experience with COSI, as an institution, and with the adult staff, transcended the typical boundaries of traditional educational institutions. When the boys began working at COSI, they were just beginning the sixth and fourth grades. When they left COSI, they were on their way to college. They left behind at COSI adults who had engaged them consistently for seven years, throughout the course of middle school and high school, something just not feasible in traditional settings.

CHURCH provided a completely different opportunity for adult engagement with the boys, one that focused squarely on the spiritual and intellectual connection. We decided to have a Rites of Passage ceremony for our sons on the occasion of their thirteenth year. We spent the twelve months prior to that birthday preparing them for that ceremony. The purpose of the Rites of Passage was consistent with our home-schooling focus of holistic balance. Their year of preparation revolved around research and writing about the past, the present, and the future of American men of African ancestry and Christian belief. During their preparation for their Rites of Passage, our pastor, Elder Eugene Lundy (a physician by training and a former biology teacher, as well as a theologian), met with the kids monthly to review their essays on specific scriptures, science topics, and faith issues. (Essentially, he committed almost two years to the effort of working with three boys, since Charles's and Damon's Rites of Passage occurred two years before Evan's.) Throughout this experience (which, of course, they hated!) they had the wonderful opportunity of working with someone who was capable of challenging them and being challenged in return. While the boys resented all the extra work their dad and I assigned them in preparation for the ceremony, they were able to recognize the enormous effort Elder Lundy was making on their behalf. They were able to engage him, not merely as the pastor of a large assembly—from their seat on the pew, wedged between their parents and grandparents—but as a man and a teacher. Most significant, they were able to have the experience of being engaged respectfully in return as he listened to them, answered their questions, and posed new questions to them. If it was a burden for Elder Lundy—if he felt bored, if he felt the boys were spiritually or intellectually beneath him and unworthy—he never gave any indication.

While many people find it odd that the boys continue to come to church now, as young adults, I don't. They have a holistic relationship there that transcends mere tradition. When the boys have had spiritual questions and challenges, they have been comfortable in going to Elder Lundy or Elder William Polley, our assistant pastor. Both men have consistently engaged the boys as young men of promise, and have encouraged their questions and inquiries. When Charles, Damon, and Evan volunteered at church camp and had concerns about the administration of the program, they contacted Elder Polley directly. They felt comfortable in discussing their concerns with him, and they seemed confident of his willingness to engage them directly and openly. Again, Elder Lundy and Elder Polley, as well as a number of other "Brothers" in the church, have been able to provide both instruction and respect in their long-term relationships with the boys.

THROUGHOUT our home-schooling adventure, we took advantage of lectures and discussions sponsored by the sizable college community in the Columbus metropolitan area. While not always enthusiastic, Charles, Damon, and Evan sat in on lectures by prominent visiting lecturers and speakers, including Professor Cornel West, Professor Henry Louis Gates, Jr., Professor Andrew Hacker, and Mr. Andrew Young, Jr. Before these lectures, we assigned specific readings so the boys would have some understanding of the speaker. (While reading one's work and listening to one speak cannot create a deeply personal relationship, it does provide a basis for understanding and connection between the student and the speaker, even if it is unilateral.) Although we took the boys to tons of lectures hosted by many different organizations, many of which were Caucasian, our consistent focus was on their exposure to African-American men and the diversity within that segment of the population.

There were two very specific, very intellectual things we wanted to accomplish through this segment of the process. First, we wanted to teach the boys to look and think past the hype, no matter who is speaking and no matter how much is true and right, and we wanted them to learn that when you hear paradox, inconsistency, and a justification of injustice, you must note it. For example, when we took the boys to hear Minister Louis Farrakhan, it was thrilling to see so many black people come together, and to hear words of encouragement, admonishment, and political theory so eloquently spoken by an obviously well-educated and well-read brother. At the same time, it was important to us that the boys identify the paradox in the minister's political commentary—the paradox in criticizing U.S. foreign and domestic policy, vis-à-vis people of African descent, while ignoring the perpetuation of the African slave trade by many Arab nations, needed to be noted. We were thrilled that our sons, while enthusiastic over the experience and the man, were able to discuss the paradox and its political implications with us.

Our second intellectual objective was for the boys to move beyond a blanket endorsement of all things academic and expensive. Everybody tenured at Harvard or Princeton or Yale is not wise. The academy is a political organization as much as an intellectual one. As the boys got older, they began to pierce the veil of exclusivity at many of the more prominent institutions, and in doing so they could analyze the cost/benefit ratio of assimilation.

Soon they could discuss the difference in the ideas put forward in the writings and presentations of different brothers, even when those scholars were at the same institutions. Over the years, they had the opportunity to compare and contrast the political consciousness of prominent scholars like Professors West and Gates, Professor Derrick Bell, and Professor Randall Kennedy. All of these men were on the faculty at Harvard, all are black, and all are at different places with regard to black consciousness. Becoming familiar with their work, and learning to appreciate the enormous efforts needed to produce such bodies of work, provided an insight for the boys that, while not based on personal interaction, was still meaningful.

In some instances, we were able to supplement the reading and lectures with personal engagements with black scholars. When Professor Tony Martin, a highly controversial faculty member at Wellesley, spoke in Columbus, he joined us for dinner at our home, and the boys were able to view another dimension of this brother beyond his prodigious scholarship as seen in his seminal work on Marcus Garvey. When Dr. John Henrik Clarke and Professor Bell came and spoke, the boys had the chance to join us for dinner and discussion later, at the home of our friends Mr. Roger Myers, an incredibly gifted jazz musician, and Dr. Linda James Myers, a professional colleague of the distinguished lecturers. The boys had been amazed by Dr. Clarke's ability to speak without notes while providing a fascinating overview of the history of Western civilization, highlighting the lessons to be learned, and responding succinctly to random questions from the audience; and Professor Bell's intellectual ability to incorporate constitutional issues into creative writing also had really impressed them, as had his willingness to leave Harvard Law School in protest over the absence of black women on the faculty. Linda and Roger's two sons, who are roughly the same ages as our boys, were also at the dinner; so, while terrific conversations were going on, the boys would sit with us a while, eat, listen, run off and play, come back, eat some more, listen, play some more, and finally doze off.

. . .

FREQUENTLY, our evenings with the Myerses would go until the wee hours of the morning. Because these were adults who cared about our boys, these were wonderful opportunities for engagement. (An added benefit is the fact that Linda is a clinical psychologist. Periodically, people would ask me if I thought the kids were okay, and I was happy to report that they were informally observed, on a regular basis, by a licensed psychologist, and I had received no warnings to hide the knives. How many people can say that?)

We maintained a similar relationship (at least until they moved) with an intellectual white couple and their children. Drs. Kevin and Martha Michael have two daughters, and a son who's the same age as Evan. Martha is an artist and was in the class behind me in prep school, and, before they moved, Kevin taught philosophy at the boys' old prep school—so we had lots of connections. But the most meaningful connection was our collective quest for intellectual growth and stimulation. Our group dinners frequently went on for hours and hours and hours, as the adults challenged one another and whichever kids happened to be present at the moment.

Ultimately, our boys grew up being questioned and engaged fully by a wide range of adults; not in the traditional forms of recitation and Q&A, but in the more Socratic form of dialogue that expands and grows with each response. Because home schooling cannot provide the parameters of specific, academic class structures, it doesn't duplicate the limitations of those structures. As home-schooled students, our sons were able to engage a wide range of people—some chronological peers, some younger kids, and many adults—in unique ways.

While it's obviously important in a home-schooled environment, I think all children need to be exposed consistently to a wide range of adults with differing intellectual and spiritual perspectives. That doesn't mean unsupervised exposure. I am a firm proponent of guided growth.

Check the various newspapers of your local colleges and universities; there are lectures being offered all over the place, and they're usually free. Once your kids are grounded in your faith traditions, help them explore the spiritual foundations of others: Attend different services and talks and presentations, not with a heart for conversion, but for understanding.

While one of the biggest criticisms of home schooling is the concern about limited intellectual exposure to the ideas and views of others, that is no less a concern in traditional educational institutions. How often are any of our children exposed to people whose social, political, and cultural views are different from those in charge? Kids need to have the opportunity to be challenged, intellectually and spiritually, and hopefully that challenge will occur in a supportive environment.

It's important to let kids see us struggle with intellectual and spiritual challenges, and political differences, so they can observe how conflict can lead to growth. It's also a good idea for them to witness that disagreements need not lead to disagreeable behavior.

15

HOW WE ENRICHED

THEM WITH SUMMER

PROGRAMS, ETC.

C. MADISON AND I love our kids and we always have, but that doesn't mean we wanted to be with them all day, every day. I don't know how old the boys were when they realized that, but we were no more interested in spending every waking moment with them than they were in spending every waking moment with us. I can't possibly know what provoked other parents to home-school, but I know spending tons of time exclusively with our kids was definitely not one of our reasons. We didn't decide to home-school to remove them from the challenges of the world or because we couldn't stand to be away from them. We decided to home-school them to control the time and intensity of those challenges, and to prepare them to meet those challenges effectively. Spending massive quantities of time with them was a by-product of our home-schooling plan, not the foundation of or rationale for it.

Even though we were able to admit that we weren't thrilled over the prospects of spending all our free time with our kids, we still weren't out of the woods in terms of peer-group condemnation on the part of many parents. Ten points were awarded for our honesty in admitting we were concerned about the amount of time we'd have to spend together, but we were still under the gun in terms of our interest in controlling the timing and intensity of certain challenges.

Conventional wisdom seems to say kids should be thrown out there, to sink or swim on their own, sooner rather than later. And when we talked about protecting our kids by controlling their environment, we got the usual flak

about being overprotective. But sometimes I think that criticism is just an excuse for irresponsible parenting. On some level, I think parenting is a lot like
gardening. In planning a garden, you have to consider the environment
you'll be working in, otherwise the plantings—the flowers, shrubs, and
trees—won't flourish. Even if you begin with hardy, healthy seeds, planted in
certain environments those seeds will need extra care to mature into healthy
plants. When Ohioans carefully cultivate new plantings indoors in early
spring, before transferring them outdoors later in the season, intelligent people don't ask why—they know a miscalculation will lead to the death of the
plantings. We felt our children needed to be nurtured in a controlled environment first—not because we intended to transfer them to a greenhouse,
but because we had seen the results of new plants put outside too soon. Our
enrichment selections were essentially part of the boys' transition from the
potting shed to the garden. We looked for enrichment activities that would
strengthen the boys' root systems before the final planting.

In that vein, we looked at a number of different enrichment programs. We
had several objectives to be met in each selection. Specifically, we wanted
Charles, Damon, and Evan to have additional opportunities to engage a
range of adults, but we wanted those adults to be part of a random distribu-
tion. We were quite curious to see how adults accustomed to interacting with
young people from traditional educational experiences would find the experience of interacting with kids from such a different background. Simultaneously, we were interested in—and somewhat anxious about—how our kids
would respond in more typical environments, where there was no emphasis
on holistic balance. There was no way we could know definitively how much
the boys were actually strengthened by their environment; we wanted to believe that an environment designed with an eye toward the development of
them spiritually, intellectually, and physically would make them exception-
ally healthy and conscious, but we had to test that belief.

WE began by compiling as comprehensive a list as possible of enrichment
programs offered across the United States. We did not want to use geography
itself as a limitation, even though we knew that the cost of travel might prove
a barrier. The downside was that by opening up for consideration programs
all across the country, we were hard-pressed even to begin the process of narrowing the list.

Due to the enormousness of the task, it made sense to cluster the available
programs by target subject first, rather than by location, cost, or age group.
Our clusters included exclusive summer camp programs, sports programs,

programs in the arts, programs in math and science, programs in the humanities, and standardized test-preparation programs. There were six different cluster groups under consideration.

We immediately eliminated three: exclusive summer camps, sports programs, and standardized test-preparation programs. Exclusive summer camps were too long—upward of six weeks—and entirely too expensive for us. The only benefit we could see would be the determination of our kids' ability to engage constructively average, wealthy white kids—the dominant demographic segment of exclusive summer camps—but we already knew the kids could engage that group; it was the group they left in prep school. We eliminated sports camps because they provided a single focus that was inconsistent with our holistic approach. Sports camps are also quite long and expensive, and our kids already knew lots of athletically talented and gifted kids—we didn't need to pay for that experience. We decided to pass on the standardized test-preparation programs for many of the same reasons: The focus was too narrow, the programs were too long, and the kids involved would probably closely match specific demographic groups our kids had already successfully engaged.

Having eliminated three categories of programs, we still had three left—programs in the arts, programs in math and science, and programs in the humanities—along with a fourth possibility: mixed programs. We asked the kids which programs most interested them and then examined which ones we could afford. The best part of this arduous process was the recognition that these were annual programs. We didn't have to try to do everything in one year.

If Charles, Damon, and Evan had stayed in private school I doubt that we would have been able to afford most of these enrichment activities. Even without the burden of private school tuition, finding the money to cover the cost of enrichment activities for three kids was a continual juggling act. We did the juggling because there are some invaluable elements of enrichment programs for any kid, but especially for home-schooled kids like ours. Some programs were designed to strengthen existing skills, others challenged assumptions about the level of existing skills, and still others exposed the student to completely new skills. Over the course of our home-schooling experience, our kids participated in each of these categories of programs.

WHEN they were younger, the bulk of their enrichment activities involved strengthening existing skills. Most of those enrichment activities were in the arts, and they were local. Mercifully, there were lots of scholarship opportunities to help defray expenses. Between BalletMet, Columbus College of Art and Design, the Church of Christ Apostolic Faith pastoral choir and teenage choir, Opera Columbus, the Columbus Museum of Art, the Davis Center, and the Columbus Arts Festival, the kids had tons of opportunities for artistic enrichment. Those enrichment experiences strengthened skills they already had.

WHILE the boys enjoyed the arts, their interests were broader than that. Their interests continued to expand and, not surprisingly, they became more costly. Early in our home-schooling experience, they decided they wanted to attend Space Camp. Space Camp represented a different kind of enrichment opportunity: It was residential, out of state, and with a distinct focus on math and science rather than the arts. It was also quite expensive. Fortunately, that year NASA was running an essay contest, with a free week at Space Camp as a prize in each category. This was a huge bonus as far as I was concerned: We much preferred the idea of the boys competing for a scholarship on the basis of merit than simply receiving a grant to go; plus, we were always on the look-out for new and creative writing assignments. NASA provided a list of suggested topics, and each of the boys picked one: Charles wrote about the biosphere experiment, Damon wrote about the development of space travel, and Evan wrote about the effects of painting in zero gravity. Wonders of wonders, each of the boys received a free week at Space Camp! NASA applied two conditions to the scholarships: The boys had to attend during the regular school year, when the most spaces were available; and we had to provide their round-trip transportation.

Luckily, we had no regular school year—the kids could go whenever Space Camp had room for them. The transportation issue was a bit trickier, but, as we were self-employed, we knew we could work it out.

There was no way we could afford to fly the three of them there, so once we found out they were assigned to the facility at Cape Canaveral, and the specific dates, we made arrangements to drive them there. I had a workshop in Columbus, so Charles drove the boys to Florida with their godfather, got them checked in, came back to Columbus, picked me up, and drove back, so we could be there for the closing ceremony and award presentation. We stayed at a Motel 6 with a Burger King conveniently located next door, and the kids had a great experience. They loved Space Camp: building rockets, doing the various simulations, and just being at a residential camp for a week. Evan, of course, felt it was entirely too much work to be called camp.

There were no other black kids there for that week, and there were no black teachers, trainers, or staff, so this was quite a different environment from what the boys were used to. Of course they commented on it, but they didn't seem overwhelmed, just surprised that everyone was so curious about them. During our debriefing with them, they described the experience as fun and all, but Evan expressed no interest in coming back.

We were able to balance their assessments with the information we received in our equally informal debriefing of the staff after the awards program. The staff who worked most closely with the boys expressed interest in the home-schooling situation, particularly with regard to what they saw as a high level of interest and confidence on the part of the boys. The staff seemed surprised that the boys didn't feel uncomfortable being the only black kids there. However, they also expressed some concern over the boys' comfort in one another's company, and wondered if their relationship had a chilling effect on their interest in building relationships with other kids. On the other hand, the most consistent observation involved the boys' uncanny ability to get along extremely well with virtually all the other kids in the programs, seemingly from the very first day. (These core observation themes were repeated, in different variations, in the debriefing from virtually every enrichment program the boys attended over the years.)

BICYCLE and generic summer camp, sponsored by the YMCA, was the next enrichment program the boys picked. This was a classic mixed program, with Charles and Damon opting for the bicycle component and Evan selecting the regular summer camp component. The camp was a one-week residential program in Bellefontaine, Ohio, with the bicycle component requiring ten to fifteen miles of riding each day. Charles and Damon were excited by the prospect of the physical challenge, and Evan was just curious about summer camp. Charles and Damon thoroughly enjoyed this experience, and Evan, predictably, did not.

When we went to retrieve them, we were removed from the line of other waiting parents and sent to the director's office. Palms sweating, I waited, wondering all the time what Damon (of course I knew it was Damon!) could have done that was so serious that the director was involved. The director arrived and confirmed that, indeed, she did want to talk about Damon, but also about his brothers. She told me she had never seen kids so tolerant and embracing of others, even others typically spurned by the group. She said that, initially, a few counselors had brought Damon and his brothers to her attention, but that by the end of the week all the counselors were discussing them. The director wanted to know how we had instilled such a sense of joy and compassion about life. Their environment had, indeed, translated into healthy relationships with others!

ENGINEERING camp for Charles and Damon was the next big enrichment experience. (Needless to say, Evan was not interested in attending.) This was a classic, academic-challenge camp, where the student's skill assumptions are put to the test. It also challenged our checkbook! Luckily, it was at OSU, so there were no travel expenses, but the residential camp itself was about a thousand dollars per kid. The program was open, by invitation, to Ohio high school juniors able to meet the competitive entry requirements. Invitations were issued based on PSAT scores. If interested, the student then was required to submit grades, recommendations, and an essay. Charles and Damon presented something of a challenge, as the program had never admitted any home-schooled students, nor was there a lengthy history with twins or African-American students! At first, their admission looked unlikely, until I pointed out that, as state residents, the boys' status as home-schooled students was irrelevant—assuming all the other entrance requirements were met, which they were. Charles and Damon were accepted for the three-week residential program, which covered an entire college quarter's course in engineering— complete with a full quarter's college credit!

When we arrived for orientation with the other parents and kids, many of the other attendees seemed shocked to see black people. Given the less than warm greetings, and the pointed questions about PSAT scores and grade point averages and who planned to apply to MIT, etc., it appeared as though they might have been laboring under the assumption that Charles and Damon were unqualified affirmative-action participants. (In all fairness, I couldn't really criticize, as I was working through my own set of negative assumptions. Honestly, when we walked in, I thought I was at a geek convention! I looked at some of these kids and I said to myself, "Gee, I really hope they're smart, since an active social life seems highly unlikely.") This unpleasantness was an important experience, however, because Charles and Damon needed to experience that challenge before they went to college.

The other great thing about this enrichment program was Dr. Frank Croft, one of the engineering professors at OSU and the person in charge of this particular program. He unwittingly verified several of the key premises of our home-schooling experiment. One premise was that youngsters brought up in an affirming, holistic environment would become so healthy that they would attract like-minded souls. Another premise was that such an attraction would create an environment of expectation of excellence, leading to strong, positive performance. At the end of the program, Dr. Croft (who's white, by the way) told us Charles and Damon were two of the most remarkable students he had encountered in his fourteen years of running the program. He said he felt blessed to have met them. He also found Damon to be one of the hardest-working students he had ever seen. The correlation between expectation and performance would be illuminated by the sharp contrast between Damon's experience with Dr. Croft and his subsequent experience with faculty at Princeton.

The final benefit from this enrichment was the verification that neither of them had any business even thinking about majoring in engineering. You know how sometimes we can become enamored of a thing without really grasping its true nature? Well, engineering was one of those things. For some unknown reason, Charles and Damon had decided they wanted to major in engineering. As their parents and teachers, we knew that was a mismatch. While they both have enormous intellectual curiosity, neither of them had shown any remarkable love for or aptitude in mathematics, a critical component of engineering. In contrast, both had shown an amazing intellectual gift for deep inquiry, analysis, discussion, debate, and writing, which would seem to point toward some branch of the humanities.

Nothing we said had any real impact, so we decided to let them go to engineering camp. Happily, they set off for life in a dorm with white roommates; lectures; precepts; problem sets; study groups; exams, including a midterm and a final, all accompanied by no sleep, no parties, and no fun. When engineering camp was done, so were they!

They still harbored silly notions that the hard sciences are better—meaning more important—than the humanities. Home schooling notwithstanding, Charles and Damon still were heavily influenced by the quantitative nature of our society. Even within the ranks of tenured faculty at colleges and universities, by and large those teaching in mathematics and the sciences are paid more than those teaching in the humanities. It took us several years to convince them that hard sciences are not hard to people who love science, any more than philosophy is hard to people who love thinking. (Yeah, I'm biased. After all, I was a philosophy major.)

THE third kind of enrichment program focused on exposure to new environments and new skills. The Institute for Oceanography at Seal Harbor, Maine, provided just such a program. This two-week program included all forms and aspects of oceanography and marine biology. Evan said it was really a sociological experience, what with white kids from the East Coast with their class issues and vices.

Officially, the program was designed for the kids to spend a lot of time in and on the water (much farther out at sea than I would have been comfortable with, but, fortunately, I wasn't there). They went whale watching, built saltwater aquariums, attended lectures, and participated in discussions and debates on the environment and the challenge of balancing the needs of humans with and against those of other life-forms. Oceanography camp provided, among other things, an opportunity to engage people with very different philosophical and spiritual beliefs in a structured and constructive environment. It was expensive (again, that magical thousand-dollar-per-kid figure), but it was well worth it.

The expense is the primary reason most parents cite for a lack of participation in enrichment activities. There are a couple of ways to approach this situation. First of all, there's no getting away from the fact that a lot of enrichment programs cost a lot of money. And if you've got more than one kid, and you're not very well off financially, the cost can be prohibitive.

Creativity is always a plus, but it's a necessity if you don't have tons of disposable income. Start off with a list of enrichment programs that excite you and your child. Avoid the temptation to obsess over one or two to the exclusion of the others. You may not be able to afford the two programs you love the most, so work at keeping a high level of enthusiasm for whichever program you can work out for your kid.

Now that you have a list of options and know there aren't any bad choices on the list, you can start looking at the money. Calculate the real dollar costs of each program: fees, transportation, supplies, spending money for snacks, etc. Now you have two elements to use in prioritizing the list: content and cost. If your first content choice is also the most expensive, look down the list and see if there's something similar in terms of content that is less expensive. This is a great opportunity for you and your kid to further explore what you each really want and are expecting to get from each program, because that's really the only way to prioritize the list accurately. Once you have completed reviewing the list, check the bottom line and see what the real dollars are.

Ideally, this process should be happening around January, so that you and your kid have all winter and spring to try to make the money work. Obviously, it would work even better if you did it in November, because then you could tap all that holiday-shopping money from grandparents, aunts, and uncles. But whenever you go through this process, use it as a teachable moment for your kid. There really aren't any free lunches and anything worth having is worth working and, yes, sacrificing for—and it's never too early to make that point. The fact that you make the point doesn't mean the point will be absorbed, but that's not your responsibility—your job is to put it out there.

Sit down with your kid and determine together where there's some give in the budget. Is it pizza and hamburger money? Maybe at your house the give is in the snacks and pop budget. Take a hard look at the entertainment budget. What do you guys spend on cable, video games, and going to the movies? Maybe your family's big expense is clothes and shoes. It really doesn't matter what it is—cell phones or cigarettes—money that's being expended for fungible consumer goods is money that could be applied to enrichment programs.

We opted to compare the long-term value of enrichment activities to those of other kinds of family/kid-related expenditures. A simple $60-a-month cable bill equates to a $720 expense annually. Add that to a couple of pairs of $120 sneakers, and that's $960. Without getting into a huge debate about the insanity of paying to provide free advertising—i.e., logo-infested clothing for children and teens—a simple reduction of 30 percent in status clothing probably would bump up that $960 to a nice even grand. There's one enrichment program paid for, and we haven't even begun to tap the beauty salon, fast food, or non-matinee movie money that is flowing like water through malls all over this country.

Focusing disposable income on enrichment rather than frivolity is no absolute guarantee of your kid's continuous commitment to live as a holistically healthy person. You can spend tons of time and money creating the ideal environment, and your kid can still reach late adolescence and make a series of ridiculous and irresponsible decisions.

Regrettably, it happens. Remember the story of the Prodigal Son? He grows up and decides to break his father's heart and become an idiot for a few years. But after a while, he "came to himself." That story is a confirmation of the scriptural admonition and promise, "Train up a child in the way he should go: and when he is old, he will not depart from it." Notice the compelling silence bracketing the space between childhood and old age. A lot can happen in those intervening years.

Enrichment programs can be a vital part of your kid's training, but they can't preclude the possibility of a misstep between childhood and old age. But at least you'll have the consolation of knowing you left no stone unturned in your quest for parental excellence. And if your kid grows up and opts to become a bum, you will have the admittedly minor pleasure of being able to look him squarely in the eye and say, "You know better."

16

HOW WE

EXPANDED THEIR UNIVERSE

THROUGH TRAVEL

ONE YEAR, WHEN the boys were still in school, I was able to score some tickets for a dress rehearsal of a ballet or opera. (I honestly can't remember which, because my anger at the school was so intense it must have seared some of my memory neurons.) When I sent a note, in advance no less, explaining the boys' future three-hour absence, with one of those hours being lunch, I was told by the head of the Middle School that the boys would not be allowed to attend. Can you believe that? I was shocked, but hardly speechless. After I explained that the kids were neither wards of the state nor the school, he amended his statement—the boys' absence, while not forbidden, would be *un*excused. Of course, we went anyway. I was fine with the unexcused part. I knew the boys would have to make up any work they missed, and any tests or quizzes would not be repeated for them. I understood that those were administrative decisions for the school administrator to make. However, the decision about what the children did or didn't do, that was for C. Madison and me to decide as parents, and while we might need administrative information to make those decisions, we certainly didn't need administrative permission.

Part of my initial and consistent enthusiasm for home schooling was the ability to remove myself from the administrative police. This was key to the design element of the expansion of our home-schooling experiment beyond our front door. I absolutely loved the fact that I didn't need to clear anything with anybody. All outings, trips, and extracurricular activities would be designed, executed, and approved by us—C. Madison, me, and the boys. We were free! Until that moment, I don't think I recognized how constricted I had felt, trying to enrich my kids' lives within the narrow parameters of school.

Okay, I'm not totally dense. I knew home schooling meant we were calling the shots. But honestly, when I realized that I'd never again have to jump through any hoops with school administrators, I felt like doing the happy dance. So I have to admit that this one part of home schooling, at least, was as much for my benefit as for the kids.

There—I admit it—I have been a selfish mother. And while that's certainly not my greatest asset as a parent, I think I can honestly say that my selfishness has not injured Charles, Damon, or Evan, at least not in any significant way.

But this component of home schooling was about more than my selfish desire to free myself of the yoke of school administrators. I wanted the kids to be free, too. C. Madison and I wanted the boys to experience more than the widely touted academic freedom, which apparently only flows to faculty members. We wanted our boys to experience the exhilaration of spiritual, intellectual, and physical freedom along with the accompanying burden and weight of responsibility.

As we were free and mobile people of color, home schooling for us could not mean staying at home. In fact, it didn't mean staying in Columbus, staying in Ohio, or even staying in the United States. C. Madison and I knew that reading broadly across cultures was critical to our kids' intellectual growth and development. Similarly, we knew that travel, while more costly, was no less critical in terms of intellectual stimulation. We decided early on to use travel as an educational tool in the spiritual, physical, and intellectual growth and development of the boys. This was to help prepare them for their responsibility as part of the next generation of free people of color. So that's the bulk of the design issue of not staying at home. There was also a series of issues—of circumstances.

Circumstantially, we couldn't afford *not* to travel while we were home-schooling. We still had a business to run, and we couldn't run it profitably in Columbus. Some of that was and is due to the economic environment of Columbus relative to small, black, female-headed businesses. (C. Madison is the technical wiz of this firm—he handles all the statistical analysis and number crunching—which leaves me as the one out front, and that's not much of a problem anywhere except Columbus.) Bottom line? We had to travel to work, and we had to work to eat, and we had to eat to live—the connections were obvious. So while home schooling was a big change that necessitated a lot of adjustments, we had to continue working, which meant we had to continue traveling. We just had to begin traveling with the kids.

The extensive traveling with the boys began as a necessity, but it rapidly grew into an immensely pleasurable learning experience that supported our holistic design perfectly. One of the most significant spiritual aspects of travel is transcending fear: Travel plunges us into the unknown and out of our comfort zones.

As entrepreneurs we were concerned about how to handle the issue of traveling with our kids while maintaining a professional demeanor. As a black woman with a self-owned business selling information—totally intangible stuff—I knew we couldn't afford the luxury of a misperception, so we were very, very careful.

Fortunately, from its very beginning, we have always maintained a fairly strict division of labor within the business, and that proved invaluable when we started traveling with the kids. I don't know why, but C. Madison thinks I talk too much to share office space with, so he works alone in the office—with all the office equipment for company—and I work all over the place, with my trusty laptop. As further division, C. Madison does marketing, sales, statistical analysis, and invoicing, while I do the presentations, workshops, and project reports. Jointly, we write proposals and consult with clients. So, while we work together, we really don't need to be physically together. That made the logistics of traveling with the boys a lot easier than they might have been, especially for the first few years.

During the first six years of home schooling, we canceled classes and took the boys whenever we had out-of-town clients. As most of our clients are not local, the boys traveled rather extensively. At last count, they had visited twenty-nine of the fifty states.

We combined education and productivity by assigning research projects as soon as we had a contract. Before departure, we expected to be briefed on the history, current population and demographics, dominant industry, employment levels, and climate (political and atmospheric) of the place we would be visiting. Not surprisingly, the boys didn't enjoy the work part of travel preparation: the research process—collecting data, organizing notes—creating outlines and drafts. They found the actual process of presenting their findings to us equally unpleasant. However, at a fairly early age, they began to see the bottom-line correlation between work product and profits. We quickly came to depend on their research as a reliable thumbnail sketch of each new area—a godsend, since we had clients in states as diverse as Arkansas, California, West Virginia, and New York.

Initially, C. Madison and I coordinated our schedules to make sure one of us was always available to be with the boys in the hotel. As the boys got older, they were able to accompany us to some sessions, especially during conferences. Soon, they became my biggest critics, probably because they'd seen me present more times than anybody else other than their dad. Pretty soon, I was relying on their observations, comments, and suggestions during the breaks. They were great at being able to tell when I was losing the audience's attention, or being too flippant with people, or when a point needed to be reviewed. Over time, Charles and Damon were able to take over the sound and systems checks for my conference presentations because of the experience and expertise they had developed during their work at COSI. This freed C. Madison to oversee other matters, and I knew my kids would go to the mat to make sure my space was set up perfectly—no small matter when you're presenting during a weeklong conference with literally hundreds of other presenters. Evan was great at reviewing the handouts and overheads to make sure they were visually stimulating—and, of course, he gruelingly critiqued my appearance.

As the boys traveled and worked with us over the years, they met an increasingly wide array of people. We never allowed them to participate in any customized training with specific client teams, but many of our clients came to know them and complimented us on the boys' work ethic. Traveling around the country, compiling research, meeting people working in and managing large public and private organizations, and editing many of our reports created an invaluable series of teachable moments for our sons. They were able to see for themselves the interplay among geographic regions, economic stability, employment opportunities, educational competitiveness, and political positions. Even more interesting, travel allowed them to examine the inextricable impact of economics, employment, and education on the interdependent issues of race, gender, and ethnicity.

Ultimately, travel provided unique opportunities for discussion as well as study, opportunities that wouldn't necessarily have been impossible, just improbable within the boundaries of traditional schooling. The movie *Gettysburg*, followed by a visit to the Museum of the Confederacy in Richmond, Virginia, undoubtedly made the economic, political, and racial issues of the Civil War, the South, and these entire United States more viable than a semester's worth of reading alone.

Once one leaves the South, the magnitude of the Civil War seems pretty much on a par with the Revolutionary War and World War I—all significant events, to be sure, but each made distant through time and space. But the Civil War feels like a real thing in the South, and nowhere is that more true than in Richmond, the former capital of the Confederacy. What was wonderful about our time in Richmond was the fact that the boys were exposed to political, historical, and social positions diametrically opposed to our own, and they were able to examine them critically. Talking about paradox and the fact that history is written by the victors is one thing; examining history from the vantage point of the defeated is something quite different. Travel affords that opportunity.

Most people are probably aware of the benefits travel affords, but within the African-American community, travel is not a favored way to spend our considerable amounts of disposable income. I absolutely understand why so many black Americans are reluctant to travel. After all, it's one thing to acknowledge the reality of racism in one's hometown—you know where it's most likely to rear up; and if you don't know, there are helpful signs. Example: You walk into a suburban ice-cream parlor with your family, and even though lots of other families are gathered there, when you walk in with yours everyone stops licking their ice-cream cones to stare at you. I think this is when the black person realizes, "Oh, I forgot—we're not supposed to be here!" Or your college alumnae group hosts a speaker from the college whose major claim to fame is "debunking Afrocentrism," and the event is scheduled during Black History Month. When you ask about the odd scheduling choice, the committee tells you they didn't realize it was Black History Month!

Oh, but when one travels, it's a whole new ball game. Who knows what might happen, what might be said, or how unpleasant it's all going to be after you've paid to be there; and the money's what makes the whole thing dicey. Racism at home doesn't necessarily require a lot of out-of-pocket funding: You can just turn around, and go home, and write a scalding letter to the corporate office or the local newspaper; or, you could even contact one of the local television stations. But when you're using up rare and precious vacation time and paying good money on travel, and then you encounter racism— well, then you're stuck. It's not really economically feasible to turn around and go home, especially since, when you're paying good money, you want to have a good time.

In light of those variables, it is not unreasonable for black people to be wary of travel, especially in the United States, because overt racism, regrettably, occurs most frequently when traveling in our actual (as opposed to our ancestral) homeland. However, as understandable as the wariness is, many black people can recite that scripture, "God hath not given us a spirit of fear." And the best way to overcome fear is to face it. We wanted Charles, Damon, and Evan to grow up not just believing, but knowing that "He has the whole world in His hand."

Yes, we had numerous unpleasant and undoubtedly racially motivated ex-periences. Example: We used our frequent-flyer miles to upgrade our seats on a flight to San Francisco. After we'd taken our seats, a flight attendant turned to another attendant, looked at us, and loudly asked, "What are these people doing up here?!" It wasn't the way we wanted to begin our trip, but we ad-dressed it immediately. And we refused to allow it to ruin the rest of the trip by musing over it. (Instead, I have learned to become a master of effective complaint letters.)

Travel also provided a wonderful opportunity to see the diunital nature of humanity. The union of opposites can be seen within the diversity of the human family. On the one hand, issues of race, gender, nationality, age, and socioeconomic status shape our experiences, and our experiences shape us. However, there are also strong familial bonds that connect the members of the human family across those differences. The concept of the union of opposites—diunital thought, the recognition that two things that appear to be in opposition can be true at the same time—was easier to "show" than to "tell." And we began the showing process within the continental United States.

Physically, we felt travel was a fun thing to do. Just because something is important spiritually and intellectually doesn't mean it can't also be a blast! Part of the fun of travel is stepping outside the box of familiarity and experi-encing the surprises, the new places, and, especially, the new people.

TRAVELING as a black family—when four of the five members are male—generates a lot of attention. But our first trip abroad as a family really showed the boys that sometimes attention is just honest curiosity.

Our first international trip was to Paris. We found an incredibly cheap hotel, right across from a Métro station with all the attendant pastries, crois-sants, and sausages—so we ate on the cheap, too. Everywhere we went, peo-ple stopped and stared, and lots of people came up and talked, and listened, politely, as we attempted to respond *en français*. The boys were able to ex-perience the exhilaration of everything new—new city, new language, new people—all the while seeing the similarities among the differences.

It was everything we had hoped for them, and more. We walked all over Paris, and hung out in museums, and played in the parks. I loved that C. Madi-son and I were able to discuss imperialist acquisition with the boys as we gazed up at the Obelisk, explored the Louvre, talked about Picasso, and roamed about Versailles. While they certainly could have taken a trip to Paris if they had stayed in school, I doubt they would have had the same lessons taught. (We balanced the academic and intellectual elements of the trip with a day excursion to EuroDisney, where we bought the obligatory T-shirts.)

OUR first trip became the model, and provided the framework, for years of subsequent travel. One key element that interferes with travel, especially international travel, is money; so, since that first trip, I collect, hoard, and track elite status with two airlines and two hotel chains.

We could never afford to travel internationally if we tried to pay standard rates and fares! Flexibility and advance planning are ways I learned to compensate for inadequate funding: Because we had the flexibility to travel during off-peak seasons, we've been able to maximize our travel options. Another compensation technique I used was to consolidate our business travel with one hotel chain and one airline, both with solid partnerships to expand our choices. I religiously sign up for all promotions, vigilantly check my account balances, and constantly watch for deals.

Points, miles, and flexibility have allowed us to continue traveling together, even after the guys left for college. (Charles and Damon have a week off at the end of every January, and it corresponds with Evan's last week of interim break. We have another window of travel opportunity during their spring breaks, which, fortunately, match up.) Since Paris, we've taken budget trips internationally to Bangkok, Singapore, Malaysia, and Hong Kong. In fact, when we took the boys to Singapore, their tickets cost $183—total—because all we had to pay was tax! The rest was covered by frequent-flyer miles— thanks to business travel! Plus, with all the business hotel stays, we've always had enough hotel points for free nights!

As our kids have aged and we have merely matured, our travel sphere has expanded accordingly. But the same principles that applied on our first road trip, to Space Camp, applied to Bangkok. Read, study, and be prepared before you go. Be open to the experience, to the people, and to the unexpected. Plan to be delighted. Never become so sophisticated and jaded that you become blinded to the beauty all around you. Pay attention: See how economics, history, and technology affect people and places.

Charles, Damon, and Evan have essentially outgrown our travel lessons. Now they clarify cultural environments for us. They're comfortable roaming the streets of foreign cities by themselves at night—something I'd never do. And, of course, the insights they derive from conversations with other young people are enlightening. We still talk about the impact of colonialism and its inherent paradoxes, it's just that now they can see the differences in its manifestations in the U.S. and other parts of the world.

It has been interesting for us to hear their comparative analysis of the long-range impact of colonialism as it is played out in different parts of the world and among different racial groups. Their observations about the difference in behavior between black Africans in Paris, African-Americans in the U.S., and native Bahamians were fascinating to us. It was also intriguing to hear their observations about the differing aspects of colonialism and assimilation in Singapore, Bangkok, and Hong Kong. A discussion about the burden of being copied and emulated—e.g., the seemingly continual appropriation of the ever-emerging African-American youth culture—and whether that burden can be felt by those who impose themselves on others, let me know they were experiencing travel on an intellectual level. Ultimately, their willingness to search for connections across the human family is one way I could know travel has been invaluable to our holistic objectives.

All families don't have the same expansive travel opportunities we've had, because every family's circumstances are different. Our consulting business necessitated a lot of domestic travel, and the frequent-flyer miles and hotel points accumulated made the international travel easier. However, with a bit of planning and creativity, I think most families can make travel possible.

Start small: Your first trip doesn't have to be a study trip to New Zealand! Think about day trips as a beginning point. Day trips give you a chance to practice traveling together, and if, initially, there are some rough patches, you're just a day away from home. I think every state has a tourism board, and so do a lot of cities—call and ask for brochures. Another good place to check for ideas is AAA. They frequently publish regional magazines with tons of travel ideas.

Begin making a list of all the neat things you and your family would like to visit in and around your state. Driving distance from your home is a logical way to organize the list. Don't make the common mistake of missing some of the great sites just around the corner. Plan trips to visit your zoo, your art museum, and your science center. Ask your local historical society for a list of places of significance. Remember to call the places you're interested in and find out which days they're open, their hours of operation, and entrance fees—and don't forget to ask if you can bring a picnic lunch. (Eating out on the road adds a big additional cost to travel, and bringing a picnic lunch for the family on a couple of trips can stretch your budget enough to make a couple more trips feasible.)

So you have three elements to use in prioritizing your list: location, content, and cost. As you look at the most distant sites on your list, keep an eye out for things that are in close proximity to each other. Look for ways to balance educational things with things that are just pure pleasure.

This is not to say that learning can't be fun, because it can be; it's just that sometimes you have to be a bit creative to see it. Doing research before the trip and having your kids participate is one of the best ways to ensure that you get the most fun and enlightenment out of the trip. If you're going to an amusement park, research its history: What's its claim to fame? What's the fastest roller coaster, and just how fast is it? How is that speed measured? What is the effect of that rate of speed on the human body, and why do most people scream? (And who's going to test your family's theories when you get there?) How many visitors does the park get each year? Based on the cost of admission, what's their gross revenue?

Some locations, like science centers, make the connection between fun and education simple and direct. Other locations require more effort. If you're planning to tour a historical building, do as much research as possible before you go, so you know what to look for and why the building is significant. Often, historical buildings and government buildings offer tours—whenever possible, go. They're usually fairly short, and they highlight all the important things; and if you've done your research, your kids will be excited when they hear the tour guide explain things they've already read about.

Another thing to remember in planning traditionally educational trips: Set a reasonable time limit and stick to it. Don't expect young children—or teenagers, either, for that matter—to be excited about spending all afternoon in a museum. Two hours is usually our rule. If it's that interesting, you can plan another visit.

Remember that each trip sets the tone for the next one. If you push your kids too hard—say, you stay five hours at the museum—and everybody's whining or pouting by the time you finally leave, expect resistance the next time you mention an outing.

Another tip I have found to be useful: The more intellectually rigorous the trip, the more important lunch is. When Charles, Damon, and Evan were young boys, I was on the Thurber House picnic committee. Only one of the picnics was billed as a family picnic, but we took the boys with us to all of them, even though it can be hard for kids to sit and listen to someone read aloud, especially when they're not reading children's literature. So I always packed a huge hamper of food, complete with all their absolute favorite snacks (repackaged in plastic bags to cut down on the noise).

A final tip in terms of getting the most from each trip concerns recording. Just *as the research is vital before the trip and helps set the tone, recording after the trip helps solidify the experience. Try to take tons of pictures (and if you forget your good camera or you want everybody to participate, those small disposable cameras take great photographs). Talk about the trip afterward, and help your kids feel free to reference the trip and the things they saw. When you get the photos back, you may want to assign a photo-journal project. (I'll admit we weren't that creative when our guys were smaller. We just assigned essays. Writing is always good, but if I had it to do over again, I would definitely opt for the photo journal, because now all our pictures would be organized instead of in envelopes, inside shoe boxes, stacked in shopping bags, etc.)*

I think the most important thing to keep in mind is that travel is for fun and enlightenment. It's not a life-and-death situation, and everything doesn't have to be perfect—because it won't be. Be flexible and try to relax. You're setting the tone for your kids. Help them maintain a spirit of discovery, and the excitement that comes from discovering new things, new people, and new places.

17

WHY WE

INCLUDED RITUAL

RITUALS SIGNAL THE importance of both the event and the people in-volved. Their encompassing potential is what makes them such valuable components in family and community structures and functions. Rituals can mark passages from one phase of existence to another, they can celebrate life's victories, or they can just create an opportunity to pause and reflect. So often, life can whirl past in a blur of obligations and responsibilities, and long, long after the fact, we realize, too late, that the much-touted *good old days* passed us by without any acknowledgment or even recognition. I didn't want that to happen to us, so I looked for occasions for rituals. I knew we couldn't duplicate the environment of school, and I knew that meant there were some things my kids would miss because they didn't attend school, including some rituals and traditions. But I also knew we could create our own, and that with some careful attention to detail they could have as much meaning if not more.

In developing rituals, our principal goal was to be both affirming and in-clusive. We looked for ways to acknowledge and reward accomplishments in the broadest way possible. I have learned that honor and recognition are not diminished by being shared.

Birthdays are a simple example of this. Our extended family in Columbus has an unfailing ritual for birthdays among the fourteen of us. Each person's birthday is celebrated on the Sunday immediately following the actual birth date. First we do the whole cake thing: When everyone is assembled in the

dining room, the lights are dimmed, the candles are lit, and the singing begins. We clap and sing the *regular* birthday song and then we clap and sing
our *special* church birthday song. (We are all loud, strong singers, and we sing
each song with gusto!) After my mother carefully collects the candles—so she
can wash them and put them back on the special candle shelf—we continue
the rest of the birthday ritual with the cards. While there are always a few
gifts—my parents and my sister, Cheryl, can always be counted on for good
loot!—a definite highlight of the celebration is the cards. Everyone brings a
card to the birthday person, and each card is read aloud. We all laugh and clap
and "ohhh" and "ahhh" over each card, and then we pass it around. The significance of the birthday ritual is not lessened because there are a lot of birthdays (and there are!). And it's not lessened by the fact that everybody applauds
the time and effort expended to pick out just the right card for each person.
The ritual celebrates everybody—that's what makes it so wonderful. I took that
lesson into the planning process for our home-schooling rituals as well.

THE first big, formal, totally independent ritual we planned was a Rites of
Passage for Charles and Damon. It was roughly a year-long process that focused on the significance of their passage from childhood into young adulthood. Before developing our own ritual, we read a lot of books on African and
African-American rites of passage and also attended several bar mitzvahs. Ultimately, we developed a ritual process that combined the history of the
African diaspora, the role of Christianity, and the future of African-American
men as the focal points. We developed an extensive reading list for the boys,
which included biblical texts, scientific journals, and African and African-
American political writings. They read Proverbs and Isaiah and Romans
along with works by Dr. Martin Luther King, Jr., Nelson Mandela, Stephen
Biko, Malcolm X, Marcus Garvey, and Frantz Fanon. We assigned articles
from *Scientific American* and other periodicals, on DNA, mitochondrial genes,
and the migrations of humanity from Africa. Each reading assignment was
followed by an essay assignment, because talking about what they read was
one thing—and it was a good thing—but we wanted them to go through the
process of writing, to process the body of work holistically and determine
what they thought and believed for themselves. We critiqued their writings
and discussed their assessments, but our purpose was not to try to change
their minds about any of it. A key design element of the ritual was their responsibility for the development of their own beliefs, based on their own
work, prayer, research, writing, and discussions.

The year of work on their Rites of Passage ended with a ritual ceremony at church. Charles and Damon each presented their essays on the past, the present, and the future of African-American men. The ceremony ended with each one's presentation of his final essay, "What I Believe." During the ceremony, their grandparents, great-grandmothers, aunts, uncles, pastor, and assistant pastor spoke, the choir sang, and many people cried. The ritual did not have tradition; its value lay in its acknowledgment of all those who had helped Charles and Damon in the journey of discovery. When we went through the Rites of Passage two years later for Evan, the process was just as rewarding, and the ritual was just as moving, if not more so—because this time it had tradition.

OTHER organizations helped us with rituals by including Charles, Damon, and Evan in those they already had in place. COSI hosts recognition programs for its volunteers to mark each milestone during the year. The Albert Schweitzer Award, the "1,000 Volunteer Hour Badge" Award, the Gold Star Award: Each of these events was celebrated at COSI, and we tried to attend every one.

These kinds of community rituals create an opportunity for bonding. I think those kinds of connections ultimately are more important than the particular award or certificate or plaque received. I doubt that Charles, Damon, and Evan even remember what they received at any one of those award ceremonies, and I'd bet money that they have absolutely no idea where any of the plaques or certificates actually are. But I'm certain they remember the sense of belonging and the sense of being valued as contributing members of that community.

Similarly, I loved the way our local NAACP/ACT-SO (Afro-Academic, Cultural, Technical and Scientific Olympics) chapter chair, Ms. Sybil Edwards McNabb, made the local awards ceremony an exciting community ritual, just like the real Olympics, with the awarding of the bronze, silver, and gold medals, complete with soaring music in the background. The national competition and awards ceremony was another amazing event. Even though C. Madison and I attended every national competition for the six years any one of our kids participated, we never got tired of going and cheering, even if none of our kids won. It was just wonderful to see hundreds of black kids gathered together and cheering one another for their work in science, math, and the arts. Although Evan was the only one of our sons actually to win at the nationals, every year was an exciting ritual.

OUR biggest ritual was graduation. None of the kids wanted a graduation because, as they so eloquently put it, "We're not *graduating* from anything!"
True to form, I listened to their concerns very carefully and continued with
my plans. We were *going* to have a graduation, I decided it was *going* to be at
church, and I was *going* to mark this passage! (My sons, like their father, have
no conscious awareness or appreciation of the significance of ritual, but that's
okay—they have me. What I know about ritual is that it's not just about the
person at center stage. There aren't any truly significant events that occur singularly; one purpose of ritual is to take the time to acknowledge the assistance, confidence, and support of all the other people who helped.)

The graduation ritual focused on the recognition of all the members of our
village who had made this journey possible. Of course, the graduation was a
celebration for Charles and Damon, and I was certainly proud of them, but
the graduation was also a celebration of others.

We had Charles and Damon make a list of all the adults who had worked
to help them achieve this milestone. Each person on that list was individually
invited to the graduation, and each received a Certificate of Appreciation.
More than one hundred fifty people came to the graduation. Dr. Samuel M.
Nabrit (BS Morehouse '25, PhD Brown '32)—Uncle Sam—agreed to come
and give the commencement address. I don't think either of the boys really
grasped what a momentous event it was, until they began calling the names
of the recipients of the Certificates of Appreciation. As person after person
came forward, hugged them, told how much they had enjoyed being a part of
their lives, the magic of the ritual occurred. Charles and Damon saw themselves within and as a part of the holistic circle of community populated with
Sunday School teachers, choir directors, librarians, tutors, coaches, and community activists. We concluded the ritual with a reception at church for
everybody, and then a barbecue for family and the boys' friends. (Of course,
I had the whole thing videotaped, and I made two scrapbooks, in case they
forget any of the details!)

Our last big home-schooling ritual was Evan's graduation. The critical aspects of the ritual were heightened by the presence of our recent alums,
Charles and Damon, and the friends they brought home from Princeton to
celebrate with us.

---

*Rituals aren't just about creating drama for nothing. I think rituals create the
opportunity to pause to reflect on and celebrate life while it's happening. Rituals also provide an opportunity to acknowledge, to ourselves and to others, the*

critical role our families and friends play in our development as holistically healthy people.

We don't have to save rituals for extreme events like graduation, marriage, and death. Life is too extraordinary to limit reflection and celebration to those few occasions. Be creative, and celebrate the things that matter to you and to your family. Help your kids appreciate the opportunity to create and to cele-brate the events in their own lives and in the lives of others. If you're having dif-ficulty in coming up with ideas for rituals, check out The Heart of a Family: Searching America for New Traditions that Fulfill Us, *by Meg Cox.*

PART IV

THE

COMPARATIVE

ANALYSIS

TEST

18

HOW WE

MEASURED THEIR

PROGRESS

I REALLY DID have a lot of confidence in my ability to tell how the boys were doing. Years ago, when we lived in Jacksonville, I received some real wisdom on this point from Dr. Wright.

Dr. Wright was an older sister—a black woman I hired to look after the boys and keep house for me while I was at work. (The boys started calling her "doctor" because she wore a white lab coat, just like their pediatrician.) Dr. Wright was amazing. When I'd come home, the house was immaculate; the children were clean, dressed, and rested from their afternoon nap; and dinner was ready. When I say ready, I don't just mean cooked: I mean the table was set, the iced tea was in the refrigerator, and a freshly baked pie or cake was cooling on the counter. (Sister girl knew how to run a house!)

Dr. Wright found my domestic skills sorely lacking, and she didn't mind letting me know that such ignorance was not cute. In her opinion, there were certain things any self-respecting woman should know, especially about her own children. Dr. Wright checked the boys' stools regularly and could tell when one of them was coming down with anything—and she insisted that I begin doing the same. During our time together, I learned to check the boys' breath, their eyes, and their fingernails to determine their state of health, and I learned how to keep them as healthy as possible.

Dr. Wright confirmed my mother's opinion that a sick child often is the sign of a lazy mother. Like my mother, Dr. Wright was not impressed with degrees and professional status—those things changed nothing. If you had a dirty house, you were just low-class, period! The rule with them was simple: Clean your house, thoroughly, on a daily basis, if you want to have healthy kids.

Further, healthy kids require daily naps and regular bedtimes, along with daily outdoor exercise. (Dr. Wright didn't believe in kids sitting around watching television for hours. She'd open the door, say, "C'mon, you need to go outside and play," and out the boys went.) She also believed in regular, balanced meals, planned and prepared by responsible adults. (As she told me, "Whoever heard of asking a child what they want to eat?")

So my boys ate what and when they were told, they had at least one nap every day, they played outside daily, and they went to bed at seven-thirty P.M. And yes, they were very, very healthy, and I knew it, because I learned to pay attention to details before there was a problem. Learning to pay close attention to the smallest details of my kids' health, and developing confidence in my ability to detect and deal with potential problems, proved to be an invaluable lesson in preparing me to evaluate their progress once we began home schooling.

While I understood other people's skepticism about my assertions that the boys were doing well, it didn't change the fact that I knew they were doing well. Intuitively, I could tell they were progressing wonderfully. And when I had doubts, I kept hearing Dr. Wright asking, "Well, who else ought to know? You carried these babies!" And she was right: I did know my own children, jointly and individually. The challenge in the evaluative process in home schooling was to observe their individual and collective development simultaneously, but that's a consistent part of the evaluative process for any parent with more than one child.

CHARLES, Damon, and Evan are three distinctly different people. Sometimes that statement seems surprising to people who don't know them or us very well. Because we've made a number of collective decisions concerning the boys, including about home schooling, it may appear that we don't know that Charles, Damon, and Evan are distinct and different individuals. But parental, collective decision making isn't a sign of disavowal of each child's individuality. Even within the context of collective home schooling, we have acknowledged and addressed their individuality. We didn't really have an option, given the objective of holistic growth. While it was a challenge, in some ways home schooling may have made it easier than traditional schooling. Home schooling forced us at least to speculate on the possible outcomes as we made our decisions. Had the boys remained in school, many aspects about the intersection of their individual and collective development may have been missed.

One obvious issue in monitoring their development is the fact that Charles and Damon are fraternal twins with enormously different personalities; an equally salient issue is the fact that Evan is only twenty-seven months younger, and altogether different from either of his brothers. Due to their proximity in age, comparisons among the boys were seemingly unavoidable when they were in school. Home schooling allowed us to monitor their individual development without relying on comparative analysis.

So once we started home schooling, when people asked how they were doing, I was able to respond individually and collectively with a degree of certainty I didn't have when they were in school. Sometimes it seemed that the closeness in their ages and their shared experience of home schooling led people to assume a higher degree of similarity than actually existed. Charles, Damon, and Evan hold values that are conspicuously similar and holistic, but their methodologies are distinctly personal. They each exhibited intrinsic and very individual strengths from the very beginning. Consequently, they each progressed during our home-schooling experiment, but at wildly different rates.

CHARLES, the eldest twin by one minute, and slightly more than six pounds at birth, came to us perfectly proportioned and strong of limb, with beautiful, fat curls and an unblinking stare. An analytical thinker and academically gifted child, Charles is the fairest of our children in terms of complexion, a factor that had great significance when the boys were in school. From the beginning, our challenge was to help Charles develop and express comfortably a genuine sense of compassion for other people.

Home schooling was an especially difficult transition for Charles for a number of reasons. Right off the bat, Charles has never assumed anyone, including us, necessarily knows more than he does. Charles is also the most traditional of our children, so embarking on something so far from the mainstream was bound to be disquieting to him. A further complication is the fact that Charles is the most likely of our children to worry, and home schooling gave him a lot to worry about. He worried that he was not being adequately educated in a general sense, especially as the form of the educational process was so far from the established norm. He worried that he would be behind in certain specific academic subjects, especially math and science. (His concern on this score, coupled with our own, was the reason we used outside tutors in these areas.) Charles worried that without an accredited high school diploma he would be unable to go to college, and he worried that he would forever be unemployable because he wouldn't even have a high school diploma. Until the actual college acceptance letters arrived, Charles was worried, convinced that he and his brothers were doomed to a life of menial labor, chronic underemployment, and poverty because of our ill-conceived, irresponsible educational "schemes."

We knew the only way to address Charles's worries and concerns was to give him as much objective and positive reinforcement as possible. Every enrichment experience helped to assuage some of his concerns, as he was able to examine and evaluate the responses he and his brothers received from adults who regularly encountered young people. While we focused almost exclusively on individual excellence, Charles really needed to see his performance relative to others, and we looked for ways to help him get that.

Charles began our home-schooling adventure as a strong student academically, but one not necessarily given to questioning established truths. Over the course of our experience, we were able to observe Charles grow intellectually and spiritually in ways that enabled him to question everything presented to him. Charles moved past the point of needing a subjective grade to determine if his work was well done. He even moved beyond needing constantly to view his work through the prism of comparative analysis. Through the course of our home-schooling experience, I saw Charles emerge as a deeply spiritual person, comfortable with intuitive knowledge and able to engage within traditional academic parameters and outside of them. I saw him develop as a person of deeply felt, if not openly articulated, concern for others.

I am certain Charles would have developed these wonderful qualities eventually, even if he had attended a traditional secondary school. The difficulty with school was that everybody there thought he was just wonderful, especially in comparison to Damon, so there were very few opportunities for Charles to be challenged. Further, the areas in which we most wanted to see growth were fairly underdeveloped within the school. It just didn't seem likely to us that the school as an institution could facilitate the growth of a child in areas in which the institution itself was stagnant. We felt that the school's comfort with issues of classism, in particular, rendered it incapable of helping Charles develop the sense of connection we wanted to see in him. We also felt that the school's comfort in traditional academic work, and busy-work, would make it difficult to help Charles grow intellectually. Finally, given Charles's size (unfortunately, none of our sons inherited their father's six-foot-three-inch, two-hundred-fifty-pound stature), it just didn't seem likely that school would provide him the range of physical activities he might want. So for us, home schooling allowed a level of holistic growth and development that we were able to tailor specifically for Charles; and the results have been phenomenal.

DAMON came to us as a wild, dark, and primal being, slightly more than five pounds, covered in fine, straight hair, with dark, piercing eyes. Intensely sensitive, deeply spiritual, and comfortable with intuitive, empathetic knowledge, Damon sensed things about people, and would scream when certain people entered the room or tried to touch him. Our challenge was to help him develop a sense of discipline and patience, with an understanding of boundaries and limitations.

Damon was out of control in utero. His heartbeat dropped off the fetal monitor during labor, and as they wheeled me in for an emergency C-section, the doctors told us he was either already dead or would be severely brain damaged at birth. Damon emerged healthy, alert, and all the way live! He nursed every two hours, around the clock, for the first six months of life, with the intensity of someone on the very brink of starvation.

Damon couldn't wait for anything. At six months, he was flinging himself out of his crib and falling down the steps in an effort to walk. At eighteen months, he had been trapped behind the refrigerator, had been caught by his overalls on the top of our six-foot privacy fence, and had taken the screens out of an upstairs window to sit on the ledge of the roof with his arm around Charles. He had escaped to the playground, twice, and I didn't even know he was gone until one of the neighbors brought him home. (Charles and Damon were a dastardly duo, and when Damon would escape through the front door while I was in the bathroom—even mothers have to go sometimes!—Charles would relock the front door and go back into the playroom to watch and wait for my reaction.)

In many ways, Charles and Damon are flip sides of the same coin. Their individual strengths and weaknesses are as polarized as their pigmentation, yet they bring out the absolute best in each other. This made it much easier for us to help them develop within our home-schooling experiment.

In school, Damon always had a difficult time. His energy, his assertiveness, and his color combined to create an almost intolerable situation for him, his teachers, and the schools he attended. For one thing, Damon could never let anything go. If he thought something was wrong or unfair, he felt obligated to intervene. The fact that the situation did not involve him directly was irrelevant to him. Damon had almost no intrinsic regard for position or status, so of course he struggled mightily in a hierarchical structure like school. He didn't understand that some kids were doomed to be ostracized and ridiculed in school, and that to try to include them would create problems for him. He didn't understand that teachers and administrators don't like to be publicly questioned about their conduct and their motives, and that to do so would create problems for him. He didn't understand that verbal violence, teasing, and taunting were acceptable, but physical violence was not. He didn't understand why people thought he was too close to his brothers, and that constantly standing with them against anyone and everyone would create problems for him. Damon just didn't "get" the culture of school, so he was always having problems. So while Damon didn't love being home-schooled, in many ways it was a much easier adjustment for him than for Charles.

Another advantage Damon had was his complete and unwavering confidence in his father. Damon is that rare kid who actually thinks his father is someone worth listening to; even when he disagreed with him, Damon always listened, very carefully. Damon also wants to be obedient; it has always been extraordinarily difficult for him, but he consistently tries.

For Charles obedience was almost a moot issue; his temperament was such that he naturally was a well-behaved child. But Damon? Damon was always wild, and being obedient was difficult because it required a disciplined approach that was inherently alien to his nature.

While all our kids openly hated being home-schooled, Damon was the first of the three to tell us that he understood why we did it. In assessing Damon's development in home schooling, I could examine the reduction in daily conflicts. Suddenly, Damon had all this extra time and energy to devote to his holistic development instead of the institutional development of the school.

Damon was never a strong student academically, primarily because he couldn't segment his intellect the way Charles could. When they were little boys, if you asked Charles to name the first settlers in Jamestown, he would give you the textbook answer with a big grin and not a moment's hesitation. If you asked Damon, he'd hesitate, look very worried, and then ask for clarification: "Do you mean after the Indians?" On some level, he knew what was being asked, and he hated to disappoint, but he just couldn't separate the academic answer from what he knew to be the truth. In home schooling, he was never asked to do so, and that made both the academic and the intellectual work a lot easier.

Damon's biggest challenge in home schooling centered around our refusal to accept any level of nonperformance from him. Damon's frustrations with our expectations were something we noted, but they didn't change anything. In school, there was very little evidence of a belief in or commitment to his development academically or intellectually; very little was expected of Damon, because he was not considered to be as intelligent as his brother Charles.

This opinion was voiced originally when the boys were in kindergarten and was repeated in some form or another every year they were in school. This difference in ability was cited as the core reason why they should never be in the same class: It would create a hardship for Damon to be constantly compared to a brother who was "so clearly" smarter. What was odd about that pronouncement was the fact that none of the IQ tests Charles and Damon have taken has shown more than marginal differences in their scores, and Charles's scores have not always been higher than Damon's.

We had early signs that the difference in their pigmentation might have social implications. One hint was on the very first Sunday we took them to church, when several people indicated their preference: "Oooh, I like the light one!" (I was shocked, but C. Madison wasn't; he simply explained that he didn't want any ignorant people breathing on the babies.) By the time they started school, the color difference was a definite issue, compounded by the fact that nobody at school would even consider the possibility that it could be an issue.

Home schooling allowed us the privilege of circumventing the entire issue of color. This allowed us, and Damon, to focus our energies squarely on his spiritual, intellectual, and physical development.

EVAN came right on schedule, fully developed—fat, at slightly more than eight pounds, and the happiest baby I'd ever seen, at least initially. Evan turned out to be very demanding, headstrong, self-aware, and intellectually gifted—an artist. Our challenge was to help him develop tolerance for others and an understanding of his place in the universe.

Although Evan and I are probably most similar in our personalities (or maybe because of those similarities), he was, in many ways, my most difficult child. Added to the difficulties in his personality, and his absolute refusal to make any effort to please us in any way, Evan's intellect proved quite challenging. Charles and Damon were extremely bright children, and their intelligence was expressed in fairly normal ways at a relatively early age: They learned to count, read, spell, and follow directions when they were quite young, and it was so much fun to show off with them!

See, I'm healthy enough to admit that's what that is—showing off. But what's really being shown is the parent's amazement. I was truly amazed at the things Charles and Damon could do, and the things they knew and could talk about when they were just toddlers. I really never thought about how the parents of less "outgoing" children felt; at least, not until we had Evan.

Evan apparently could retain no information whatsoever. No matter how often I worked with him, he learned or remembered no data: not his numbers, not the alphabet, not the days of the week—nothing. Yet he was obviously very bright and alert, and his observations and comments about the things and people around him were astonishing to me.

Around age three, he started telling me that he wouldn't be going to school—no, not ever, not even to kindergarten. He said it sounded too unpleasant—and, as it turned out, school was quite unpleasant for Evan. A classic Evan story will help clarify this.

When we lived in Florida, psychological testing was recommended for Evan. The public school he attended for first grade was certain he had fairly serious learning disabilities, but no one was certain which ones he had. First, they thought he had hearing loss (Evan is very good at ignoring people). Then they thought he was having peripatetic seizures (Evan can ignore you for a very long time, thereby creating the illusion of a trancelike state). Next they thought he had reading comprehension problems, when Evan answered every question on a multiple-choice test, "Not here." (When I asked him why, he said, "I was pretending I wasn't there.")

I went to school to discuss the testing process with Evan's teacher, the principal, the school psychologist—all white women I knew, liked, and respected—and the district's psychologist—an African-American woman I had not met, who would be administering and scoring the test. I felt reasonably comfortable with the people and the process. I took Evan out into the hall with me, begged him to cooperate, kissed him goodbye, took him back inside, and left.

Two weeks later—the weekend before the scheduled meeting to discuss the test results—the district's psychologist called to speak confidentially with me. She told me Evan's score was quite high, clearly in the gifted range, which explained some of his more eccentric behavior. However, she also told me that this district, like most districts around the country, was very reluctant to classify black children as gifted, especially black boys. She wanted me to know that she would present her findings, i.e., the test scores, but she would not be able to act as an advocate for Evan during the meeting. She advised me to go to the library and do the necessary research so that I would be able to discuss the options indicated by Evan's test scores. She explained that the small percentage of black children in gifted programs across the country was directly related to the reluctance of school districts to identify them as gifted and the corresponding lack of information on the part of their parents. She concluded the conversation by telling me what an enormous professional risk she had taken by calling, and that she hoped I would show my appreciation by not commenting on it during the meeting.

I was stunned. We spent the weekend at the library and completed a crash course on IQ testing for young children. While far short of becoming an expert in the subject, I at least felt competent to discuss the range of scores and their implications.

Monday, when I arrived at the meeting, the district psychologist acted as if she barely remembered meeting me. She presented her findings—basically, Evan's scores on each section of the test—and then left. I was so thankful she had given us a heads up, because, otherwise, I would have been completely unprepared for the meeting.

The rest of the committee said they felt the results were inconclusive. While Evan certainly was capable of performing the work required in first grade, he needed more discipline.

Again, I was shocked. The scores absolutely showed he was gifted, and the school had a gifted program. Yet they had not mentioned moving him into that program—so I did. I suggested we hold off examining the discipline issue until after he was in the gifted program.

Everyone readily agreed, and the matter was settled. But as happy as I was about the resolution, I was chilled when I thought about how it had come about. What if the sister hadn't called? What if we hadn't been able to do the weekend crash course? How many other kids slip through the cracks? And why was it seemingly so much easier to presume Evan had a series of learning disabilities and disciplinary problems than to consider that he might be gifted?

Not surprisingly, we went through a similar situation when we moved back to Columbus: Evan's last teacher recommended testing for him to determine the extent of his as yet unnamed learning disabilities. After almost six months of testing, and meetings with the school psychologist, it was determined that the problem was that Evan was gifted!

Home schooling allowed us to help Evan learn to bring discipline to his intellect. In spite of the difficulties we had encountered, regular school had taught us an invaluable lesson: no matter what academic or educational environment was selected; no matter how much it cost, how selective its admissions policy, or the credentials of its faculty; we had to pay very close attention to each of our sons. That realization was a boon as we went through the process of evaluating our home-schooling experience.

CHILDREN did not come easily to us. We had two miscarriages before we were blessed with Charles and Damon, and two more miscarriages before Evan. By the time we actually had them, we were so thankful that we never had the chance to get really sick of taking care of them. Waiting to become parents made the joy of it almost tangible. Every aspect of the kids was a source of true wonder and fascination for us. We didn't know it at the time, but in a very real way, this waiting helped prepare us for home schooling: The waiting forced us to move past a sense of entitlement to one of privilege about the whole thing—conception, gestation, labor, delivery, and parenting. The process of waiting awakened a deeper sense of wonder and responsibility in us. So, in that sense, the evaluative aspect of home schooling was a relatively easy thing to incorporate: Because we had thought about them and observed them closely from the moment we knew of their conception, we had a clear evaluation benchmark as we began home schooling.

The bulk of our ongoing home-schooling evaluation was an assessment of each child's holistic development. Each year, their level of self-awareness expanded, and it was thrilling to be able to observe and assist in that expansion. We knew their moral and ethical development would be our best indicators of their spiritual growth, so we watched for those signs. We paid close attention to their ability to handle what we called the micro challenges; we weren't tracking their ability to resolve macro challenges—in other words, we were far less interested in their ability to engage in moral reasoning with hypothetical fact patterns than we were in their ability to "play nice."

Anyone with adequate academic training, having read the dominant philosophers of the Western world, can engage in moral reasoning. Ethics is, after all, an academic discipline. It's a field of inquiry wherein one examines what is right and how right is defined. And that's interesting. But we were much more interested in our sons' ability to live a moral life, and, even more important, their desire to do so. So, we paid a great deal of attention to the micro stuff like good manners, polite speech, cooperative play, and genuine consideration for others.

We looked for signs of their ongoing awareness of the limitations of the physical universe. As we watched, listened, and talked to them, we could see their progress. Others saw it too. It was phrased differently, of course. I mean, nobody said, "Gee, your kids seem deeply spiritual. What kind of incense are you burning at home?" But, invariably, people would comment on how different they were, how the difference was difficult to name, and how they were just "so nice." The difference was real enough for people to ask us how it had been achieved.

So we knew the boys' spiritual growth and development was very strong, but we also knew they couldn't put that on a college application. Their progress had to be evaluated on a quantitative level. Toward that end, we relied heavily on standardized testing, specifically, the SAT.

. . .

OUR first quantitative testing as home-schoolers was administered by Dr. Julia Butler, an older African-American psychologist in Columbus. We specifically looked for a licensed psychologist who was African-American, because, based on past experience and information, we knew the process of psychological evaluation was highly subjective. And, again from past experience, we knew the element of race was a variable in the evaluative process, and that the weight of that variable is increased if the person doing the evaluation isn't even aware of the variable and therefore cannot objectively quantify its impact. We really wanted to begin this process with an objective evaluation, including racial objectivity. We felt Dr. Butler's professional training, maturity, and racial identity, coupled with her experience with African-American males (clinically, and as a wife and mother), provided a solid foundation for her work with us.

Dr. Butler tested each boy on separate days at her home office. She spent over an hour before the examination just chatting with each one over cookies and milk. By the time she was ready to administer the test, each was quite comfortable alone with her. (She allowed me to wait in the living room so I could overhear her questions and their answers.)

The results from that test established a baseline for our home-schooling experience. Dr. Butler gave us quantitative results that, while slightly higher, were in line with earlier IQ test results, so we knew we had a solid foundation. What was just as helpful was the qualitative advice she gave in terms of each boy's learning style, and ways to assist each to reach his potential.

WE did not include any additional testing for almost two years. During that hiatus, we focused our energies on intellectual stimulation rather than academic work or objective testing. Our internal evaluation of the boys' work was based on our assessment of their relative mastery of the work assigned.

The issue of mastery was relative to their ages: As our curriculum in most disciplines did not change from year to year, we often explored the same texts. So, for example, their mastery of Countee Cullen's poetry definitely was relative to their age and maturity. Their grasp of the work at fifteen was markedly different than what they exhibited as twelve-year-olds.

One significant marker for our evaluation was their ability to see, grasp, and understand relationships; to see the reality of Einstein's theory that everything is relative. C. Madison and I viewed their ongoing ability to see and understand relationships as the chief indicator of growth. As we continued to study world religions, for instance, we listened for their analysis of the relationships between man and man, man and nature, man and intellect, and man and God. We were especially pleased to witness their ability to see the relationship between the human desire to know God as expressed in Christianity and how it's expressed in other religions.

In examining current events, we listened for their analysis of the relationship between politics and economics. Current events also gave us an opportunity to monitor vocabulary and reading levels.

Listening to the boys read aloud provided an opportunity for us to evaluate the growth and depth of their vocabulary. Listening was also a skill we were working to develop in them.

One technique for monitoring their growth in this area was taking them to lectures by visiting professors. Very quickly, they were able (and willing) to initiate commentary with us about their assessment of what they had heard and observed. Their ability to recognize the deference afforded facile ideas when expressed by people from elite institutions was a sure sign of intellectual development.

Places like The Ohio State University, Otterbein College, and Capital University provided tremendous opportunities for us to observe and evaluate our kids and their intellectual abilities in a comfortable, noncompetitive fashion. They read books, listened to authors, and watched group discussions. And when we got home, they told us what they thought.

It was a lot like church: You basically know the text before you get there; you listen to a presentation and discussion of one part of it; and then, if you're lucky, you have someone with whom you can discuss it. But to do so, you first have to have listened.

As their progress continued intellectually, we expanded their academic workload with an eye toward SAT preparation. When Charles and Damon turned thirteen—right after their Rites of Passage—two things changed: We began to add traditional academic work to their schedule, and we began a process of regular SAT examinations.

We were convinced standardized testing did not measure intelligence. We were also convinced that, while they might not be accurate predictors of academic success in college, they absolutely were a potential barrier to getting into college. More than anything else, we felt standardized tests measured the success of the test-preparation process.

We began our process of test preparation by making the entire test process as familiar as possible. When I, like most people, took the SAT in my senior year (decades before there was anything like an SAT II), I thought my entire future was riding on the outcome of that one Saturday afternoon. My headmaster and most of the faculty had helped me reach that conclusion. Everyone in my class probably felt that our performance, individually and collectively, would be a reflection on us, our teachers, and our school. But more than that, I felt my performance would be seen as a reflection on all black people everywhere. The pressure was enormous, and I don't think it helped my performance.

C. Madison and I made a conscious decision to demystify the entire ACT/SAT/SAT II process. We talked about people we knew who blew the SAT out of the water. We talked about people we knew who actually had scored a perfect 800 on one or both sections, and how some of those perfect people didn't graduate college in four years—some never graduated at all. We talked about people we knew who didn't do that well on their standardized tests, but excelled in college and, more important, in life.

We looked at the demographics of the advertising for and location of test-preparation centers and their clients to illustrate the inherent bias in the exams. After all, if the tests really measured past academic performance and potential, kids from the wealthiest public and private schools wouldn't need to take the prep courses, and the fact that the vast majority of kids in the prep courses were in that demographic pool helped prove our point.

We wanted Charles, Damon, and Evan to understand that standardized testing simply creates the dual illusion of objectivity and a level playing field. This was an important first step in helping them prepare psychologically for testing.

Our next step was to help the boys become accustomed to the testing process well in advance of the test having any real impact on their future college acceptances. Preparing for the SAT before it counted also allowed us to take advantage of the various programs offered by the Educational Testing Service (ETS). The most helpful was the question-and-answer service (the SAT PrepPacks). This program, modestly priced at a mere ten dollars, returns an actual copy of the test with all the student's answers. Incorrect answers are identified along with the correct answer and a notation of the type of question missed. So, on the mathematics section, an incorrect answer would be identified as an algebra or a geometry question, while in the vocabulary section an incorrect answer could involve reading comprehension. This service really helps in the preparation process, because it identifies very specific areas of weakness. Using the program in advance helped take a lot of the mystery out of the process for our sons.

By the equivalent of Charles and Damon's junior year, C. Madison and I felt we had maxed out our ability to assist the boys in SAT preparation. We re-searched the various SAT preparation programs available commercially and selected the Princeton Review, because of the private-tutor option. This was quite an expensive option—fifteen hundred dollars a pop!—however, we knew the scores on the SATs would be outcome determinative for African-American male home-schooled students.

If the boys were to achieve the goal of Ivy League college acceptances, we knew we had several negative presumptions to overcome, namely, race, gen-der, and the fact that the boys' grades could not be validated objectively. We knew the exceptional nature of their home-schooling education, but, for col-lege, we knew everything was riding on their board scores. So, with that as a backdrop, we were ready to get serious about SAT preparation and the entire college search-and-admission process.

There are any number of ways of evaluating your child's progress, and the form of much of that analysis will depend upon what is being evaluated. In a purely academic sense, there are nationally standardized tests for certain grade levels, e.g., fourth grade. Those tests are administered by local school districts, and even if your kid is home-schooled, he or she can still sit for those tests, and you can receive the results for evaluation. SAT and ACT exams are another set of standardized tests that are available.

Most school districts have some sort of evaluative process available to home-school parents. And if you hire independent teachers or tutors, they can provide evaluative progress reports.

We didn't rely on a lot of testing until almost the end of our home-schooling experience, and then it was for the sole purpose of college admissions. I have never been particularly impressed with testing, test results, or projections based upon testing. I have similar concerns about grades.

We evaluated the boys' work on a daily basis, as it was turned in, and when we saw areas of weakness, we addressed them. We offered a very limited and un-varied curriculum, so we were able to assess their progress fairly easily. We were comfortable with repetition, and encouraged their tutors to review and repeat material if there was any question about full comprehension. We tended to focus on mastery of thought and the ability to convey those thoughts in a way that was both comprehensible and creative.

19

HOW WE DID

THE COLLEGE SEARCH

BECAUSE THE BOYS hated home schooling and felt we were so unreasonable in pursuing it, we made a deal with them: If they made a good-faith effort to cooperate with us in home schooling, we would support them in whatever college choice they made, when it came time.

I thought that by the time they were ready to go to college, they'd be so impressed with the job we'd done that they'd want our help in making such an important decision. Okay, that was naïve and stupid: Of course they weren't impressed with us, not even a little bit.

By the time they were ready to apply to college, they still hated the very idea of home schooling, and they were still mad at us for making them do it. Needless to say, they held us firmly to our promise, which just added another dimension of pressure to the college search process for C. Madison and me. We had to remind each other constantly that the boys were making an important decision, and while it could be life altering, we were confident that it wouldn't be life ending—as flippant as that sounds.

After accidents and homicide, suicide is the third leading cause of death for college students. Kids who come to college unprepared for the totality of the experience can be at risk. College is that marker in time when issues of holistic health and balance take on pragmatic dimensions; yet, consistently, this critical issue is ignored. So much attention is placed on the quantitative indicators of academic readiness that, when kids score well on those all-important SATs, it's pretty much the end of the discussion.

We knew Charles, Damon, and Evan were strong and healthy spiritually, intellectually, and physically. We didn't know how they'd adjust to college, or whether they'd be happy or popular. We didn't know if they'd flunk out, barely graduate, or graduate with honors. We didn't know if they'd play intramural or varsity sports, or if they'd earn a championship ring. What we did know was that they'd survive college, and we knew they'd leave an indelible mark wherever they went. And I knew that might prove to be quite unpleasant for them.

Overall, I was thankful to know that no college or university environment could warp or destroy them. And while lots of parents may not actually articulate an awareness of that thought, the fact is that some kids are consumed and destroyed by the post-secondary institutions they attend. The sad irony is that the parents of those students probably saved for years, and spent a lot of money, for that shattering experience.

So, while I had general concerns, I was thankful to feel enormously confident.

But that confidence didn't mean that I didn't think the boys needed my assistance in making a good decision. After all, I was still their mother, for God's sake. How could I not think they needed my insight?!

DECIDING where to go to college is unquestionably important. By default, that means trying to make an intelligent search is important as well. But the fact of the matter is that it's not really a life-or-death decision, and we refused to allow the boys to behave as if it were.

We struggled throughout the process with keeping the search and the search objectives in perspective for the boys and for ourselves. The boys needed to determine which of the seemingly infinite number of post-secondary institutions available would be good choices for them. And since neither penal nor mental institutions were among the choices, there wasn't any danger of them making a truly horrific choice.

We tried to relieve some of the pressure of the search by reminding them that there were no perfect colleges, so they didn't have to sweat the possibility of missing that perfect selection. No matter which college they picked, there were going to be some serious and significant challenges, most of which wouldn't show up on the radar of any kind of search. They'd have to wait until they enrolled to find out.

There's no search engine to identify the prospective students who will be there at the same time, shaping the tone and tenor of the campus, much less the roommate who might determine which of Dante's nine circles of hell you'll inhabit during that critical first year. There's no search mechanism to measure the quantity, quality, or sincerity of faculty involvement with under-graduates, and, no, student/faculty ratio really isn't a reliable indicator of such factors. There's no search for the actual quality of classroom teaching, either; and while lists of faculty credentials and publications can be comforting and impressive, they provide absolutely no clue about teaching ability.

These unsearchable, invisible, and intangible elements form the foundation of the quality of life in a liberal arts institution. What we tried to point out to the boys was the fact that the college search is best at highlighting the visible, tangible, and quantitative aspects of any institution—so, make the best of it. The search process has some limitations, and we tried to help the boys identify them, but we also encouraged the boys to pursue the search with gusto and vigor.

WITH enormous enthusiasm and excitement, we began the active, physical college search relatively early, when Charles and Damon were thirteen. On a larger scale, the passive components of the college search had been life-long.

We began the indoctrination process early. Charles, Damon, and Evan knew as toddlers that going to college was not optional; it was an exciting thing to look forward to in their future as "big boys." It was something each of them was going to do, just as their parents, grandparents, and great-grandparents had. College was a foregone conclusion that didn't require discussion; the only uncertainty was which college, and what they'd do when they went there.

Many people accused us of brainwashing, as though we would deny it, in shame. While I prefer to see it as indoctrination, rather than as brainwashing, the truth is I felt I had the right and the responsibility to impress our values upon our kids.

The corresponding allegation was that such indoctrination shaped their perspective and inherently limited their choices. And in the way of all values, principles, and ideals parents try to inculcate in children early, it may have limited their choices, but I prefer to think we helped them make informed choices.

Either way, I have absolutely no remorse about it. Every option in every situation is not worthy of weighty consideration by children, which is one reason why I never asked my little ones questions like "Do you want to get dressed?" or "Do you want to eat breakfast?" or "In what room do you want to eat breakfast?"

For God's sake, no four-year-old should be so burdened: Lay out the kids' clothes the night before, wake them, fix breakfast, and serve it in the kitchen — end of story. Even with adults, everything in life need not be subject to mind-numbing analysis, or prayer, either, for that matter.

In this society, in this time, for young black males with the abilities manifested early, as in my sons, the question of whether or not to go to college is a classic no-brainer. It no more needed analysis than it needed prayer.

When it's freezing outside, you don't need to analyze or pray about wearing a coat. If it's freezing outside and you're blessed to have a coat available — wear it. Wear it even if the coat's the wrong size, the coat's ugly, and you hate it. The important thing is: You need a coat!

For us, going to college was analogous to wearing an ugly coat or having to get inoculations. Vaccinations are not pleasant, but they are infinitely better than contracting the various diseases they ward off. By the same token, college can be unpleasant in many respects, but it is better than the alternative.

Now, of course, these comparisons are not universally true. Some children have had extremely adverse, even fatal, reactions to some vaccines, and, similarly, some students have had extremely adverse, even fatal, reactions to college. But those unfortunate situations are the exceptions, not the rule.

The only choice that existed about college for our boys was which college they would attend. I think the kids knew that by the time they were five.

Two of the biggest challenges in the college admissions process that a lot of kids face are figuring out if they want to go and feeling confident enough to apply. Those issues complicate the challenge of creating a sense of optimism and confidence in the process. These are fairly passive, subtextual challenges, but fortunately we addressed them so early in the boys' lives, they almost became nonissues.

The boys knew they wanted to go to college, and, initially, they felt very confident about their ability to get into good, competitive colleges. Of course, all that confidence evaporated in the midst of their home-schooling experience. So we started with college as a foregone conclusion—a huge asset— only to lose momentum because of a lack of confidence in home schooling. By the time we were ready to begin the college search in earnest, the boys were only confident of two things: They were convinced that their father and I had absolutely no idea what we were doing, and they were convinced that our inflexibility (and stupidity) meant they would never be admitted to any accredited college in the United States.

So, in the context of passive preparation, half of the job was done: Charles,

Damon, and Evan each eagerly wanted to go to college, and each felt confident of his ability to be reasonably successful in college. However, their confidence in their competitiveness, notably, was absent, and we had to move forward with *our* confidence as a substitute for theirs. We then moved to the active part of the college admission process.

The first active thing we did was to build side trips to area colleges into our upcoming business trips with the kids. By adding college visits onto business trips, we were able to take the kids to a wide range of schools. Ultimately, we visited colleges as diverse as Amherst, Berkeley, Brown, Case Western, Columbia, Dartmouth, Harvard, MIT, Morehouse, Northwestern, OSU, Princeton, the Rhode Island School of Design, Stanford, the University of Michigan, Williams, Wittenberg, and Yale.

We used a number of factors in selecting which schools to visit. Geography played a big role in some selections: We always visited nearby colleges when we had business trips; that's how we saw Stanford. Geographic diversity also played a role in the selection process: We wanted the boys to see and feel the geographic differences among schools in the South, the Midwest, and on the East and West Coasts; hence, visits to the University of Florida at Gainesville, Northwestern, and Yale. We also looked at some schools based on specific interests, size, and race; hence, RISD, Wittenberg, and Morehouse. Our objective was to allow the guys to see as wide a range of colleges and universities as possible, so that they would have the best chance of making a good choice.

Let me interject one area of surprise for other parents: I found visiting colleges to be arduous work, and nothing that could be confused with fun or having a good time. The romantic notion of traveling with one's child to visit various colleges is wildly exaggerated. Knowing one of those places will be that kid's home for the next four years creates a certain distasteful pressure. And being there for that all-important, mutual, first impression—the whole thing was quite stressful, and not nearly as wonderful as I thought it would be. The kids frequently were cranky during these trips (the strain, no doubt), and, of course, since they believed we, their parents, knew nothing, and were single-handedly responsible for their noncompetitive status, much of their crankiness was directed at us.

This undercurrent of resentment would flood to the surface each time we got ready for a campus tour and interview. Our sons thought these were "come as you are" gatherings. Judging by the appearance of lots of the other hopefuls, they thought that, too: They were all caught up in the myth that appearance has no impact whatsoever. So I had to be "mean" and morph into my own mother as I told them, "Rich, white kids can afford to dress like that.

No one will assume they don't know any better. They simply will appear too sophisticated and jaded to be bothered with appropriate attire. That must be very convenient; however, *you're not white!*"

Our kids saw us as pathetic, and painfully bourgeois, middle-class parents from the Midwest when we forced them to dress appropriately in a blazer, shirt, and hard shoes. But we really didn't care. We were content, with the smug satisfaction that comes when you know you're right and it's confirmed by objective third parties.

At almost every interview or tour, someone on the admissions committee commented on how nice it was to see a student who cared enough to clean up before the meeting. Admittedly, this was not the confirmation I was hoping to receive; I was secretly hoping that, at some point, preferably during one of the tours, one of our sons would look at the two of us and emit one of those 1950s platitudes, something like "Gee, Mom and Dad, there's so much to think about. I'm sure glad you're here. You're the greatest!" Of course, I wanted this to be followed immediately by a sincere and spontaneous hug. Nothing even remotely like that happened.

The process quickly became an "us" versus "them" kind of issue. While there was no clear conflict of interest, there were competing issues. Our understanding of the terms of the promise we had made was that the boys would make the ultimate choice of which school to attend; consequently, we had an interest in the selection and visitation process. The kids acted as though the terms of the promise meant that they would have the ultimate choice about *everything* involved in the college choice.

We definitely had competing issues about preparation. They wanted to just be "open" to the experience; we wanted them to be prepared. C. Madison required the boys to compose questions, some general and some specific, for each college to be visited, and to go over those questions with him in advance.

We really wanted the kids to understand that this was not just a process of a college accepting them. The student/college selection process ideally is a bilateral kind of thing. Our view on this score highlighted another area of competing interest: We wanted—in fact, needed—the guys to see how much they had to offer. In a way, that qualitative validation of themselves was as important to us as the quantitative validation of college admission.

The guys differed with us on this point. They did not seem to feel they were on a par with the institutions examining them. So we were forced to require a level of preparation that would have been unnecessary if the process weren't ultimately going to be bilateral.

We were confident that the boys would have some choices to make, so they needed to determine which college they would accept. Part of our concern on this score was that we did not want all the qualitative gains from home schooling to be reversed during the college application process. It was critically important to us that our sons realize what contributions they would be making to any college they attended, and we were convinced that the preparation of questions in advance would help them solidify their thoughts on that issue.

Too often, the college application process is like a wedding. When planning a wedding—that one-of-a-kind picture-book fairy-tale wedding—it's easy to get so focused on that perfect, magical day that the marriage itself becomes an afterthought. I think college admissions are subject to the same kind of myopic thinking. So much attention is focused on getting into college that it's easy to forget about surviving in or even staying in college, and some places are more difficult to live in than others.

We really tried to push the boys to look beyond the challenge of acceptance toward the challenge of living at these different places. It was hard to get them to consider this perspective, because, like so many applicants (and parents, grandparents, teachers, etc.), it was easy for them to assume that if these colleges were so competitive and expensive, they must be great.

Of course, nothing weakens a person's sense of self like the vagaries of the college application process, and those vagaries made it difficult to evaluate these institutions with any degree of objectivity. Our sons were so anxious about the impact on their competitiveness of being home-schooled, it was hard to convince them that they would be accepted anywhere at all. Charles the younger kept telling me how irresponsible we had been. His consistent question was, did I think fulfilling my "dream" of home schooling was worth relegating him and his brothers to a lifetime of fast-food service?

We, along with the boys, kept fairly detailed notes about each college, and tried to visit most of them more than once in an effort to gain a clear sense of each institution. We discovered this was an ambitious goal, because, after a while, so many schools look the same, the admissions officers ask the same questions, and you end up seeing a lot of the same people—i.e., parents and kids—over and over, as if you're trapped in the Twilight Zone.

The college visits supported the research C. Madison had the boys do in between our road trips. He really made sure that the boys made the most of library and online information. We talked about comparisons among different geographic, racial, social, and academic environments. While the boys didn't need to select a major, we did feel it was important to determine whether they wanted a technical or liberal arts experience.

As unpleasant as much of it was, it proved very valuable. By the conclusion of the search process, two important things had happened. The boys had a lot of comparative information well in advance of what was the equivalent of their junior year, which helped narrow the actual application process. And the boys knew that, with few exceptions, college admissions officers were familiar with home schooling. None appeared horrified. No one kicked the boys out of group interviews. No one stated any negative assumptions. Even better: The admissions officers from some of the most competitive colleges were quite interested in speaking with us about the process! As they reviewed the boys' abridged bibliographies, which they brought to each interview, many admissions officers openly expressed their admiration for such broad-based study.

Charles, Damon, and Evan really needed to hear someone they assumed to be knowledgeable and objective say what we had been saying all along, namely, that they were more than qualified to be competitive in the college admissions process. After the first confirmation, the boys returned home with a real sense of confidence in home schooling, and we rode that through the ugly applications process.

While there is no guarantee that college visits will result in a perfect selection, it certainly helps facilitate the process. There are several key points to emphasize:

First of all, college visiting is one of the few situations where less is not more. I think it is vitally important for students and their parents to see as many schools as possible. Sometimes the easiest way to clarify what you want is to see what you don't want. With that in mind, don't make the mistake of forgoing visits to local colleges and universities, even if you know your kid isn't interested in attending. Also, don't assume because a school is close by that you or your kid knows everything (or anything) about the institution. Use those nearby institutions as test runs for longer, more expensive visits. Try out your questions, estimate the time requirements, see what's missing from the campus tours, and talk to students and faculty. You'll be able to approach subsequent visits with a greater sense of confidence and efficiency.

Along with quantity of visits, the timing of visits is also critical. Whenever possible, try to visit while school is in session, and if multiple visits are possible, try to make sure at least one of those visits happens in bad weather. Every campus looks beautiful in the spring and fall; to get a real feel for the totality of the environment, try to schedule a visit in January or February so you can see what the place looks like in the dead of winter. Winter's also a great time to view student life during the doldrums of midyear, when the enthusiasm and optimism of September is long gone—and the excitement of spring and the anticipation of conclusion is a long way off.

Once you've sat down as a family and discussed which schools to visit, contact those colleges. We found colleges and universities to be very helpful about letting you know the best times to visit, when tours are offered, and when overnight stays are available.

And speaking of overnight stays: While sometimes inconvenient, they can be deal-breaking events. Most schools insist that overnight stays include a weekday, so interested students can attend classes. This gives prospective students an opportunity to experience the academic as well as social dimensions of the institution, which is invaluable, because while a tour is a good way to get an overview, nothing compares with attending classes and spending a night in a dorm.

Finally, there's the question of when the visiting process should begin. I think seventh or eighth grade is an ideal time to introduce this experience. Granted, a seventh- or eighth-grader is too young for an overnight experience; regardless of how mature the student is, I think there are some things a twelve- or thirteen-year-old shouldn't experience firsthand. However, visiting campuses, having lunch in the student center, and going on a tour are valuable experiences at almost any age.

Middle school can be an ideal time for these visits, because it can help the student clarify the necessity of maintaining high academic standards and making good course selections as they enter high school. Too often, middle school students are mesmerized by the social prospects of high school—e.g., driving, dating, proms, athletic events, etc.—and it's easy to lose sight of the fact that the decisions made in high school will determine the availability of choices for college.

It's heartbreaking to see kids reach their senior year in high school, only to find that poorly thought-out decisions in high school have created almost insurmountable obstacles for college admissions choices. This is not only very sad, but also completely avoidable.

Whether or not you choose to home-school, take responsibility for assisting your kid in preparing for the next stage in their academic career. Too often, parents with kids in traditional educational institutions assume that their guidance counselors are responsible. Technically, that's true; however, most guidance counselors are extremely overburdened, with more students than they can handle with the level of individual attention the counselor would like to extend.

Further, guidance counselors are human. They frequently have certain students whom they prefer to work most closely with, and generally these are the students with the greatest possibility of success in the college admissions game.

Parents have to make sure that their kids get the guidance and information that is so critical to making good decisions about this next step. If the guidance counselor has the time and the inclination to be a partner in that process, so much the better. But even if that's not the case, your kid still needs and deserves all the assistance that can be provided, and if that means you have to be the prime mover, do it.

Whether the information and assistance comes from the guidance office or from you, the important thing is that your kid gets the information, and college visits can provide a vital component of that information.

20

HOW WE SURVIVED

COLLEGE ADMISSIONS

WITHOUT A GUIDANCE

COUNSELOR

ONCE UPON A time, in a galaxy far, far away, C. Madison and I thought the college search process was the low point of our home-schooling experience, but we were so wrong, and oh, so naïve. The search process was difficult, but the applications process was hideous. C. Madison and I both agree that if we'd had more than three kids in this family, the rest would have had to forgo college. I don't think we could survive it again. But here's how we did it (and no, it really wasn't easier with Evan).

The process of getting into college is based on a series of formalized procedures with students, guidance counselors, teachers, secondary schools, admissions officers, and, of course, parents. In our case, all we had were the students, the admissions officers, and ourselves, the parents. Let me tell you, when you're outside that carefully constructed structure, with no guidance counselor, teachers, or secondary schools to help you through, it can feel like a free-for-all.

I realize not all guidance counselors do a good job, but, believe me, going through the college application process with no guidance counselor at all was not a pretty sight. Part of what's truly evil about the whole college applications process is the needless complexity of the thing. This process was a nightmare—and a multistep nightmare at that. C. Madison and I went to college, and our siblings, friends, parents, and grandparents went to college. Despite all that experience, we were completely unprepared for helping our kids through the process of getting into college.

For one thing, the process has changed significantly since the early seventies, when C. Madison and I last participated in this cruel dance. For another thing, much of what I remembered about the process had less to do with the actual application and more to do with my feelings about going to college—getting out of prep school and leaving Columbus. Essentially, my memories were too vague to be of any assistance at all. But by the time I realized that, we were well into Charles and Damon's junior year. The ordeal was under way, and, ready or not, we had to deal with it.

The good part? Well, for one thing, all the boys got into great schools. And for another thing, we got confirmation that the college application process, like so many things, is as much about form as it is about substance.

A big part of the multistep nightmare was the fact that at every turn I was discovering something important, even critical, about which I knew very little—and I hate that. I don't mind learning new things; what I hate is when you need to know something right now, but you're just at the beginning of the learning curve. Fortunately, we began this project in a relatively timely fashion, so we were able to segment the entire thing into smaller-project pieces.

The wisdom attributed to Lao-Tzu—"a journey of a thousand miles begins with a single step"—really can be applied to the college application process. Much of it seemed overwhelming, but with a lot of prayer and the knowledge that it was, indeed, possible, we persevered. I just kept reminding myself of all the people I knew who got into college, and all the people I knew who helped them. I figured all of them couldn't be smarter, or more organized or disciplined, than we were.

Throughout this ordeal, we had the added pressure, and the incentive, of public scrutiny. If we ever wanted our kids to forgive us, if we ever wanted our parents to forgive us, if we ever wanted our friends and associates to look at us with anything other than the special contempt one holds for irresponsible parents, our kids had to get into school. And not just *any* school. They had to get into a G-R-E-A-T school. Our redemption hinged on their acceptance by at least one exclusive, competitive, Ivy League college or university. Talk about pressure—it was enormous!

One of the worst aspects of the pressure was the lack of equally miserable comrades. We had no one with whom to complain and commiserate. Every time we mentioned the horror of the thing, people would give us that patronizing look and the reminder comment, "Well, you wanted to home-school," or, "Well, you don't have a guidance counselor, so what'd you expect?" Also, it was interesting to note how many people felt the irresistible urge to tell us how unreasonable it was for us even to think that our kids could get into an

Ivy League college. I was surprised to learn that, apparently, several people assumed we had decided against college altogether; otherwise, we wouldn't have risked home schooling. These kinds of presumptions didn't help.

Early on, we decided to approach this project by separating, as much as possible, the emotional energy from the administrative details. Given the enormous time constraints, focusing on the emotional-energy issues before we were finished, and the boys were safely ensconced in school, was a luxury we just couldn't afford. Plus, dealing with the administrative details proved so humbling that, after a while, the emotional stuff became less and less significant.

Very rarely have I heard anyone say anything particularly good about guidance counselors, but this experience certainly has made me reevaluate the difficulty of the job. I cannot imagine going through the administrative nightmare of college admissions every year. I hated the process when the participants were my very own sons—flesh of my flesh, bone of my bone. I cannot imagine going through this for somebody else's child.

RIGHT off the bat, Charles and Damon had to decide which schools they thought they might want to apply to, and then they had to request that school's application for the upcoming year. If you try to be an early bird and collect applications in advance (I thought I was very clever!), like in the sophomore or junior year, forget it: Every year there's a new application. We didn't know that. So, while we thought we were just the tiniest bit ahead of the game, we were actually behind right out of the box.

Once the various applications arrived, we photocopied them before they got messed up. I could see no point in pretending that somebody wasn't going to spill something on one of those applications before they were completed. Plus, as the applications were so complex, it was unrealistic to think that any one of them could be completed in one sitting. We set up a large, alphabetized accordion file so we could keep all the applications—originals and photocopies—in some semblance of order. We used the copies to practice on and saved the originals for the final submission.

Next, we had to check for the various application deadlines. We got one of those gigantic, erasable whiteboards to keep track of all the various deadlines for all the various sections of all the various applications. (That's right: Each application is in separate parts, and many of the parts have specific deadlines.) Getting the whiteboard turned out to be one of the best administrative-support decisions we ever made. We used it for everything: the application deadlines, financial aid deadlines, SAT schedules, college visits, and alumni interviews. I honestly don't know how we would have made it without the big board.

The next issue was how to apply. Charles and Damon had to decide if they wanted to apply Early Decision or Early Action. And, no, those are not different terms for the same thing, which originally is what I thought.

When I applied to college, back in the previous millennium, the choice was simple: regular decision or Early Decision, period. Early Decision meant you knew there was only one place in the universe you could spend four productive years as an undergraduate, so you applied in November and received your answer in December. You didn't apply anywhere else, and if that blessed place accepted you, you would never be so unfaithful even to consider looking at any other school. Good news meant you could remind everybody you were already in, while they spent Christmas completing the hideous process, waiting in agony for April. If the news was bad, you got over the embarrassment by quickly applying somewhere else before the traditional, let-us-blow-your-entire-holiday-season December 31 deadline.

Early Decision still means pretty much the same thing. Early Action is different, though. With Early Action, you still apply in November and find out in December, but there's no binding agreement between the applicant and the school. So you can apply only to one school under Early Decision guidelines, but you can apply to more than one school under the rules of Early Action.

Next, filing questions: Which colleges have rolling admissions? Which require all admission materials by December 31? Which colleges have a January 1 deadline and which accept applications until February 2? And here are a couple of critical questions: What time does the post office close on December 31? If the postmark is late, will the college still accept the materials? (With Charles and Damon, we were at the post office at ten P.M., December 31. I am ashamed to admit that it was even later with Evan's applications.)

Then there was the issue of recommendations. Who's going to write them? Every applicant needs more than one. And if you're home-schooled, it's probably a good idea to have at least four lined up.

This was something we had been thinking about, actively, throughout most of our home-schooling experience. Of course, we knew the kids' applications wouldn't receive the serious consideration they deserved if we wrote their recommendations ourselves! This whole issue of recommendations and what they needed to illustrate for home-schooled applicants was something C. Madison and I discussed with the admissions officers at every college we visited. Those discussions were very helpful, because we found out exactly what issues most needed to be addressed.

Overwhelmingly, admissions officers expressed concern about evidence of overall successful socialization for home-schooled students. Specifically, they wanted evidence of the home-schooled students' experiences with adults and peers outside the home-schooling environment.

When we began trolling for recommendation writers, we knew what we needed from each person. As we broached the question with each potential writer, we were very candid about what was needed. One of the really great things about our home-schooling experience was how incredibly helpful and supportive lots of people were. For every group of vocal naysayers, there was always at least one person who went out of his/her way to encourage and help in very tangible ways. Virtually every person we asked to write a recommendation immediately agreed to do so. Not only that, each one asked specifically what they could best say to solidify the boys' applications, and quite frankly, if you're not seriously committed to helping the student's chance at being admitted, why bother writing a recommendation?

Although most of the colleges the boys were interested in requested three recommendations, we decided to err on the side of excess, and in almost every application we supplied five.

As the people most familiar with the applicants, we had to provide the guidance counselor recommendation. The problem was that we knew better than anyone how wonderful, bright, and well educated the kids were, and what a dynamic contribution they would make to any college. Yet, because we were their parents, we knew it would be exceedingly difficult for any admissions committee to believe our statements. So we added two academic recommendations, a volunteer/community service recommendation, and an athletic or arts recommendation to both balance and validate the guidance counselor/parent recommendation.

In prioritizing the recommendations needs, we put the academic recommendations requirement first. We knew the primary academic recommendation needed to come from someone with typical teaching credentials and experience. It needed to be from someone the admissions committees would view as worthy of consideration.

For Charles and Damon, we asked Dr. Frank Croft, from OSU's engineering program. We figured that, having taught both college and high school students for more than a couple of decades, he could evaluate Charles and Damon objectively in relation to their chronological peers. We felt his affiliation with a recognizable university further validated his assessment. As a bonus, Dr. Croft not only taught Charles and Damon, but he actually took the time to know them as separate people.

With Evan, we were fortunate to be able to have Mrs. Searles, from Westerville North High School, agree to write one of his recommendations. After Charles and Damon left for college, Evan requested, and we agreed to allow him, to take two courses at our local public high school, and one of those courses was Latin. While Charles and Damon were understandably furious about our decision to allow Evan this opportunity, in every instance we tried to make decisions based on our assessment of the best interests of each kid at that particular moment. In Evan's instance, we felt that continuing to home-school him, in the absence of his brothers, was a significantly different arrangement, and one that required an adjustment. One hour of Latin each day was part of that adjustment.

Mrs. Searles was Evan's Latin teacher for the two years he attended our local public high school as a part-time student. She is the epitome of the ideal teacher. She demands and gets excellence by being clear, firm, and deeply caring. She was able to evaluate Evan objectively in relation to his high school peers, based on her observations of him in class and supported by her twenty-plus years of teaching Latin to middle and high school students.

This was extremely fortunate, as there was absolutely no possibility of Evan applying or being accepted into the summer engineering program at OSU! And both Dr. Croft and Mrs. Searles commented on their positive assessments of the boys' socialization skills within their peer groups.

For the second academic recommendation, we asked the boys' biology tutor, Mr. Charles Morgan, to write for Charles and Damon. Mr. Morgan received his master's in education, with a focus on science and mathematics, the same year Charles and Damon "graduated." Having done traditional student teaching, he could evaluate the boys objectively. Having taught them biology at our kitchen table, complete with four-hour labs and dissections, he could talk about their genuine enthusiasm for learning.

We asked Ms. Angela Whitaker, their mathematics tutor, to write Evan's second academic recommendation. Angela highlighted Evan's consistent efforts in mathematics, even though he really hated the subject and did not excel in it.

Our second recommendation topic was volunteer work and community service. We relied heavily on Ms. Jan Davidson from the Center for Science and Industry. Ms. Davidson oversaw COSI's entire student-volunteer program and designed its home-schooling segment. So Jan was in the unique position to comment not only on the boys' long-term commitment to volunteer service but also on their socialization skills relative to other student volunteers and other home-schooled students. Plus, since Jan first met Charles and Damon when they were twelve and Evan when he was ten, she was truly qualified to assess their long-term development and maturation.

We focused on athletics for Charles and Damon's third recommendation, and on art for Evan's. In the case of the athletic recommendation, we went to Charles and Damon's fencing coach, Mr. Michael Shearer, whom they met at Fedderson Recreation Center. Along with his work through Columbus Parks and Recreation, he also was an assistant coach for OSU's fencing team.

During their two years in the program, Mr. Shearer was able to observe the boys in intensely competitive situations. (Since their "school" didn't have a fencing team, Charles and Damon had to practice at home. My only requirement was that they leave the protective tips on their foils, and that under no circumstances were any weapons to be used against me or aimed in my direction, ever, even in jest.) Coach Shearer considers fencing to be the athletic equivalent of chess. He succeeded in individually addressing the boys' physical and intellectual agility, and their ability to respond positively to high levels of stress while simultaneously supporting other members of the team.

Evan's art recommendation was, in many respects, the easiest one to request. Dr. Roman Johnson had been Evan's mentor since Evan was thirteen. Roman became a dear friend and educator to our entire family during those years. Roman regarded Evan as a fellow artist, and trained him in the classical tradition of the old masters. Roman was delighted to write Evan's recommendation, and his praise for Evan's work was enormous. (We also submitted slides of Evan's work, which helped to validate Roman's accolades.)

As we organized our thoughts and plans regarding the recommendations, we also had to factor in the issue of timing: The recommendations needed to be completed and ready to submit with the applications, so we asked everyone to return their recommendations to us. While this is not customary, no one seemed troubled by the request.

I feel strongly that if one is not able to write a glowing and 100-percent-supportive recommendation, one should decline when asked. The traditionally secret nature of recommendations always has left me cold. When I was a student member of the admissions committee at Wellesley, I saw hideous secret recommendations that left me wondering why the person involved agreed to write the recommendation in the first place. When I taught as an adjunct faculty member at the University of North Florida in Jacksonville, and Franklin University and Columbus State Community College in Columbus, I made it a point to address this issue candidly with students. There were occasions when a student asked for a recommendation, and I felt obliged to say I could not write an unqualified endorsement. Sometimes, the student desperately needed a recommendation and had run out of people to ask, which was unfortunate, but at least the student was not deceived.

In any event, in this situation everyone was extremely gracious about completing the recommendations on time. Charles's and Damon's recommendations were particularly burdensome, because we had to ask each writer to do two. And each recommendation needed to be uniquely applicable to each boy. Amazingly, everyone did a wonderful and detailed job. Another bonus for us was reading how other people saw our sons. It was enlightening to see which aspects of each one's personality most struck a chord with the writer. As home-schooling parents, we were given that rare opportunity to see our sons described with detail through the lens of someone else.

I WOULD say that test scheduling and reporting was the next step, but that would imply that these were consecutive steps, which they weren't. That's one of the hidden mysteries of this multistep nightmare: These critical steps are not consecutive, they are simultaneous, and each is somewhat tedious and time-consuming.

We couldn't afford to focus on any one step to the exclusion of all the others. While we were figuring out due dates and who would write recommendations, we also were figuring out how many standardized tests would be needed. And what about all those various tests? Some schools accept the ACT; others prefer the SAT. If a school requires the SAT, that means the SAT I and at least two of the SAT II subject tests. Which of the sixteen SAT II subject tests does this or that college require? All the schools our kids applied to required one SAT II subject test in writing and one in mathematics. All the required testing—in our case, SAT I and SAT IIs—had to be completed and scores received by the various application deadlines. So our next step was to check the ETS testing schedule.

There was a prescribed limit on how many tests could be taken in one sitting, so in order to have all the testing completed, with enough time for multiple testing and repeat testing, we had to begin the serious testing early. Fortunately, the boys had had previous experience with the SAT; so, by their junior year, we were able to move past comfort and familiarity issues to focus on scoring.

I didn't know how costly the whole process could be! Granted, no individual test is that expensive. However, by the time you tack on late-registration fees (hey, sometimes those dates just get away from you!), question-and-answer-service fees, fees for extra score reports (lots of kids apply to more than four schools!), and fees for early score reports (sometimes you just can't wait to find out how your kid did!), the process can be quite costly indeed.

Then there was the seemingly endless array of questions: When's the test registration cut-off date? What's the late fee if you miss the registration deadline? Where are the tests taken? Not every SAT exam is offered for every test date, at every school. And without the registration card in hand, the student will be unable to take the test. I also didn't know that, for an extra fee, test scores are available over the phone, weeks before they arrive by mail.

The answers to all those questions were fairly easy to find, but it was the sheer volume of unanswered questions that initially felt overwhelming. So, as we plodded along looking for answers and checking application deadlines, recommendation requests, and test schedules, we also had to begin the next step: that delightfully provocative piece, the college-application essay.

Some of the suggested topics and questions for the essays ranged from the sublime to the ridiculous. Evan looked at some of the essay questions and said any college asking these questions is too stupid to attend—hardly the most scientific way to narrow the search! But the worst part was that they each required some degree of creativity, and we all know how hard it is to be creative on demand. Nevertheless, the boys plugged away at their essays, even though they kept telling us that they had nothing even remotely interesting or intelligent to say.

Meanwhile, we still had the whole transcript-and-résumé thing to handle. All of that needed to be organized. We created a transcript based on the curriculum we had developed. Because the core curriculum didn't change from year to year, and because we had maintained copies of the boys' work and a fairly detailed bibliography, it was relatively easy to create a transcript and post the boys' grades.

Grading had never been a significant component of our home-school experience, but the tutors we hired diligently assigned grades for the vast majority of the coursework they supervised. With the traditional humanities courses, grading was easy, because all work was judged on mastery rather than proficiency; in other words, until we felt the work was excellent—i.e., worthy of an A—we didn't move forward. Because the core curriculum was limited and the school year was a full twelve months, the idea of mastery was workable.

So we had the grade thing worked out, but we still needed to figure out the administrative requirements about transcripts. How many copies of the transcripts were needed? Did the copies have to be certified? Who certifies transcripts for home-schooled students? For Evan, I had to find out what

Westerville North charged for transcript copies, and how far in advance I needed to request certified copies.

And then there's that extracurricular-laden résumé. Our kids had no idea how many hours each week they each had spent on each activity since ninth grade! And I had no idea they would need to know that, just as I didn't know some colleges require applicants to prioritize all those activities!

Fortunately, I maintained obsessively detailed day planners every year, so we were able to go back and reconstruct their schedules. Also, COSI maintained extremely detailed records as well.

So, the boys took all the necessary tests, filled out the applications, completed the essays, and got their recommendations. It looked like it should be over. It *felt* like it should be over. But it was not over—not by a long shot. There were still financial-aid applications to complete and dozens of scholarship applications to submit. By the time every component of every application was completed, the right to privacy had ceased to exist for us. With all the information it was possible to glean from this paper labyrinth, we might as well have submitted to a cavity search.

Finally, it was done. Every application packet had been completed, postmarked, and received. We knew they had been received because one of the zillion forms required is a self-addressed, stamped postcard that the colleges return when your application is received. This procedure prevents neurotic students (and parents!) from calling admissions offices around the clock with the same question: "Is it there yet?"

I'M certain the process of waiting for the answer—the big evaluation—is different for every student and every family, so I won't pretend that our situation was anything but personal. I think the waiting was hardest on Charles the younger. He undoubtedly had the least confidence in the process and the most clarity about what was at stake. Plus, Charles tends to worry.

I think the waiting was hard for Damon primarily because he could see how upset Charles was. I think Damon could have been quite happy going to Ohio State, and while I think he knew Charles could, too, Damon knew Charles wanted to have a choice about where he went.

Evan may well have had the most ambivalence, as he was facing what might arguably be the most difficult change. Charles and Damon were Evan's closest friends and his classmates as well as his brothers. I know he was happy for them, but their departure would mean he'd be stuck here, alone, with us—not a pretty picture.

So we all waited, each with different views on this collective experience we hadn't quite finished, but had essentially reported on and submitted for a comparative evaluation. During the three months we waited for responses, we continued home schooling. And, finally the big packages came.

In the world of college admissions you know the kind of news you're getting by the size of the envelope that arrives. A thin, business-letter-sized envelope usually contains the we're-sorry-we-couldn't-accept-everybody response, and a big, fat envelope contains the congratulations response—and the next batch of forms to be completed.

When Charles and Damon got their big, fat envelopes from Dartmouth and Princeton, I jumped up and down and screamed in the living room until I was hoarse. C. Madison wasn't at home to restrain me, so I—as we say in the black community—performed. I made Charles and Damon grovel, and admit that we had been right and that they had been wrong to doubt us. All the while, I was gloating and hollering and calling everybody—I was beside myself! And then, thoroughly hoarse, I was able to sit down and reflect on the enormousness of what had just occurred.

That evening, the five of us sat down and really talked about what had been accomplished, and why it might be that God had allowed Charles and Damon to be accepted when so many other equally deserving kids had not been. While it was certainly tempting to pretend that we had known all along we'd be successful, and that we'd known they would get into some of the best colleges in the world, that would have been a lie—a comfortable and satisfying lie, to be sure, but a lie nevertheless. Such a statement would have been a lie because it's fraudulent, even though it contained bits of the truth.

Legally, fraud is defined as the intentional misrepresentation of a material fact. Bits and pieces of the truth can be found in a fraudulent statement, but the significant facts—the material facts—are intentionally misrepresented. Given that context: Yes, we'd had faith that our home-schooling experiment would yield positive results, including college admissions, so I guess you could say we'd "known" all along, on some level. But the truth is that we were really proceeding, literally day by day, on faith.

We had had no way of knowing the outcome. There are people running the best secondary schools in the country who cannot state with certainty that any given student from their school will be accepted at Princeton or Dartmouth or Amherst, and they certainly cannot state that 100 percent of their graduates will be so fortunate.

I think God wanted to remind us—this family, and maybe other people and other families as well—that, just as they say in church, "He's able!" So for me to say now, after the fact, that this was our plan, our idea, and that the boys' college acceptances were the culmination of our vision, without acknowledging that we were merely trying to follow instructions, would be fraudulent. We tried to impress upon the boys that no matter how intense the flow of congratulations and accolades became, for them and for us, it was critically important for us to give credit where credit was due.

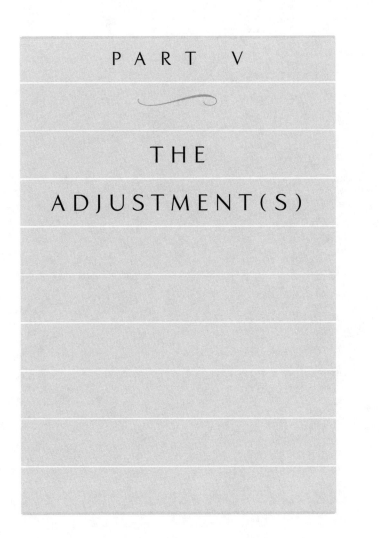

PART V

THE

ADJUSTMENT(S)

HOW THEY'VE ADJUSTED

(SO FAR)

I THINK COLLEGE IS an adjustment for everyone, including people just moving up the Eastern Seaboard from prep school dorm to college dorm. So we knew college would be an adjustment for our sons. We prepared to observe and evaluate that adjustment and its implications from the same holistic perspective we used to create our home-schooling environment. And while it's a process that will remain ongoing throughout their undergraduate years, and possibly beyond, the adjustment from home schooling to a larger, less-controlled environment is worth discussing.

The most frequent home-schooling question is about socialization. While I think that's the least informative issue, it's probably a good place to begin the whole college-adjustment discussion. Interestingly, the purely social dimension, in its narrowest definition, probably was the easiest and the quickest adjustment for each of our guys. By narrow definition, I mean casual, social encounters: chats in the dorm, over meals, and at parties. Meeting, greeting, dating—those things have always appeared fairly easy for each of our sons. So while Princeton University (which Charles and Damon attend) and Amherst College (where Evan is enrolled) are different-yet-similar institutions, Charles, Damon, and Evan, who are different-yet-similar people, have had fairly consistent socialization experiences in that regard.

I think Charles, Damon, and Evan appear different from other young men in a somewhat vague, almost amorphous way to lots of people who meet them.

Home schooling clearly created a different kind of socialization process, and I think that's pretty obvious to people, right off the bat. Interestingly, that difference seems to attract, rather than repel, people, at least initially. There is no way to validate this observation, but I also think the boys' inherent kindness—the moral and ethical dimensions of their individual personalities—makes them somewhat appealing in a way that is hard to pinpoint. Another possible factor is their obvious sense of self-worth and identity, which, while not always appealing, does seem to attract the attention of others. Then, of course, there's the whole issue of their appearance: They are quite handsome—and, no, my bias as their mother does not invalidate my observations about their appearance! My comments are much more tempered than many I have heard, like, "Oh, my God, they're gorgeous!" or "Paula, your sons are so incredibly good-looking!" No one has actually invoked the name Adonis to describe any of them, but I have seen women old enough to be their mother forget themselves!

So socially, they're fine. They have decent manners, can engage in reasonably intelligent conversation about a host of issues, including the different styles of hip-hop (no, it's not all the same), and they have wild hair with coordinated clothing. And, I must admit, I am very happy and relieved to see the ease with which they have adjusted to the social demands of college. No one has called home crying, or depressed about the difficulty of meeting new people or making new friends. When we have visited, the guys have not shown any of the telltale signs of being social pariahs—e.g., bowed head, rapid walking, aversion to eye contact—and we have observed tons of the required colloquial greetings and hand signals. I am happy to say that lots of people on campus acknowledge them, and no one seems uncomfortable being seen speaking with them in public. Finally, the ultimate proof of social adjustment: They are almost never in their rooms when I call (and their grades indicate they cannot possibly be in the library all that time!).

Now, that's just my assessment of the narrow social dimension. An additional component of the socialization question is the cultural-adjustment angle. Here, the results have been a little less enjoyable for C. Madison and me as outside observers. Part of our difficulty is in knowing that the boys' difficulty is directly attributable to their home-schooling experience.

The foundation of our holistic home-schooling experience was premised on race-and-gender identification. It was about the relationship between the boys, as African-American male students, and their tutors/teachers—Africans and African-Americans, the majority also male. Our thought was that the boys' growth and development would be enhanced in an environment that valued them, and where that environment mirrored their spiritual, intellectual, and physical foundations. And we were right: The environment we created really worked for our kids. So I hate to describe such a positive environment as a problem, but once they left that environment, I'm not so sure how well prepared they were for the antithesis of it.

Neither Princeton nor Amherst is traditionally a black university or college. Surprise! So, it's not as though we were expecting an abundance of black faculty. But the dearth of such faculty has been a disappointment for our sons. It's also a tremendous loss for those institutions, although I have seen no indication that they are aware of any serious intellectual deficiency as a result of it. So, culturally, our sons left an environment populated by older versions of themselves and entered into environments where there are very few Africans or African-Americans, and many of the few who are there seem consumed with the effort to achieve complete and total assimilation. You know: "Don't think of me as a *black* professor. Think of me as a *professor*."

The guys have emerged into a broader cultural universe, which is great, but there has been a definite loss of African-American cultural engagement, which is regrettable. The best thing I can say about this situation is that at least they have experienced such cultural engagement, and the fact that its loss is palpable proves its value. I think it's like that old saying, "It is better to have loved and lost than never to have loved at all." It is definitely better for a student to have been immersed in an environment that supports every dimension of that student's identity and then to lose that support than for the student never to have experienced it at all. Time will tell whether I'm rationalizing, and if the foundation was strong enough to support and guide the guys in the larger universe.

I AM observing the boys' spiritual adjustment with that same optimism, but for somewhat different reasons. Unlike the cultural component of their home-schooling environment, we purposely did not select tutors whose spiritual beliefs and experiences mirrored ours. So, in that respect, the spiritual adjustment to college has been far easier than the cultural one.

One really great advantage of the environments our kids have entered is that they unintentionally have forced the guys to deepen their individual spiritual existences. Supportive, holistic environments don't always force people to see the light; in fact, sometimes the comfort such an environment creates can dim one's awareness of the need for a meaningful spiritual life. Conversely, there's nothing like the WWE-type "SmackDown" of a covertly racist, nonresponsive institution to show one the need for prayer. Plus, it's great to be right, even about something this wrong: I definitely can see the validation of their African-American, spiritual tradition of Christianity as a theology of liberation.

During our home-schooling epoch, the boys often accused us of outdated racial views and perspectives. Because their own environment was so well designed, I sometimes felt they actually thought blatant racism was a thing of the past. It was something they had not witnessed or experienced on a daily basis, certainly not in a way that significantly affected their lives. I don't think they thought we were lying—they just thought we had been so damaged, we just couldn't get past it.

I know I routinely dismissed 50 percent of my parents' admonitions and warnings, especially about issues of race. When I was in prep school, my dad warned me direly, "You're there to get an education—period. Those people are not your friends. Don't let 'em lull you to sleep!" And I would look at him and think, "Daddy was really damaged by the 1940s." My mother would come to me quietly and remind me that my father was a very smart man, and that he knew something about the world. And I would look at her and think, "Gee, do you have to agree with everything he says? You guys don't know anything about prep school. You don't know these people. How can you say they're not my friends? This is the sixties!" I didn't really get it until the end of my tenure there, and then it was like my parents had been the ghosts of prep school future.

This race thing is like a hot stove. Sometimes you just have to touch it yourself to believe how hot it really is. And it can be quite confusing. After all, everybody white isn't like that, but in the face of civilized behavior it can be confusing for a teenager to distinguish between patronizing and polite behavior. In the face of my own past confusion and hardheadedness on the subject, I couldn't very well blame my sons for their reticence.

So great was their desire to believe that blatant racism, as a 24/7 kind of thing, was principally a relic of the past, even other respected adults had a hard time convincing them otherwise. Their maternal grandfather, their maternal uncle, and their godfather all echoed everything their father told them, but it was still hard for them to grasp. These were, without a doubt, the most influential men in their lives, men they loved and men they knew loved them. These were men from different generations and different geographic origins. These were men the boys played with and respected. Yet the eternal optimism of youth was right there at the ready.

Their tutors unequivocally reiterated the same truths, from a global perspective; yet, the boys had no real, daily, tangible, experiential perspective with which to validate them. So they went off to college and discovered the practical implications of racism for themselves.

And in the midst of that discovery came a renewed spiritual commitment. The boys discovered for themselves that if God is for you, no man can successfully stand against you. That is the spiritual truth uncovered by African-Americans throughout our collective experiences in this country. In that regard, Princeton University and Amherst College have provided our sons with an invaluable knowledge base.

INTELLECTUALLY, the college adjustment has been equally enormous, but much of that also is linked to the nature of the boys' home-schooling experience. As home-schoolers, they really experienced almost continuous intellectual stimulation. Our program was designed to follow the guidelines of upper-level, undergraduate seminars. We focused on enormous quantities of reading, writing, and discussion across the curriculum. Frequently, class discussions—including biology labs and mathematics—went well over schedule, and that was not a problem. In fact, we were delighted when that happened. We saw such overruns as indicators of intellectual stimulation and encouraged them with the boys and their tutors.

In retrospect, I realize that probably was not the best preparation for the academic discipline and time constraints of typical college environments. It also has been somewhat difficult for the boys to develop the same level of personal rapport with full-time faculty and TAs that they enjoyed with people who, essentially, were private tutors.

There is a great deal more individual responsibility on the part of the student to develop such relationships in college than existed in our little home-schooling experiment. And, quite frankly, I'm not certain our sons always have put forth the effort necessary to develop those relationships.

In the absence of such personal relationships, I think the opportunity for true intellectual stimulation is diminished. I can't say the boys have not experienced any intellectual stimulation in college, because they have. But it seems that much of it continues to transpire among themselves, even across campuses, rather than between them and the faculty members at their respective institutions. I am saddened by that, but I hope the situation will improve over time, both for the sake of my sons and for the colleges they attend.

PROBABLY the most significant observation I can make about the boys' adjustment to college is that it is in process. College is something they never had experienced previously, and their adjustment to it, in all its myriad forms, probably will continue.

I can't help but compare their adjustment to college to my own, and, in that context, they definitely aren't having the blast I had, and I'm sorry about that. But, by the same token, my sons entered college at a very different place intellectually and spiritually than those where their father and I were when we left for school.

I entered Wellesley having finished four years as the only black person in my class in prep school, a school with no black adults in any positions other than food service or janitorial. From that perspective, Wellesley felt like heaven. Many of the issues and concerns our sons raised as first-year students didn't even enter my consciousness at Wellesley on any serious level until my junior year.

When Evan told me recently that the biggest problem with college was that it was, and I quote, "an artificial construct," I was fascinated. It's not that I didn't know that small, elite, exclusive colleges and universities were artificial constructs; it's just that I didn't figure that out until I was almost finished with law school. I didn't know until I was well into my twenties that my presence had contributed something of spiritual and intellectual value to the institutions I had attended.

I guess my experience validates the theory that ignorance may be bliss. At the very least, when I compare the boys' experiences with mine, it certainly illustrates the fact that there are no free lunches—everything costs. For Charles, Damon, and Evan, it appears that the cost of their healthy, holistic, home-schooling experience sometimes has been a very difficult and painful adjustment to college. But while I am certainly sorry they're not having the wonderful time I had, I can't say I'm sorry for the advanced level of wisdom and insight that they brought to college with them.

ULTIMATELY, we miscalculated the force of their "reentry." The move from a holistic home-schooling environment to a traditional, academic institution requires a substantial adjustment. Charles, Damon, and Evan have each had their own adjustment issues. Some have been pretty generic—new places, new people, new levels of independence—and others have probably been the inevitable result of strong and fairly independent individuals moving into strong institutions steeped in traditions.

Essentially, their adjustment is part of a fluid reflection on the quality of their home-schooling experience. If their overall adjustment is positive and healthy, that would be another validation of our endeavors with them. If, on the other hand, their adjustment is negative and unhealthy, that would invalidate those endeavors. Which leads to the inevitable issue of definitions for positive, healthy adjustment and negative, unhealthy adjustment.

A positive, healthy adjustment to college is not one devoid of conflict. I am convinced that an absence of conflict signals an absence of growth, which is why I was never overly concerned about the level of conflict we experienced as a family as we journeyed through the home-schooling experience. It has been said that every seed bursts its container, and I think that's true. And while the bursting part can't be fun for the seed or the container, it's essential, and the alternative—stagnation and complacency—while commonplace, is tragic.

The proverb "Whatsoever a man soweth, that shall he also reap" takes on a whole new meaning when you have actually sown and reaped. Through gardening, C. Madison helped the boys to see that some seeds are annuals, so, even if it's a mistake, you only reap for that one season; but other seeds are perennials, and they return to be harvested season after season after season. Gardening also showed the boys that some things are easy to grow and produce very large harvests—so don't plant a lot of tomatoes or zucchinis unless you're sure you really love them, because, even when you're sick of them, they're still there and they still have to be picked. Finally, they learned that growth is a struggle—it takes time, and when those first tiny shoots begin to appear there has to be a breaking apart of the surface soil.

So what does this have to do with their adjustment to college and my assessment of it? Well, it has been a struggle, and there has been conflict, and some of it has been enormous. They each have made their own mistakes and, hopefully, most of those have been of the annual rather than perennial variety. At this moment, I would define their overall adjustment, though complicated, as positive and healthy.

I would define a negative, unhealthy adjustment as one that includes a loss of the sense of self, spiritual alienation, and intellectual regression. Of course, nobody walks around saying, "Hi! I'm suffering from a loss of the sense of self, spiritual alienation, and intellectual regression!" So how would one know the adjustment process has become negative and unhealthy? This is part of the challenge facing colleges and universities as they try to create and support healthy academic environments; yet, even with substantial institutional resources, they often fail to see the signs. (The alternative theory is that the signs of a loss of self, spiritual alienation, and intellectual regression are so common within such institutions, they no longer generate any attention or concern.)

With regard to my own sons, what I looked for as signs of negative and unhealthy adjustment included avoidance of past relationships, substance dependence, and shallow, unquestioning academic work. More simply stated, I watched to see their interest, or lack thereof, in maintaining connections with people from their past.

I think a loss of the sense of self can be manifested by a marked discomfort in the presence of people "who knew you when." This can be particularly troubling with African-American students who attend elite institutions. It can be difficult to maintain relationships with the "regular" black folks left at home, the ones who have not and will not have such educational opportunities. It takes an effort, a reciprocal effort, to maintain those relationships, and sometimes it seems easier simply not to make the effort. But the danger with such a position is the temporary and somewhat artificial nature of elite institutions. The effort to create a new identity in such an environment, without the tempering effects of past relationships as a balance, can lead to a loss of a sense of self, of one's true identity.

This was one of the first things we looked for in the guys. C. Madison and I are very aware of this loss of a sense of self, because we saw it happen with a number of people we knew in college. Fortunately, we have seen absolutely no evidence of this at all in our guys. They still love to hang out with their cousins David and Samuel, probably more than anyone else on the planet—they're always eager to have David and Samuel come to visit. And when Charles, Damon, and Evan are home, their first stop is at their Uncle David and Aunt Sonjia's house—to see Joseph, Benjamin, and Alexandria, their younger cousins—before they take off with David and Samuel.

What I especially admire about these five young men—Charles, Damon, Evan, David, and Samuel, all born within thirty months of one another—is their consistent, collective effort to maintain what has become a long-distance relationship. They each make the effort, including taking the time to stay connected with, involved in, and aware of one another's lives. As they grow and mature, they continue to allow their collective to be a touchstone and a lighthouse. None has lost his sense of self. Charles, Damon, and Evan continue to return home, willingly, on breaks, and I know it's not because they want or need to see me. Coming home seems to be part of the way they maintain a sense of connection with who they were as they continue the process of becoming.

Another area of concern in identifying a negative, unhealthy adjustment is the issue of spiritual alienation. By spiritual alienation, I do not mean a withdrawal from attendance at regular religious services. (Don't get me wrong: I wish the boys would each go to church, religiously, every Sunday. But I know they don't and I'm probably more okay with that than they would assume, because I know regular attendance doesn't mean spiritual alienation hasn't occurred.) What I am most concerned about in terms of the boys' adjustment is not how regularly they attend services but how regularly they make time in their lives for prayer and meditation.

It is vitally important that they work to maintain and deepen the personal relationship they each had with Jesus Christ before they left home, because that is the source of their strength. Spiritual alienation becomes a particular concern in academic institutions because spiritual consciousness is so often viewed as primitive and anti-intellectual. In monitoring this risk factor, I looked for signs of the boys' ongoing spiritual maturation, and there have been many. I have been pleased by the boys' ease in addressing spiritual concerns and their willingness to ask for prayer. I am satisfied that their spiritual relationship, while far from perfected, is definitely in process.

The evidence of this spiritual stability rests in their responses to the constant pressures in the material universe of college life. Regrettably, C. Madison and I have had a great deal of experience in observing substance abuse, and we have a very good idea of the telltale signs. Fortunately, we haven't seen them in any of the guys.

Another indicator of spiritual alienation is severe, relentless depression. While it is perfectly normal to have bad or off days, the pharmaceutical industry certainly wants us to believe that clinical depression is somewhat normal, common, and treatable. But the fact is, "Thou wilt keep *him* in perfect peace, *whose* mind *is* stayed *on thee*: because he trusteth in thee" (Isaiah 26:3). I know this statement of belief will annoy the you-know-what out of people, but there it is: I believe that depression is the direct result of incorrect thinking. Perhaps a more tenable way to state this would be to paraphrase the Buddhist position that all illness is the result of incorrect and inappropriate thinking, and the desire for things that have no intrinsic meaning or worth. So allowing knowledge of the academic to supercede knowledge of the divine; allowing the desire for grades, social status, and dates to supercede the desire for peace, tranquility, and joy—such misalignments and incorrect thinking will lead to spiritual alienation, which will result, inevitably, in depression. And the signs of depression are strewn all over college campuses across this country, in the form of repetitive binge drinking; regular, abusive use of all manner of illegal drugs; and a seemingly total dependence on a whole range of pharmaceutical products.

Here's a news flash: Humans should not have trouble sleeping; they should not have chronic headaches; they should not have chronic heartburn, acid indigestion, or flatulence. Humans should be able to eat, digest, and eliminate food without pharmaceutical assistance. And humans should be able to meet and interact with others of their species without the need for alcohol or cigarettes.

Fortunately, I do not see signs of depression in Charles, Damon, or Evan. This is not to say that I think they have never smoked or drank or relied on caffeine to regain consciousness. What I mean is that when they are off their feed, so to speak, they know how to right themselves, because they are spiritually connected.

I would include intellectual regression as a signal of a negative, unhealthy adjustment. If either Charles, Damon, or Evan had ceased to think for himself in college, I would consider that to be a sign of intellectual regression. If they began to rely solely on the thoughts and writings of others—if they began the annoying habit of constantly quoting their professors without any critical analysis—that would be a sign of intellectual regression. Fortunately, we have seen none of that evidenced.

Consequently while their adjustment has been chock-full of conflict, I think it has been positive and healthy. That collective part is fairly easy to comment upon. What's more difficult is the assessment of their adjustment individually.

THE challenge with an individual assessment is the issue of privacy. Talking about our collective past is one thing—after all, C. Madison and I were primary players in that drama, so I feel comfortable writing about it. The boys' individual adjustment, however, does not really involve me other than as an observer (and an infrequent—but very loving, and only when asked—adviser or assistant).

With that as a disclaimer, here's the bottom line on the boys' adjustment to date. As of this writing, Damon has left Princeton, permanently, and will not be receiving his degree there—he is currently working for us, doing marketing, sales, and some research; hopefully, he will graduate from somewhere at sometime before his thirtieth birthday! Charles will be graduating from Princeton a year late, in 2003. Evan has done well academically, and will graduate from Amherst on time, in 2004.

In an academic nutshell: Evan has performed very well, Charles's performance has been adequate, and Damon failed to perform. Because it's easier, I'll start by delineating the individual shortcomings of Charles, Damon, and Evan as students, rather than the institutional shortcomings we observed at Princeton and Amherst.

The enormous range in performance levels among the three of them has not been totally surprising to us, given the differences in their individual temperaments, coupled with the differences in the institutions they selected. Charles is probably our most idealistic and, arguably, most intrinsically naïve son. He adamantly wanted to go to Princeton despite our rather dire predictions and unflattering commentary about the institution, and its history and reputation of racial bias. Charles absolutely did not believe racism would be a problem for him, and was stunned and sorely disappointed to find that institutional racism was an issue at Princeton and, inevitably, was an issue for him. Institutionally, Princeton, with its university setting, is not designed to provide the kind of individual attention we felt would have been invaluable to someone making the transition from the nuclear environment of home schooling to college. Objectively, we felt this was a variable for consideration regardless of the race of the student in question. We felt the impact of the variable would be intensified for an African-American male student, particularly at Princeton, where a tradition of institutional commitment to the success of individual black students appeared to be lacking.

Damon, our most sensitive and undisciplined son, was almost immediately overwhelmed by the Princeton profile. He sorely missed, and desperately needed, more personal involvement and interaction, especially with African-American males as professors and advisers. We definitely felt a college, rather than university, environment would have been a better choice for him, but he wanted to go to college with Charles. With complete abandon, Damon threw himself into the social arena of Princeton—an unwise but somewhat understandable effort to make up for what he felt he had missed by being home-schooled. There were predictable and disastrous academic results to that decision.

Evan had the advantage of observing his brothers' first two disappointing years in college before he set off on his own adventures at Amherst. He also had the advantage of being our most independent and self-confident son. Evan, with the strong urging of Charles, wisely selected a college, rather than a university, to attend. While he has encountered his fair share of racism at Amherst, he seems to be more annoyed than surprised or hurt by it.

C. MADISON and I are certainly saddened and disappointed by the quality of each of our sons' college experiences. Given the enormousness of their individual and collective challenges and adjustment struggles, we have sorely questioned our decision to home-school them. We see instances in which Charles, Damon, and Evan have exercised poor judgment, and in some cases have made repetitive errors. We have observed a seemingly fierce resistance to specific issues of timeliness and general issues of structure, and we have struggled to understand their complaints about both: "They care more about the day you turn in the work than about the quality of the work"; "The problem is that college is an artificial construct." While we certainly know there is truth in both those statements, they seemed somewhat obvious, superfluous, and therefore confusing to us.

Of course timing is critical in college—it's an institution! And while I guess we always knew it was somewhat artificial in its design or "construct," I don't think we ever considered that as a problem. Home schooling may well have induced an unrealistic expectation of tolerance for individuality, and flexibility, that simply could not be realized in a broader, institutional environment.

Fortunately, however, home schooling also provided an intellectual foundation for critical self-assessment. The boys—especially Damon—have shown an unwavering ability and willingness to acknowledge their individual failures and shortcomings. This has been heartening to us. College has provided a series of classic, teachable moments, and the boys have just begun to synthesize all the life lessons to be gleaned from them.

However, these difficulties and failures have not been unilateral. Individually Charles, Evan, and especially Damon have been guilty of missed opportunities; most important, they know it. I wish they had learned some of those lessons earlier in the process, but college is part of the ongoing process of learning. So, in that regard, I have to quote my tax professor again: "Never complain when wisdom comes late, because sometimes it never comes at all." Which brings me to the other part of this bilateral failure, namely, the institutional part.

Charles, Damon, and Evan came to their respective institutions eager, excited, and very well prepared, albeit in a nontraditional way. While this was, for each of them, their first individual experience with college, it certainly was not the institutions' first experience with undergraduate students. When an undergraduate student fails to manage his time, stay on task, and follow the stated rules of the institution, the student is exhibiting irresponsible and immature behavior. Such conduct cannot be condoned, or mediocrity and complacency then takes hold. Institutions are adamant in their refusal to tolerate such departures from their stated standards of excellence.

Yet when, in the first month of his first year, Damon was stopped by four campus police officers at ten A.M. and required to show proof of ownership of his bicycle, Princeton wanted us to understand. They acknowledged the poor judgment exercised by the institution, but they wanted Damon to be flexible and understand that everyone makes mistakes, including, sometimes, racial-profiling-type mistakes. Such so-called isolated incidents have marked each and every semester Charles and Damon spent at Princeton.

Damon continued to behave, individually, in ways that were academically ill-advised and irresponsible, and he was asked to withdraw. The severity of the consequence for him, as an individual, illuminated the teachable moment. Conversely, Princeton continued to behave institutionally in ways that were academically ill-advised and racist, but there was no consequence. So while the individual and the institution participated in a bilateral failure, the institution missed the growth opportunity that an acknowledgment of failure can provide.

The development of a community committed to the life of the mind requires a willingness to stretch and to fail. At least one definition of the intellect includes the ability to perceive and understand relationships. Whether a relationship thrives or fails is a reflection of the commitment of both parties; and throughout the life of the relationship, demands are brought to bear on both sides. Sometimes those demands exceed the normalcy range of one party or the other.

For example, Evan just finished his second year at Amherst College as a Fine Arts major. He was invited to cohost an art show at the University of Massachusetts Amherst with a senior there, and he was understandably excited. While I was delighted for him, I tried to warn him that the faculty at Amherst might not be pleased at the prospects of him hosting his first show off campus. Evan thought I was projecting anti-intellectual pettiness, and he went on with his plans. The show was marvelous. My parents, my sisters, Charles, Damon, C. Madison, and I all attended, as did a great many of Evan's friends. Despite the invitations he sent to his professors, his deans, his adviser, and even the college president (Evan is *very* proud of his work!), no one from the faculty or the administration at Amherst College attended the opening. I think Evan learned a valuable lesson from his failure to comply with the traditions of the institution. I am not sure what, if anything, the institution learned by disappointing an individual student.

In any event, I think Charles, Damon, and Evan were initially overwhelmed with the challenge of synthesis when they entered college. Not to get bogged down in the Hegelian dialectic, but home schooling, as we created it, was the thesis of holistic health. The premise of the thesis was that the simultaneous focus of attention on spiritual, intellectual, and physical health will lead one to excellence. College represents an antithetical premise, namely, that a narrow focus on academic achievement will lead to excellence. Neither the thesis nor the antithesis is wrong; the challenge is in the synthesis of those competing ideas.

It may not have been possible to do it better, but we obviously did not do an adequate job of preparing our sons to perform their own synthesis within the institution. The other thing we learned is that, no matter how much an institution may profess a commitment to diversity, and no matter what the numbers state, diversity of thought and being can be very difficult to absorb for institutions and the people who populate them.

We did not do an adequate job of preparing our sons to cohabit constructively with diverse ideologies. As one of the administrators at Princeton said to me, Charles and Damon did not appear fully to appreciate the opportunity that had been presented to them, and that absence of obvious appreciation was annoying. Oddly enough, I knew immediately what she meant. Charles and Damon were appreciative, but I knew it was not in the way she meant.

We did not do an adequate job of preparing the boys to understand reciprocity of need. Elite institutions need validation and evidence of appreciation. The absence of that is interpreted as arrogance. Help your home-schooled student understand that institutions, like individuals, have needs that must be met. Once your student understands that and can identify what those needs are, he will be in a much better position to make a solid decision about whether the institutional needs will mesh with his own. We failed to perform that critical function in advance.

If you choose to home-school, what can you learn from our painful lessons? Here are a few things we learned.

First of all, we grossly underestimated the force of institutional reentry. We failed to account for the obvious fact that we are shaped by our past experiences; therefore, if a student is home-schooled, the past experience will be significantly different from that of almost everyone else in the institutional environment. This may cause grave difficulties.

At the same time, I have to say that those difficulties may not prove significant to everyone. There was another home-schooled student who entered Princeton with Charles and Damon, and I believe she graduated with a class standing of number one! Obviously, reentry is a different experience for everyone, so definitive suggestions won't be that helpful.

There are a great many promising students, many from great preparatory schools, who head off to some of the best colleges in the country, and some of those students never graduate. My guess is that there are a multitude of reasons for those failures, but I'm certain all those failures are bilateral. So my advice is really to help your children to examine what kind of institution they need to attend.

Some students need a good deal more attention and interaction than others. If that's the case, a college is an infinitely better choice than a university.

Some institutions need students to take complete personal responsibility for their undergraduate experience and to initiate a request for faculty involvement and assistance, should the need arise. Try to help your child find out if that's the culture at any of the schools she might be looking at, and then determine if that culture will mesh well with her personality.

PROBABLY the most important thing is to make sure your child knows that college is merely the next step—it's not the last step. With or without a degree, you want your child to survive college, whole and intact.

Don't assume your children know they matter to you. Tell them. Stay in touch with them and help them put their disappointments, mistakes, and failures into some perspective.

Finally, as well-meaning as faculty and administrators are, they are people doing a job. They are not required to love the students, care about them, or even really get to know them. It is a mistake to transfer familial commitments and concern to faculty and administrators. Do not be duped by the our-students-are-young-adults argument. Remember: You're still the one getting the bill!

22

HOW WE ARE ADJUSTING

DURING OUR LAST year of home schooling, everyone kept asking us how we would adjust. And I have to admit, the issue of our adjustment always was there, smoldering at the back of my mind. I mean, everybody talks about empty-nest syndrome—that sense of emptiness when the last child leaves home. I had to assume the sense of change would have to be even more enormous to us after twenty years of parenting coupled with nine years of home schooling.

Actually, I just wasn't sure what to expect. Would C. Madison and I have enough to do and think and talk about in the absence of our sons? I could only guess, because I couldn't possibly predict our future and I honestly couldn't remember our past.

Truthfully, I couldn't remember much of what our life together had been before we had children. I mean, I was sure it had been fun, but I couldn't really remember a lot. I was twenty-one and C. Madison was twenty-three when we married in August 1976. We immediately moved to Buffalo, New York—hardly the fun capital of the universe—where C. Madison was working for IBM; and after one long, horrible, snowbound winter, we returned to Columbus and I started law school—another fun escapade. We had Charles and Damon in 1980, after six months of bed rest for me—also fun; and, after one more year of law school (yes, it took me four years instead of three), I graduated in 1981—that *really* was fun. After a bout with pneumonia—yet more fun!—I had Evan in 1982. When Evan was about fifteen months old,

C. Madison took a job with AT&T's divestiture/transition team and began commuting between Columbus, Ohio, Piscataway, New Jersey, and Jacksonville, Florida—which lasted for the next nine months. I can't begin to say how much fun that was! We had three little boys, all under the age of four, and C. Madison was only home for forty-eight hours each week! Finally, we all moved to Florida. I took a job with the same company as C. Madison, and we both began that blue-suit, silk-tie, corporate grind. In 1986, after two years of major good times and insights (I'm not a team player), I left and started PN&A, my own business, and we've been self-employed ever since. In the midst of the growth and development of our entrepreneurial dream, we began home schooling.

All that's just to say that C. Madison and I have been pretty much working our behinds off, nonstop, since we were in our early twenties. I'm not complaining, because everything we did—marriage, law school, kids, corporate jobs, commuting, self-employment, and home schooling—was stuff we wanted to do, so that's cool. What's even cooler is the fact that most of that hard work, especially the day-to-day parenting part, is now over and we're still relatively young. I'm pleased with where our lives are at this point and I know it's all part of a process, but when I look back on the process, most of what I see and remember is work.

So when I tried to imagine what my life with C. Madison, sans kids, would look like, I couldn't really rely on my memory, because I can barely remember when we didn't have kids. The last time I didn't have any kids around, I was just past being a kid myself. Oh sure, I used to tell the kids, all the time, that they were not the center of our universe, that their dad and I had had a delightful youth and marriage and life even before they existed, and that we weren't defined by them. I told them, all the time, that my name was not "Charles-Damon-and-Evan's Mother." Both those statements were made to illustrate a point, like my bumper sticker that said, "Because I'm the Mommy . . . That's Why!"

I never wanted Charles, Damon, or Evan to think that they were the center of the universe, our universe, or my universe, either, for that matter. I think everyone needs to know that there really is an ecosystem at play, and, consequently, everyone needs to know where they fit in the big food chain of life. It was also important for me to remind myself where my kids fit in my own life.

C. Madison and I worked very hard to keep our lives and our relationships in balance. He gave me a small banner once that read, "The greatest gift a father can give his children is to love their mother." We kept it hanging in the family room for years, because it was such an important message. Similarly, it was important to me that he and the boys know that he came first. So when the boys complained about things like "Why do we have to eat in the dining room? Daddy's the only one who likes to eat in the dining room!" or "Why are we having that for dinner? Daddy's the only one who likes that!" I would gently remind them that Daddy was the man, the only man in this house, so Mommy does what Daddy and only Daddy wants. I would tell them that, maybe, when they grew up and became men, if they were blessed to have their own wives and their own homes, then, maybe, their wives would make an effort to accommodate them the way Mommy and Daddy accommodate each other. In other words, don't think more of yourself than you ought, and don't assume a greater degree of significance than you actually possess.

Nevertheless, the boys really were a very big part of our existence, and I did have some curiosity about what their daily absence would feel like to us. So, for the entire last year of home schooling—as we helped Evan through the morass of the college application and selection process—I kept wondering and remembering, and imagining the future in our empty nest. And now that future finally is here.

I ALMOST feel guilty admitting it, but for C. Madison and me the adjustment has been wonderful! It's been exciting! It's been glorious! For one thing, we are adjusting to a previously experienced, if not-quite-remembered state of being. We were married and living together, quite happily I might add, long before we had any kids. So I'm finding that being alone together is not a new thing; it's just a thing we haven't experienced in a while. And, yes, twenty years is a long time, and everything and everybody changes, but, still, it feels like a return to something wonderful. I know there's some truth in that old song, "Everything Must Change," but sometimes the dynamics of change can move people forward and closer together, rather than further apart.

Since we've been alone together, I haven't felt a moment's sadness, not even when we left Evan at Amherst. It's kind of embarrassing to admit, but on the very last day of the family orientation activities, a woman at the financial aid office asked me if I was Evan's mother. I happily hugged Evan across the shoulders and said, "Yes!" She told me I was the happiest mother she had seen all week!

The fact is, I was happy—very happy. I didn't have any sense of sadness or even any nostalgia. One of the unexpected benefits of our home-schooling experiment was that we felt we had had more than enough time with each one of our sons. Our time together as a family had not rushed by in a blur. I didn't have the overwhelming sense of inquiry about where all the time went.

I had no feeling of urgency about things I might have forgotten to say. There really was nothing I could think of to say that had not been said, whispered, yelled, written, or demonstrated, repeatedly, in every way imaginable. We weren't one of those little family clusters holding on, heads down, rapidly repeating mantras of love and concern and confidence. We were done talking. Plus, Evan was happy and confident, which, of course, made the entire process easier. He was so ready, so in the "now-ness" of the moment, so psyched to be in college, and so very ready to be done with us, how could I be sad in the face of such eager anticipation?

His reaction wasn't a complete surprise. We had been down this road before, with Charles and Damon. They, too, were elated to have reached that time in their lives; and they, too, seemed enormously conscious of the momentous nature of our collective transition as a family. The biggest difference was my reaction. When we left Charles and Damon, I actually cried. I'm not naturally a crier—my kids have probably seen me cry fewer than five times in their lives—but I cried when I said good-bye to Charles and Damon at Princeton. It wasn't a monumental crying jag, complete with sound effects— nothing you could nominate for an Emmy or an Oscar—but there were multiple tears shed at one time. The entire outburst lasted about two minutes—just long enough to convey my deep love, yet not so long as to make a spectacle of the boys or myself.

I think those tears were an almost-reflexive reaction to having achieved an enormous goal, while still knowing I had miles to go before I was finished. I was tired, but I knew we had two more years of the home-schooling process to complete with Evan. So maybe I was crying because I wasn't finished!

When we left Evan, although I felt reflective, I didn't feel any tears. Of course, in the midst of that reflection, I might have been reminded of our first school transition, the one to kindergarten.

When Charles and Damon began kindergarten, I cried when we left them, and I spent the rest of the day crying or at least tearing up at regular intervals. It was ridiculous, but I couldn't seem to stop. Two years later, when I took Evan to his first day of kindergarten, he stopped me on the steps of the school and said, "Let's say good-bye here, so you don't act up." I was furious, but, appropriately chastised, I did not shed a tear, at least not in his presence.

So, subconsciously, I may have been reacting to Evan's somewhat inflexible persona by not crying when we left him at Amherst, but I don't think so. It was a momentous occasion in its own right, but it occurred in the midst of another momentous occasion—C. Madison and I were celebrating our twenty-fourth wedding anniversary.

In the midst of family orientation at Amherst, C. Madison and I enjoyed a quiet anniversary dinner—all dolled up in moving clothes. It was obvious that we were at a crossroads. On a surface level, we were experiencing an ending and a beginning, but, really, it felt more like a transcending experience than anything else. It was as if we were all at different stages of being, and becoming more of what we had always been. The only real change was one of location. Evan wasn't about to become a new person at Amherst any more than Charles and Damon became new people at Princeton. C. Madison and I certainly weren't going to become new people in their absence.

Knowing that made the beginning of our adjustment easy and exciting for me. During that informal anniversary dinner, we promised ourselves that the next year, for our twenty-fifth anniversary, we would have a "knock-down, drag-out party" to celebrate us, and if that meant the kids had to go back to school late, so what? We decided to dedicate 2001 to us, our twenty-five years of marriage, and our fifteen years as business partners. It didn't mean we were going to disown our kids or move away and not leave a forwarding address; it just meant we were going to begin putting ourselves first.

We left Evan, drove to Princeton to drop off Charles and Damon, and then began the trek home . . . alone.

So now we've passed a major milestone, and things definitely will be different around here. In fact, they already are. The first night back after depositing our sons at their respective institutions of higher learning, I slept better and more soundly than I've slept since I gave birth to the lot of them! I was stunned, and, at first, I thought maybe it was the onset of mild depression. Since everyone had told me how hard an adjustment it was, of course I was expecting the worst! It was just like when I was pregnant. So many people told us how awful labor and delivery had been for them. Women asked me if I was carrying twins (I looked like I was carrying a hippopotamus!) and when I said yes, so often they shook their heads and told me how sorry they were. One woman told me she was sure she would have died from the pain if there had been a second one. Acquiescently, I murmured "thanks" while wishing I had the capacity to jump up and run away. But at my size, that was quite impossible! So I merely sat, hummed to myself, and tried to not absorb any of it, but it was futile. I entered the labor and delivery room prepared to die and be resurrected. I was so happy to discover that, yes, it most certainly was painful, shockingly so, yet at no time did I think I was going to die.

You'd think I would have learned something about assuming that other people's experiences would be an accurate predictor of my own, but I didn't—not completely anyway. So I came home from dropping off our boys, expecting to be depressed. And when I continued to sleep soundly over the next three nights, I wondered if all the sleeping was symptomatic.

During my morning prayers, I had the proverbial epiphany. This was the first time in years I was sleeping without worrying about the boys, listening for them, or anticipating their needs. I was sleeping soundly because they were gone, not because I was depressed that they were gone.

For the next four or five weeks, I kept waiting for the depression, or at least the sadness. I would wander down the hallway to their rooms and peek inside. I waited for the feelings of loss to overwhelm me, but it never happened. All I felt was disgust; they had left their rooms a mess! Finally, I overcame that bad vibe by simply shutting their doors. I don't know why I didn't do that in the first place! It was perfect! When the boys were home, they kept their doors shut all the time anyway. So, except for the delightful sounds of silence emanating from behind those closed doors, it didn't look or feel that different.

Now it's just the two of us. That's the thing I think about in the mornings when I wake up: It's back to just the two of us, and it feels great! Oh, sure, I miss my sons. But I talk to them regularly, and we see them frequently, what with parent weekends, fall breaks, Thanksgiving, Christmas, semester breaks, spring breaks, and summer recess. So it's not like they have left the country.

The truly delightful aspect of this is that the boys are as comfortable with the change as we are. We're still very close, and we're pretty much always happy to see one another. We keep each other informed about our lives.

We are close in spite of the miles that separate us. Maybe if we felt distant, this adjustment would be hard. But it feels right, for them and for us.

The adjustment is as individual a process for the parent as it is for the student. I think everybody involved experiences the adjustment differently.

Probably one of the best ways to prepare for the empty nest is to live each day in recognition of the fact that an empty nest is what you're aiming for. As parents, we all want our kids to be able to live holistically healthy and independent lives.

23

WHAT WE LEARNED

OBVIOUSLY, EVERY FAMILY is different, and what works for one will not necessarily work for another. But, having said that, I still think there are a lot of things we learned that could be used by other families, whether they home-school or not. I know home schooling is a viable educational option, but I also know it's not the only option. Therefore, whether a family chooses to home-school or use traditional public, parochial, or private educational options, I think some truths cross all those boundaries.

1. *There are lots of choices.* Not only that, there's probably more than one viable choice during the educational lifetime of a child. Looking back on it, I can't believe how many times I really stressed over an educational decision, primarily because I assumed I couldn't change it later. I was so wrong. I have learned that if an educational idea or program isn't working, I need to do something about that. Moreover, as disruptive as a change can be, that disruption probably is far less damaging than continuing down a nonproductive road for the sake of continuity. I'm sure my parents were apprehensive about sending me to prep school, but they looked at the choices and felt that that was the best one at that time. And maybe that's the point: Parents need to look beyond the traditional choices — the neighborhood public school, the highly touted magnet school, the church-sanctioned parochial school, and the expensive, exclusive private school — to figure out what's best for the specific child at that specific moment in the child's education.

2. They're our kids. Okay, so maybe having a child no more makes me an expert than having a violin makes me a musician. But I care deeply about my children (I think most parents do!) and have some genuine insights into what they need. The biggest mistakes I made were the ones in which I completely dismissed my instinctual response to what was going on with my kids. I'm not advocating instinctual knowledge over professional training and expertise, but there needs to be a balance. Being a trained professional does not equate to having perfect knowledge and understanding of what is best for each child. Parents have the right and, in fact, the responsibility to question everything having to do with their children. I think that means that if your kid goes to school, any school, no one should have to beg you to be involved actively in the PTA. Parents shouldn't assume that any teacher, administrator, or institution cares more about the welfare of their kids than they do. Similarly, parents shouldn't allow themselves to feel their very presence, participation, and assistance at school somehow is a nuisance. I think more parents need to feel greater confidence in their position as parents and their genuine commitment to the welfare and well-being of their own children. Because, in the final analysis, whose kid is it, anyway?

3. Take responsibility. Charles, Damon, and Evan are our sons, and we knew we were responsible for them. It's not that I was unwilling to share that responsibility with other members of the community, but that the principal responsibility rested with us as their parents. I was always very uncomfortable thinking, feeling, and behaving as though what was happening to my kids somehow was out of my control and, therefore, beyond the limits of my responsibility. While we certainly didn't plan on it initially, C. Madison and I were willing to take on the full responsibility for our sons' education. And that's not to say that we weren't responsible parents before we began home schooling, because we were. However, when we saw that the traditional education route no longer was viable for our sons, we were willing to take on the full weight of that responsibility. We were willing to accept the responsibility for their academic, intellectual, and spiritual development. I do not think home schooling is the single hallmark of parental responsibility. In fact, there are instances I have observed in which home schooling appears to be quite selfish and irresponsible. But I do think that more parents need to take a greater degree of responsibility for their children in every dimension. As taxpayers, we all have a right to expect solid school services in exchange for our financial support. However, no amount of tax support can replace parental responsibility. Parents may not be responsible for the actual process of teaching, but they are responsible for ensuring that learning occurs in their child's life. I don't think any parent should be comfortable with fully abdicating that responsibility to any educational institution. As home-schoolers, of course, we knew what subjects our kids were taking, we designed the curriculum, and we taught most of the courses. Again, parents of kids in regular schools still have a responsibility to know what's going on, what subjects their kids are taking, and how well they're doing. And if they're not doing well, parents have a responsibility to find out why and to help find a solution that will work, even if it takes two or three grading periods or the entire academic year.

4. *Face the hard stuff.* "Life is hard and then you die." I used to tell my kids this when I felt they were whining about stuff that I felt wasn't worthy of any legitimate complaint. The fact of the matter is, some things in life are hard. Life is hard by design. I've learned that facing the hard stuff actually is easier than fighting it or pretending that it doesn't exist. It was really hard to accept the fact that our sons' tenure in prep school was over. It was hard to accept that we had made some rather severe miscalculations regarding the nature of our relationships there. It was hard figuring out how we were going to home-school the boys. And it was very hard knowing they didn't like it and that they didn't think we knew what we were doing. Yet, in the face of each of those hard things, I found that dealing with each difficulty really did make us stronger, individually and collectively. I think that we, as parents, need to embrace the hard stuff and admit to our kids how hard that stuff really is. I think parents need to understand how important it is for kids to see that life is difficult for everybody, including adults. I think parents need to be less afraid for our kids to see us struggle.

5. *Stop lying—nobody's that busy!* When we first decided to home-school, I really couldn't imagine how we'd find the time. After all, we were busy entrepreneurs, trying to make it, trying to grow the business, blah, blah, blah. It's such a growing status thing to talk about how busy we all are, because being busy seems to equate with being important. But like every other carbon-based life-form on the planet, we get twenty-four hours each day—no more, no less. What we choose to do with that time is just that—a matter of choice. We had to choose how we would distribute our existing twenty-four hours to free up more time for our kids. Almost everybody has this as an option. We all have a certain number of disposable hours. Some people use those hours for television, some for volunteer work. Some people use that time for high-profile board positions while others use it at the hair salon. Community activism consumes a lot of time for some people, while others use up all their extra time at church. Obviously, some uses are more commendable than others. However, if *any* use

means that the parent has less than forty-five minutes with the kid per day, that disposable time is not well spent. Whether kids are home-schooled or attend traditional schools, they need and deserve at least forty-five minutes a day with their parents. Anybody who is too busy to spend at least forty-five minutes a day with a kid is too busy to have one.

6. *Family time is not optional.* It really makes a difference when families spend time together, eat together, and end the day together. Sure, our kids had lots of friends and various activities, but we made it a point to eat at least one meal together daily. Have you ever seen kids who never seem to be at home, or even to want to be there? Something about that seems off to me. It's like that line in the movie *Beloved* when Beloved asks, "Ain't you got no people?" C. Madison and I made it clear by our actions that we and the family we had created came first—before our careers, before our friends, before our community-service obligations. Home was a place we wanted to be, and the people in that home were people we wanted to be with—family time was not optional for us. Relationships are consistent in terms of what is required for success, and familial relationships are no exception. I am amazed when I listen to people explain why they do not have time for meals with their family, but they can find time for a breakfast meeting, a lunch meeting, a dinner meeting, and even a board meeting, all in the same day! It's not a question of time, it's a question of commitment. No one wants to admit that lots of other things take priority over family commitments, but the evidence of that fact is everywhere. I think more parents, whether they home-school or not, seriously need to reexamine their priorities and stop using that pathetic line, "It's not the quantity of time, it's the quality." That is not true! It is absolutely the quantity of time, just like it's the quantity of time for any other successful relationship. No one actually expects to be successful in any professional relationship by putting in an occasional appearance. I think more parents need to bring the same kind of strategic-planning skills to their family lives that they bring to their professional lives.

7. *Siblings can be friends.* Our sons are very good friends. Two of them attended the same college, and the three of them spend a great deal of time together in spite of distance. People often comment on their closeness as a potential problem. As Charles, Damon, and Evan were home-school classmates as well as brothers, their friendship is a particularly strong one. I think sibling relationships are important and should be encouraged. I always think it's weird when parents tell me their kids are closer to their friends than to each other. Sure, there's a lot of stuff to be worked through and worked out in sibling relationships. These are the

people who truly knew you when, and every effort should be made to build, strengthen, and sustain those relationships throughout childhood and adolescence. After all, those familial problems that don't get worked out by the end of high school often end up resurfacing later in therapy. Strengthening sibling relationships does not require home schooling, nor does it require a limitation on other relationships. But I think parents need to do a better job of pointing out the lifelong nature of sibling relationships. Long after that best friend from tenth grade is married and living in another state, your sibs are the people you'll be sharing turkey with on Thanksgiving. I think more parents need to do a better job of integrating the various threads of the family's life. Right off the bat, everybody's bedroom doesn't need to be an oasis; in fact, everybody doesn't need his or her own room. Privacy is good, but so is sharing. I think there should be one communal television and a definite limit on independent, nonacademic computer time. Furthermore, every kid cannot be in every activity; otherwise, everybody just gets dropped off, and nobody gets supported. Finally, a lot of parents need to examine their own sibling relationships to see what kind of example they're setting.

8. *Summer is too long to be idle.* Summer can and should be a time for more than just getting a minimum-wage job to cover the cost of summer entertainment and back-to-school clothing. Granted, some families really need the financial contribution from summer employment, but not every family is facing such dire straits. To give the extra flexibility we needed, our home-school program went all year. We did not have summers off. I know lots of people think that's extreme, but I don't. I realize everybody doesn't home-school, and traditional schooling does provide a three-month break. I still think more parents should work with their kids to find some exciting and enriching things to do for at least part of the summer. I think more parents should encourage their kids to consider summer as a great opportunity to try something new, something different. Summer comes the same time every year. More parents need to begin discussions in January about what might be fun to do in June. Advance planning also helps identify alternative funding sources in enough time actually to apply for it. Really, there are tons of terrific summer possibilities, complete with tons of scholarship dollars to help offset the cost. Early planning gives a winter window for the kid to work and earn the balance. Also, the extra impact of those creative enrichment activities on college applications often is overlooked. Part of the responsibility of parenting is to prepare the kid for real life and, sorry to say, in real life very few of us get the summer off.

9. *Cable TV and videos are evil.* Okay, not really. I don't really believe

that MTV is the portal by which evil enters the universe; however, I do think television—and especially cable television and video games—create an unmerited distraction for children and teenagers. I am not in favor of censorship, but I am in favor of parental control and integrity. From that first captivating episode of *Sesame Street*, it became apparent that TV was a powerful thing. It can be such a pleasant distraction, and, let's face it, how many of us, even as adults, really prefer reading to watching movies or music videos? I'm not advocating the abolition of television or even cable television. I just think that during the formative years—meaning until high school graduation—cable television can be a major distraction. Regular commercial television is so boring that it's almost no distraction at all, so it's far less of a problem. But cable coupled with video games does appear to be a deadly combination. I think more parents need to face the music and just say no. Step up, do what's best, and even if you're wrong (worst-case scenario), can a kid really be damaged by restricting the daily dose of cable and video games? I think not. Conversely, is there a potential benefit in removing these mind-numbing devices? Yes. If all there is to do is watch three channels of commercial TV or converse with family members, read, and do homework, commercial TV rarely will win out. As home-schoolers, each of our sons found it fairly easy to get in two hours of quiet reading daily, especially without the distraction of cable television and video games. Our kids acted as if they were going to die—they were angry and they pouted—but they survived and excelled. (And now that they're gone, we have cable, and I love it!)

Here are some other things I've learned:

- Use your time wisely.
- Education is more than academics.
- The idea of parent as teacher doesn't have to end at kindergarten.
- The family is our introduction to community.
- Extended family is a safety net.
- Yes, kids really do better in environments designed for them.
- Travel is an education.
- Athletics is more than competitive sports.
- Everybody you deal with doesn't have to be your age or even your peer.
- The secret to SATs and ACTs: Test early and often.
- Get used to diversity.
- It's okay if your kids get angry—they'll get over it!

24

SO HOW IS THIS RELEVANT

IF I DON'T CHOOSE TO

HOME-SCHOOL?

OBVIOUSLY, HOME SCHOOLING worked well for us, and we are pleased with the results. However, home schooling is not for everybody; it's just one of the many educational options currently available. And, quite honestly, I am convinced that none of those options is perfect. In other words, whichever option you pick, be prepared to supplement it. Public, parochial, or private, any or all of the above will require some parental supplementation, spiritually, intellectually, or physically, before the first twelve years of education are finished. Once I began thinking about education in that context, it became easier to think about how some of the ideas in this book might work for families that choose to exercise other educational options.

Much of what I now know to be a good education—one that really prepares a student for life—is that it includes compromise and flexibility, along with a willingness and ability to take full advantage of options and opportunities. Home schooling provided that for our family, but, with a little creativity, the fundamental ideas of freedom, flexibility, and compromise can be used in any educational environment.

In the spirit of flexibility and compromise, these ideas aren't presented in any order of absolute priority. Realistically, I couldn't possibly present a priority list for families I've never met. What makes more sense is to try to explain the ideas in my "To Do" list. Every family can decide which ones (if any!) might work for them. (You'll notice right away that much of the infor-

mation on the list pertains to parents, because parental involvement is probably the most distinguishing factor in home schooling.)

*1. Perform an intellectual, spiritual, and physical assessment. Determine areas
of weakness and develop a strategic plan to address them.*

This doesn't have to be anything deep and esoteric; it just needs to be honest. Where are you and the rest of your family on these key elements of holistic health? Where are you intellectually? Does your answer include anything
beyond quantitative, academic analysis? Do you and your family discuss literature, history, science, philosophy, etc., just for fun? What about a spiritual
assessment: Does the analysis extend beyond religion? Do you acknowledge
moral and ethical dilemmas, or do you pretend they don't exist? What about
the physical component of holistic health: Does your family discuss that?
Does your family embody the elements of good physical health, adequate
sleep, nutritious diet, and consistent exercise?

It really doesn't matter what the answers are to these questions, because
there's always room for improvement. The key here is simply doing the assessment: taking the time to examine areas of relative strength and weakness.
The next step is the development of an action plan. While the school and the
community at large can certainly assist in this area, the fundamental responsibility for the holistic health and wellness of the family rests with the family.

*2. Make family time a priority. It should be as important as work, school,
church, sports, lessons, or extracurricular activities.*

As often as the phrase "family values" is touted, one might be persuaded that
we live in a society that actually values families. Unfortunately, that doesn't
always appear to be the case, and our allocation of time highlights the deficiency. As simplistic as it sounds, we make time for the things we truly value,
or have been taught to value. Often that translates into spending time doing
anything and everything except spending time with the other people in our
family. Interestingly, we seem to understand that anything worth having is
worth working for, and we apply that to professional and career goals. The entire time I was in law school, I certainly heard people complain about the
work, but nobody seemed ready to throw in the towel under the theory that
three years was just too long. Quite the contrary: I watched classmates spend
tons of money and what seemed like every waking moment working, reading,

writing, going to class, studying, worrying, and generally obsessing about law school. I've observed the same thing in people I know who went to medical school. Variations on that theme are played out daily in organizations, as people carefully craft career strategies that span decades.

How sad that we rarely see that same level of devotion directed to the development of strong, healthy families! When it comes to family time, people are quick to recite the smug mantra, "It's not the quantity of time, it's the quality of time." Can you imagine anybody trying that tired line in professional school, or after being promoted to an executive position? If it's true for our families, why isn't it true for our careers?

The fact is that it isn't true in either environment. Success in any arena requires a serious and consistent commitment of time, time, and more time.

Our families deserve the same serious strategic planning that we bring to our careers, and the same kinds of sacrifices. The functional dimension of making one's family a priority will take on different forms for every family, and even within the same family the prioritization will take on different forms at different times in the family's life. However, there are some consistent features that can serve as guideposts.

Intellectually, what draws a significant percentage of my thoughts, dreams, and creative energy? Spiritually, am I praying, meditating, and seeking wisdom on how to be an asset to my family and the people in it? Physically, do I make time for activities with my family on a daily basis, or do I fit them in when I can because I know they understand I'm working this hard for them?

Too often, our intellectual, spiritual, and physical energies are directed to our work rather than to our families. We expect our families to succeed on a fraction of the resources we make available to our careers. This is an unrealistic expectation.

If your family hasn't been a priority, start out with one new idea, e.g., maybe setting an expectation of having dinner together and then figuring out how to make it happen. Maybe you'll have to go into the office earlier or shorten lunch in order to get home in time for dinner. Maybe you'll have to take a dinner break and then finish up uncompleted work. Maybe your kids will have to examine how many extracurricular activities are really manageable. Maybe you'll have to become a bit "cosmopolitan" and have dinner later; say, maybe at eight. It will take some adjusting, but, hey, you adjust in order to get to work every morning!

Actually, the biggest adjustment is probably a mental one. Once you begin thinking about your family as a functional priority, not just something that is theoretically or verbally valued, it will be easier to find creative ways to accommodate your family's unique needs.

3. Add twenty minutes a day of quiet reading time for every family member. (Note: The comics and TV guides don't count!)

Okay, this is a big one, so let's start with the obvious stuff. Reading really is fundamental. Almost every college admissions person we spoke with told us that admissions committees pay particular attention to verbal scores on standardized tests because it's very difficult to catch up on verbal skills. A child with ability can be tutored to cover a lot of ground in mathematics in a relatively short period of time, but verbal skills are best developed over a kid's lifetime. When that hasn't occurred, there is a serious deficiency that is very difficult to overcome.

With that in mind, one supplemental educational idea would be to focus attention on reading, broadly, on a daily basis. How do you do that? Well, first of all, make sure your children see you reading something besides *TV Guide*. Also, look at what kind of reading environment exists at your child's school, so you'll know what areas most need to be enhanced.

Is the reading all about assignments? If so, begin the process of reading for intellectual and spiritual enjoyment—the sooner the better. If reading is associated with assignments, then what happens when school's not in session? Don't let your child—or the school, either, for that matter—snooker you into believing that academic work is the same as intellectual work, because it isn't. If the school's reading focus comes from the typical anthology series that focuses on English and American literature, then add some cross-cultural and global reading. As compelling as American and English literature can be, the world's a big place and there's a lot of great literature in it.

Newspapers are another way typical reading programs can be enhanced. If you can afford it, subscribe to a range of newspapers so your kids can see the range of views on the same series of events.

If the school doesn't have a strong reading program at all, the supplemental process will be pretty easy to fashion. First of all, make sure your kid has a library card. Don't assume that every child does, or knows where the card is! Second, make trips to the library a regular part of life so that your child feels at home there and knows why the library exists; and, no, the library does not exist as a movie-rental source!

Next, figure out where the greatest reading weakness lies. If your kid is already in the seventh grade or higher, you'll need to focus on what's commonly regarded as the classics. Any librarian can help you develop a reading list of books that form the foundation of a good, solid American education. Once you get the list, don't panic about the size of it or how many of the books on it you've actually read yourself. None of that matters. What does matter is that you and your child go over the list and recognize it's incomplete. There's probably nothing, or very little, of global literature on that list (which just goes to show you that everybody needs to read more). You and your child just need to go over the list, find a book to start with, and begin reading. Some of the stuff you won't like, but that's okay, because you'll probably love lots of it. Don't become frustrated by how long it takes to read any one book on the list; again, the important thing is that you and your child are reading. What's really important is that you're helping your child develop a habit of reading on a daily basis, and an awareness that reading is a critical component of any well-lived life. And thanks to the public library system, reading is free!

Another supplemental benefit the library offers is access to tons of newspapers and periodicals. It is critically important for children to grow up at least perusing several newspapers on a regular basis, for an awareness of the range of political and social views that exist. It's also a good idea for children to recognize that even to scratch the surface of understanding about much of what's happening in the world really requires more than the sound bites television provides, and more than the uninformed opinions spewing out across talk radio. Newspapers certainly aren't perfect, or even neutral or objective, but—and this is an important but—reading a range of newspapers on a regular basis comes closest to presenting an accurate, 3-D view. And as you and your children become more familiar with two or three publications with opposing views, you'll be able to combine them to create a whole vision of what's happening in the world around you.

An added academic benefit for your child to such a reading regimen will be the enormous increase and improvement in vocabulary and grammar. Reading is probably the easiest way to build a large vocabulary and good grammar skills, and reading is certainly more enjoyable than going over long lists of vocabulary words or doing grammar drills!

Regardless of the relative strength of the reading program, if it is exclusively secular, expose your child to spiritual and religious reading. Reading facilitates our understanding by expanding our knowledge base. Whether you're a family of atheists, agnostics, or fundamentalists of any ilk, children need to be intellectually exposed to the religious and spiritual views that shape the very existence of millions of people around the world. Such reading goes hand in hand with academic readings in moral and ethical reasoning. You don't have to sit down and try to read the Qur'an, the Talmud, and the Bible in one afternoon, and finish up the next day with the Hindu scriptures and the writings of Buddha. But reading these works, even in short pieces at a time, will add depth to the intellectual, academic, and spiritual growth of your children.

Now, I don't mean to denigrate the amount of daily academic work that lots of children have, so the two-hour-a-day quiet-reading-time requirement we had in our home-schooling program won't be feasible for everybody. But most people can add twenty minutes of quiet reading to their daily lives without too much strain. I know twenty minutes sounds like nothing, but this isn't a race or a contest, so even a small amount of supplemental reading on a daily basis will really add up over just one year.

Another benefit to parental involvement is that the reading can provide another opportunity for engagement and discussion. Oh, I don't mean the nagging "Did you do your twenty minutes?!" I mean a joint-venture approach. Try to find some things that you and your children could benefit from reading, or even rereading, at the same time. (Yeah, lots of books are definitely worth reading more than once.) The preponderance of book clubs is a testament to the enormous excitement and enjoyment that comes from sharing books. There's no reason that that same excitement and enjoyment can't be shared between people who happen to be swimming in the same gene pool. Just schedule a couple of hours once a month, get some great snacks, and have fun with it. Fight the temptation to make this an academic exercise. Don't work up a bunch of prove-to-me-you-really-read-this kind of questions. This isn't supposed to be a book report or presentation for a grade!

Try to engage your children with respect for their intellect. Engage them as people whose opinions matter to you, recognizing that they may share insights on books that you may have never considered.

4. *Discuss, and be open to debate about, the moral and ethical values that shape you and your family.*

This is one of the things that can easily result as a by-product of suggestion #2—"Make family time a priority." As you consistently spend more time together, and collectively begin the process of bringing your intellectual, spiritual, and physical consciousness into your interactions, moral and ethical analysis will occur. The Bible asks us, "Can two walk together, except they be agreed?" As your family begins viewing the life process as a path designed to be walked collectively, the moral and ethical dimensions will beg for exploration.

Too often, we limit our moral and ethical engagements with our kids to pronouncements rather than discussions. But we need to engage them in pragmatic moral reasoning, the kind of moral reasoning that helps them think about actively living a moral life. It's important to resist the pull toward what I like to call macro-ethics. These are topics like the deforestation of the rainforest in Brazil, or the use of child labor in Sri Lanka, or whether criminal charges of fraud should be brought against the officers of Enron. These are tempting topics, because, for most of us, they don't encompass our ethical or moral challenges. These topics allow us to pontificate and to feel genuinely good about ourselves, because, after all, we certainly would have blown the whistle on that whole Pinto-with-the-exploding-gas-tank deal or the Challenger with the defective O-ring. But, in fact, we all have moral and ethical challenges that we deal with daily, and if we are to have any hope of dealing with them in ways that we can be proud of, we need to discuss them.

Is cheating to help someone else as bad as cheating to get an unfair advantage? Has cheating become more acceptable, even in the presence of honor codes? Can an academic honor code have any real meaning in an environment where people are not valued or treated with respect? When does the end justify the means—never, sometimes, or does it depend on the circumstances? If the store gives you too much change back, should you return it or see it as a bonus? Is goofing off at work the same as "theft by deception"? Does it mean anything if I laugh or say nothing when people tell racial or ethnic jokes in my presence? As adults striving to transcend to a higher level, we struggle with the seemingly insignificant micro-level issues of ethics. I think it's important that we share that struggle with our children. They need to understand how much this kind of struggle defines the quality of our life process.

5. Find an inexpensive way to travel, out of town, out of state, out of the country, out of the hemisphere.

Travel creates an opportunity for amazing dimensions of growth. I say that at the outset in an effort to focus attention away from the hassle of travel. And, yes, in many ways travel can be a hassle, especially travel on a budget, with children. Maybe if money weren't an issue, travel might be hassle free. I wouldn't know. Money is and has always been an issue for us. So when money is an issue, you really have to be creative and look for ways to maximize your opportunities.

We began our travel odysseys on a relatively small scale, with road trips. When the boys won scholarships to Space Camp, we simply couldn't afford to fly the three of them to Florida. And even if we could have afforded three airline tickets, we wouldn't have felt comfortable sending the boys off alone in the care of people we had never met. While lots of people apparently think that's an extreme position, we don't: When it comes to the safety of children, it's always better to be safe than sorry. (It's heartbreaking to realize that pedophiles and sexual predators are present in our universe, but it's a reality. One way to counter that reality is to function as visibly attentive parents. Awareness and attentiveness may be the best deterrents parents can provide.)

We were thrilled the boys won the scholarships, and we didn't want them to miss the opportunity, so we made plans to drive them. We rented a van and drove them to Florida. We have also made road trips to D.C.; St. Louis, Missouri; Kansas City (Kansas and Missouri); Seal Harbor, Maine; Atlanta, Georgia; Chicago, Illinois; Baltimore, Maryland; New York, New York; Hanover and Manchester, New Hampshire; Boston, Massachusetts; Little Rock, Arkansas; Chattanooga and Nashville, Tennessee; Minneapolis, Minnesota; and St. Augustine, Orlando, and Jacksonville, Florida. Additionally, we've driven to tons of places in Ohio: Akron, Athens, Bellefontaine, Cincinnati, Cleveland, Dayton, Gambier, Springfield, Toledo, Xenia, Youngstown, and Zanesville. Some of these were short trips, like the day trip to the National Afro-American Museum at Central State University in Wilberforce, Ohio, and others were much longer.

The consistent fact is that we tried never to let money (or the absence of it) determine what the kids could see or experience. We've packed gigantic picnic baskets for the car and stayed at inexpensive motels. The important thing was the process of going, the process of experiencing different environments, perspectives, and people. First-class air travel is a blast, and a stay at a five-star hotel is fabulous, but I would never let an inability to travel on such a grand scale deter my ability to travel. Plus, I think it's great for kids to experience the sheer pleasure of travel, and to recognize that that pleasure is present whether they're staying at a roadside motel or a world-renowned resort.

Now, I realize everyone doesn't do as much business-related travel as we do, so the stratagems for long-distance and even international travel detailed in Chapter 16 aren't available to all. But I also know that with some advance planning, and a different allocation of interest and income, more extensive travel would be available to a lot more families. Travel is not always comfortable and the unexpected must be accounted for—and that alone can be disconcerting. Yet the intellectual benefits of travel, especially for children, really cannot be overstated.

Learning to place one's own circumstances into global perspective is critical to holistic development. Observing the devotion of Buddhists in the temples in Bangkok helped our sons critically examine their own Christian faith and commitment. Feeling the openness of the Midwest as we drove to Minneapolis highlighted the expansiveness of the United States. Contrasting the openness of the welcome in the museums in Paris to the disdain we experienced at the Museum of Fine Arts in Boston and other art museums in the United States illustrated the intersection between racism and classism in this country.

While travel isn't the only avenue to an expanded life experience or greater consciousness, it's a relatively easy and fun avenue. And while there truly is "no place like home," sometimes you need to leave Kansas to know that for yourself!

I also think travel helps kids (and adults!) put themselves and their situations in perspective—a perspective shaped by their own observations and experiences and thoughts; not by the labels and limitations other people chose to place upon them. My kids tend not to overreact to, or be overly impressed or overwhelmed by, things, places, and people, and I think it is precisely because they have seen so much of this country and the world.

I think the more kids travel, the more they recognize how much knowledge, beauty, suffering, and complexity exists in the world. For African-American male children, growing up in a society that openly fears and distrusts them, this is particularly important.

There's a poster that I used to see at the pediatrician's office that connected what a child experienced with what the child learned. When black boys experience fear, distrust, and minimal expectations for excellence, what do we expect them to learn about themselves and others like them? I think the benefits of broadening a child's experience beyond those limiting parameters far outweigh the costs of travel.

6. Get access to the ballet, the opera, the symphony, and the theater, as well as local art and science museums, and the zoo. Volunteer so you can get free or discounted memberships; cough up the cash and buy family memberships; or, if you have family memberships but they've expired, buy some more.

Okay, I'll admit it. This is a pet peeve of mine, especially as it relates to black parents. That's not to say that tons of white parents aren't also too trifling to make sure that their kids have the opportunity to make an informed choice as adults whether to ever attend cultural events. Obviously lots of parents—black, white, Asian, Hispanic, biracial, etc., etc., etc.—are dropping the ball on this one. But, for obvious reasons, the negligence of black parents really galls me. How do people justify not exposing kids to the arts? And, boy, do I hate that lame it-costs-too-much excuse. I especially hate it when I watch those same parents, who won't spring for the fifty dollars for a children's matinee at the symphony, blow that same fifty dollars on an afternoon at Dave & Buster's! Don't get me wrong, I too have spent a lot of time and money at Dave & Buster's. I am a major proponent of fun and good times. However, I also am a proponent of responsible parenting, and I know that if given a chance to find out, most humans enjoy at least some of the arts. I used to hate it when we'd take the boys to the ballet or the symphony or the opera and there'd be only one or two other black families there. Sure, there'd be groups of "disadvantaged" black kids, and going as a group is certainly better than not having a chance to go at all. But, come on, we can do better! And why should black kids have to go in droves like orphans, when scores of white kids are there with their parents or grandparents?

Further, I detest that excuse, "It's boring." Who cares if it's boring? Everything in life is not supposed to be as thrilling as a roller-coaster ride! But the truth is, most parents who don't take their kids have no way of knowing if the event in question is boring or not, because they've never been themselves. Plus, there are lots of things we have to do as parents that are boring, not fun, and expensive, but so what? Do it anyway—it's your job!

Life as it is lived in this industrial world is, and will probably remain, full of references to the major cultural and artistic contributions of Western civilization. No matter where your child goes in the United States, Europe, Asia, or Africa, educated people will be referencing works in the so-called classical arts. Some of the references will be based upon a genuine love for and interest in those arts, and some of them will be a ruse—a bald-faced attempt to make others feel "less than," underexposed, and ignorant. So by denying a child the opportunity to attend these events, one is not only denying them an opportunity to experience something truly enjoyable, one is also creating an unnecessary opportunity for self-doubt and discomfort.

Now that you're convinced, how does one go about paying for all this fun and culture? We started with the easy stuff—look for free events! I'll confess that I never found a cheap way to go to the zoo or the science museum—I just had to budget the hundred dollars for the annual memberships—but those were my only failures in the arts-on-a-budget crusade, and they were offset by the fact that my kids loved the zoo and the science museum. And believe me, once I paid those membership fees, we went, and we went regularly.

Almost all museums have at least one day of the week with free admission. Make it your business to be there on those days.

When it comes to the performance arts, start with the ones that are the most stimulating; i.e., opera and ballet—you get costumes, movement, and music going on at the same time. Try to avoid the dark, dreary pieces (in other words, don't try to start with Wagner!). With the ballet, go for the story ballets—Cinderella, The Nutcracker, stuff that's easy to follow. Plus, those ballets are almost guaranteed to have discounted group tickets. Get a bunch of families at your church or in your neighborhood and go together.

Years ago, when Evan danced with BalletMet, my mother began getting twenty-five discount tickets for people at our church. Every parent or grandparent who wanted a free ticket for their kid had to buy a ticket and come

with the kid. Evan hasn't danced in twelve years, but my mom is still organizing Christmas outings to see *The Nutcracker*.

If your kids are too sophisticated for storybook ballets, but money is still an
issue, check out dress rehearsals. Tickets to them cost practically nothing,
and they are fascinating to watch.

Opera is another good bet for an introduction to the classical arts. Lots of
drama, love, betrayal, and sometimes comedy, complete with elaborate costumes, great sets, and stirring music. So what if it's in Italian? There may be
subtitles, but, even without them, the stories or librettos are usually easy to
follow. And if you're concerned about total and complete comprehension,
and/or you want to expand the event, most opera companies provide a free
and engaging pre-opera discussion an hour or so before the performance. If
you bought the ticket anyway, why not get your money's worth?

My kids never took to the symphony like they did to opera and ballet, but
we went anyway—they just never go now. Almost all symphonies conduct at
least one children's concert each year, with reduced-price tickets and matinee schedules. If you have a bunch of kids or if the tickets are just too much,
try the group approach again.

Finally, if all else fails, do what lots of parents do about other child-related
expenses: Hit up the relatives—grandparents, aunts, uncles, and all those
other folks who express genuine interest in your kids and in their development. Don't be shy—it's not like you're asking for a down payment on a car!
(And speaking of cars, if you own, or are making monthly payments on, a couple of luxury cars, then you really don't have any business looking for cheap
ways to underwrite your kids' cultural experiences!)

*7. Model your commitment to community service and volunteer work, and stop
using that tired line, "I'm too busy," as an excuse. Nobody's that busy.*

Kids need to understand that community service and volunteerism are part
and parcel of being a viable member of the community. In other words, the
community does not merely exist to support them, but, rather, the community
exists to model support. And that modeled support should become reciprocal. Selfishness, self-centeredness, and self-absorption are naturally occurring
phenomena, in all of us, but they can and must be overcome. Kids should not
view community service as something one does to bulk up the college application.

Rather, commitment to one's community should be viewed as an ethical
and moral imperative. That's the reason it's so important for parents to model
that behavior. Kids need to grow up observing their parents' active concern
and involvement in their community; and there are lots of ways to do it. Some

people work for affordable housing and better public transportation, to enable people who are underemployed to get to better jobs. Some people volunteer in hospitals while others choose libraries or tutor in local schools. Lots of people volunteer at their church, synagogue, or mosque, while others help out at the local recreation center.

In the big scheme of modeling behavior, it really doesn't matter what mechanism is selected, but it probably helps if the focus is squarely on assistance to others, rather than on self-aggrandizement. There's nothing wrong with being recognized for one's contributions, but it needs to be clear to our kids that that's not why we're doing it.

There is so much focus on self in our society that sometimes it's easy for us to forget that our beliefs about commitment to community may be overshadowed by the other messages our kids are picking up. This is not the sixties, and while it's now painfully clear that much of the "revolution" was really fashion in fatigues, at least there was open discussion and dialogue about something other than self—no matter how facile those discussions later turned out to be. Compare some of the lyrics of popular music thirty years ago—even the ones about filthy lucre; e.g., "don't let money rule you"—with some of today's lyrics, e.g., "got my mind on my money and my money on my mind." I have been taught to appreciate much of today's music, and I know there are "righteous" artists out there, but I'm talking about the dominant, commercial focus as highlighted on MTV, et al.

We didn't spend a lot of time lecturing the kids about the social and political implications of continuous messages of rampant consumerism. The irresponsible and seemingly relentless images of gigantic BMWs and Benzes, palatial mansions, Rolexes, Gucci, Versace, Cristal, Moët, big cigars—and the objectification of semi-naked women—are best debunked by action and example. We wanted to demonstrate to the boys how free people of color ought to be living in community with others.

C. Madison was particularly effective in this regard. While most of my community and volunteer work was in the mainstream—United Way, Ballet-Met, the Thurber House picnics committee, etc.—C. Madison was out there doing more dramatic work. His activities with B.R.E.A.D., the local branch of a national, ecumenical organization focused on improving the quality of life for folks who are traditionally disenfranchised, has had an enormous impact on the boys. They've also watched their dad work for years on issues like expanding public transportation beyond the I-270 Outerbelt, greater accountability when corporations get economic incentives from the city, and establishing a joint city-and-county fund to create more affordable housing. But what's remarkable is that they've seen him work as diligently on those issues as on the issues of our business, and they've seen him do it from a behind-the-scenes posture. He neither needs nor seeks recognition. This is work he does because he's committed to this community.

That's why it's not surprising that each of the boys has a definite sense of commitment to community service and volunteerism; it's something they've observed in their father.

Quite frankly, if someone who's self-employed in the kind of intensely competitive arena we all live in can make time to live as a committed member of a community, then I think everyone can. Like I said at the outset, "Nobody's that busy!"

Try to find out what your children are interested in; see what social issues grab their attention. Children are aware of the vast needs that exist all around us. Sometimes we just have to help them look past the enormity of it; otherwise, it can feel overwhelming to them. Help them focus on one or two areas that they're most concerned about, and then begin a discussion about how they can help. It's important to help children realize that the fact that they can't fix something doesn't mean that they can't contribute to the process. If hunger concerns them, help them find a way to help, maybe by collecting canned goods and turning them in to an already-established collection center; or, they could find out about helping in a food pantry or soup kitchen. If homelessness is something they care about, help them collect usable clothing or encourage them to use part of their money to purchase some inexpensive essentials to donate—things like toothbrushes, toothpaste, or soap. Maybe their concern is educational: Encourage them to look for tutoring opportunities, or they might want to volunteer to read to homeless children at one of the shelters. Almost every existing community service organization needs administrative volunteers: Maybe your children can help with mailings; or, if they're older and can drive, they could offer to run errands.

I think it's important to help children understand that every contribution—financial, in-kind services, even grunt work—is important. All of it helps move us forward collectively as a community.

8. *Research and document all available resources in your area. Include things that might be too advanced right now, remembering that someday, very soon, your kids may very well grow into them.*

Once we began home schooling, knowing what was available in our community became a necessity. But, in fact, I should have viewed that information as essential even when the boys were in school. Had I really been on top of my game, I wouldn't have found myself in the annual catch-up practice every school break to try to find some meaningful activity with available spaces for three! Yet, every year, I was in the same place during Christmas, spring break, and summer vacation—looking for something constructive at the last minute. Home schooling removed the luxury of pretending that I didn't know I needed broader resources for my kids.

I began at a simplistic level, and just made a list of the things that would be helpful. Then I developed a secondary list of probable sources. I left room on both lists for the additional information that always comes when you're looking for one thing and people tell you about something else. Lots of time the unasked-for information was better than what I was looking for in the first place, since I didn't know enough even to ask the right questions!

My first list had three components—you guessed it: spiritual, intellectual, and physical. On the spiritual part I listed religious training, community service, and reading. Probable sources I identified included Sunday School, church, COSI, and the library. The human resources included Elder Lundy and Elder Polley, our pastor and assistant pastor, Brother and Sister Ragin, the heads of our children's ministry, Ms. Jan Davidson, head of the student-volunteer program at COSI, and Ms. Ruby Kyles, one of the directors of the Columbus Metropolitan Library. As the boys grew and matured, the list expanded, and then it contracted again, as the guys were able to determine where their spiritual interests lay.

Intellectually, the list was heavy on what would be labeled enrichment programs. My first list included a combination of academic and intellectual issues. Here I included the arts, science, mathematics, and literature. In terms of sources, I included colleges, universities, community centers, national organizations, church, and the library. Initially, the list was extensive and national in scope. I had everything from the American Boychoir in New Jersey to Purdue University's gifted-students program, along with tons of things offered in Columbus and across Ohio. Narrowing this list was somewhat easy, not because of a lack of interest in a lot of the resources, but because many were simply too expensive for us to consider. As we narrowed the scope, we tried to establish a balance between the expense of tutors for academic work and the expense for broader enrichment and intellectual stimulation.

In interviewing tutors, we really looked for people who could move holistically and comfortably beyond the boundaries of their academic disciplines, and we were blessed in that most of them could, and were enthusiastic about the opportunity to do so. We looked for the same openness to balance in the enrichment programs, and, once again, we were blessed. While lots of people were curious about the boys, and somewhat suspect of their social skills, at the end of each experience we received unsolicited comments and compliments about the guys. What pleased me the most were the consistent comments about the quality of the boys' character.

One of the greatest benefits of enrichment programs is the opportunity they create for a new and objective assessment of your child. I think this would be especially beneficial for kids in traditional educational institutions. Kids get labeled pretty quickly in school, and once that happens it can be very difficult to move past it. That can be a problem for kids who are excelling as well as for those who are struggling. Teachers are only human, and they, too, follow the path of least resistance. So if a kid is an A student, that kid gets A's even when A work isn't turned in; similarly, kids who have been pegged as C students get C's even if they turn in A work. That's why some kids who were stars in high school go off to college and flounder, while kids who were marginal performers in high school may go on to excel in college. Sometimes that's about the student's maturation, but sometimes it's about a new and objective environment.

We used enrichment programs to maintain a steady stream of objective evaluations of our kids. That way, we could balance the evaluations of the people we hired—the tutors—with the evaluations of people who didn't know us, wouldn't be seeing us next year, and didn't live in our community. We really wanted to see if the people we knew the boys to be were evidenced in their engagements with people outside our sphere of influence.

Obviously, we needed a lot of feedback from other people to make an accurate assessment. Some of the people who helped us included Dr. Frank Croft at OSU's engineering program, and the instructors at Space Camp, the Institute of Oceanography, and YMCA camp. Ms. Sybil McNabb, with the Columbus NAACP–ACT-SO program; Sister Paulette Thomas, who coached our church's Bible Bowl team (they were national champs!); the folks at the Davis Center, a division of Columbus Parks and Recreation; Ms. Jan Davidson at COSI; and Ms. Ruby Kyles and all the wonderful people throughout the Columbus Metropolitan Library system provided another level of analysis, somewhere between the boys' tutors and the enrichment-program personnel.

Our physical list focused on fitness rather than competitive sports. The resource list centered on the Parks and Recreation department and the clubhouse in our subdivision. Tae kwon do, golf, swimming, tennis, and fencing were the dominant activities. Brentnell Recreation Center provided the opportunity for football. The range of instructors and coaches the boys dealt with really shaped these experiences into ones that were extremely healthy. In particular, Mr. Jim Berry, the tae kwon do instructor at the Brentnell Recreation Center; Coach Packer, the football coach at Brentnell; and Coach Sherrer, the boys' fencing coach at Fedderson Recreation Center, really worked at establishing relationships with the boys.

My hunch is that most communities offer a similar range of resources, and people who are genuinely glad to assist in the holistic development of children. The hard part is sitting down to do the research, compiling a workable set of lists, and then working out the scheduling issues. The vast majority of resources we relied upon consistently over the nine years of our home-schooling experience turned out to be free. Some of the programs were available in traditional after-school segments, others were available during traditional school breaks, and some were extremely flexible in terms of scheduling. So whether or not you choose to home-school, sit down, figure out what you and your kids want, and start contacting folks!

9. Find broad-based athletic activities with wide skill-level participation.

If you've spawned the next Tiger Woods or Venus and Serena Williams, obviously this section doesn't apply to you. Giftedness on any level places an entirely different set of demands on the concept of holistic development. But most of us don't have the genetic input to produce athletic giftedness, so we don't have to worry about it. For the average, run-of-the-mill student, sports cannot become a profession.

With that as a given, I think the emphasis should be on a commitment to lifetime health and fitness. Expose your kids to a broad range of athletic opportunities. Give them the opportunity to find out what they enjoy. Give them the opportunity to stretch and struggle physically. Most important, give them the opportunity to find out that physical activity can be fun and enriching even if you're not a star! Let them experience the joy of striving for a personal best, rather than the fleeting satisfaction of beating someone else.

The hard truth is that no matter how extraordinary a talent your kid has, it's just a matter of time before somebody exceeds his or her skill level. Records— all records—will be broken; that's a fact of life. I think it's very healthy for kids to focus on the idea of a personal best, because there's no potential for a sense of loss. It's a classic win/win situation. They can be happy about the successes of others, because the concept of personal best doesn't create any kind of competitive threat to the kid's sense of self.

10. Find a place of worship and go there regularly. Nothing that important should be left up to kids to decide for themselves. It's possible for a kid to teach himself to read, but most of us wouldn't count on it.

Here's another pet peeve: parents who fail to take responsibility to aid in their child's spiritual development. It's particularly irksome when people try to elevate this failure to the status of a virtue by pointing to all the admittedly horrible things that have been done in the name of religion. Yes, many, many horrible crimes against humanity have been committed in the name of religion, or irresponsibly condoned by religious leaders. The truth of that fact in no way negates the necessity or benefit of religious training any more than the litany of crimes against humanity committed in the name of science renders science education null and void.

When we expose children to science, it isn't an act of denial of science's sometime criminal past. Rather it is in recognition and validation of what science could and should be in its purest sense. Similarly, we do not negate the benefits of a capitalist democracy because of the evidence of robber barons. Exposing our children to the economic theories of capitalism and democracy is not a validation of greed and avarice, but, rather, a validation of what can be achieved economically and socially in a healthy and competitive marketplace.

See where I'm going with this? Children need religious instruction. Religion is probably one of the easiest introductions to spiritual enlightenment. Further, a lack of knowledge of, not to mention wisdom and understanding about, religion makes it virtually impossible to understand the axiology or belief systems that govern the behavior of millions of people around the world. A conscious decision to validate a lack of knowledge can only be described as ignorant, and to transfer such a pattern of willful ignorance to one's children is the essence of irresponsibility.

I know that sounds harsh, but, quite frankly, I can't think of any other way to describe such conduct. What would we say about a parent who willfully deterred his or her child's knowledge of mathematics or literature? I think it is presumptuous and classist to look for other descriptors merely because many of the opponents to religious training are middle- and upper-middle-class.

When I talk about exposure to religious training, I'm not advocating for the blind acceptance of religious dogma. In my own faith I have had occasions, even important occasions, of disagreement with the pastor and church leaders. The Bible teaches us to work out our own soul's salvation. We will each be accountable for the deeds done in our own bodies.

For example, when C. Madison and I decided to marry, we were not allowed to be married in my church because C. Madison was a Baptist, and, in the Pentecostal Apostolic tradition, that meant we would be "unequally yoked." My interpretation of the scripture did not lead to that understanding. I think "unequally yoked" means two people with different beliefs in the identity of God. If C. Madison had been a Muslim, a Hindu, or a Jew, we would have been unequally yoked. But C. Madison was a Christian of a different denomination. After considerable prayer and fasting, I felt quite comfortable making my own, independent decision to marry him.

This, to me, is a classic example of why religious training is so important. I knew the Word for myself, and was able to bring my own wisdom and understanding to it. Further, I was open to revelation of the Word, separate and apart from the religious doctrine in my church.

Culturally, I think religious training is especially critical for African-American children. The unfortunate truth is that there are very few arenas where black children in this society will be loved, valued, and appreciated in the manner that the black church has traditionally provided. I think it is the worst kind of naïveté and neglect for middle- and upper-middle-class black parents to think that beautiful homes in exclusive suburbs and fine private schools can re-create the embracing environment that has been the hallmark of the black church.

Let me hasten to add that dealing with church folks can be extremely annoying on any number of levels, but that's true of people in general. And given the trade-off, I think those annoyances are well worth it. I know my sons have never received the kind of unconditional love and support in any institution that they have received in church. There's not a Sunday that passes in which several of the "saints" don't stop to ask after the boys or to tell me that they're praying for them, or how much they love them and how proud they are of them.

And, yes, services go on entirely tooooooo long. And, yes, there is far too much of pomp and circumstance, and titles. I mean, really, do we need eight zillion ministers and evangelists? I don't think so. And I don't think our preachers really need to be so exceedingly well dressed, or to live in such expensive and opulent homes, or to drive such conspicuously expensive cars. I don't think we need hours of "Praise and Worship" before the sermon. I don't think everybody should need to be "anointed" every other Sunday. I don't think we need a "First Lady" or a "First Family," or love offerings and anniversaries and other forms of pageantry.

Much of that stuff really gets on my nerves. I'm not blind or stupid, and I certainly see and pray about the various ways in which the church acts as a stumbling block to our development as a people. The church is an institution of people, so of course it is flawed. And since I am a conscious adult, I recognize that, as much as I wish it were not so. But, in the history of the black diaspora here in these United States, you simply cannot deny the critical role of the black church in our collective development. It is a fundamental part of who we have been socially, culturally, and economically, and black children need that foundation as they move into the larger universe, because I know of nowhere else that they will get it.

11. No more surprises: not about grades, skill level, drugs, and violence. Make it your business to know what's going on at your kid's school. Ask questions and see for yourself. Get involved, be there, and observe. Ignore your kid when she rolls her eyes or acts like you're a dork. Your job is not to be her friend or to try to impress her with how cool you are.

Home schooling forces you to be cognizant of what's going on with your kid, but, obviously, that level of awareness doesn't require home schooling for activation. All parents need to make a commitment to know what's going on with their kids. And while it certainly takes a village to raise a child, or at least a holistically healthy and happy one, the fundamental responsibility rests squarely with the parents. At the end of each school year, there are parents who are "shocked" to discover that their kid can't read, or won't pass, or can't graduate. How in the name of God can any of those issues be a surprise in May?!! You know that adage, "Always inspect what you expect"? Well, I can't think of a better application than in the education of one's child. There is no excuse for not knowing what's going on in the life of your own child, just as there is no escaping the responsibility or consequences for not knowing. No matter what your kid says or does during childhood or adolescence, at some point in adult life that kid will come to the realization that you either handled your parental responsibility or you didn't.

It's your job to know precisely how your kid is doing in school, every day. It's your job to make sure your kid's homework is done, correctly and neatly, every day. (And if it isn't, it's your job to make your kid do it over.) It's your job to make sure your child knows how to behave in school, and it's your job to know when that behavior is not up to par and to apply the appropriate discipline. It's your job to know whether or not your child is progressing, and developing the appropriate academic skills in a timely manner; and, if it's not happening, it's your job to find out why.

And if you don't agree with your kid's teacher's assessment, get a second opinion. This is *so* not about the teacher's feelings. This is about looking out for your kid. If your child needs assistance, either in gifted programs or developmental programs, it's your job to find that out and make sure your kid gets it.

It's your job to know who your kid's friends are, and it's your job to know what kind of people your kid's hanging out with and where the hanging out is happening. It's your job to talk to and question your kid about cigarettes, drugs, and alcohol. It's your job to know what parties your kid's going to, and it's your job to wait up until they get home and make sure they're clean and sober. It's your job to be the adult and to challenge your kid if you smell tobacco or reefer or alcohol on the kid's breath or clothes. It's your job to let your kid know that you're concerned about and interested in every facet of that kid's existence on the planet. And it's your job to challenge your kid when you think that kid is messing up!

It's your job to know whether or not your kid is developing into a well-rounded and holistically healthy person. It's your job to encourage and support those efforts. It's your job to be at every sporting event, every choir concert, and every play your kid is involved in, whether your kid wants you to be there or not.

Quite frankly, after about the third grade no kid wants their parents lurking around at school events, but so what? It's still your job. Just like it's your job to go on field trips and to help with the book fairs and to chaperone parties and dances. It's your job to know your kid's teachers—all of them. And it's your job to make sure that all those teachers know you are looking out for your kid's best interests and that you will settle for nothing less than the best for your kid, because you know your kid deserves it! You might be the only one who believes that about your kid. That's why it's so important to make sure you're doing your job.

Make sure you know what courses your kid is taking, has taken, and is planning to take. It's your job to start talking to your kid about college. It's your job to know when the SAT and ACT are happening, and it's your job to know how your kid did; and, if it isn't good enough, it's your job to find out what resources are available to help your kid do better.

It's your job to make sure your kids know that their potential is limitless and that anyone who tells them differently is a liar—and we all know where liars go! It's your job to make sure your kids know they're responsible for uncovering their potential and working to develop it, and not to do so is a sin before God—it's squandering a gift, wasting a talent, depriving the world of something essential and necessary; otherwise, it wouldn't have been placed in them.

It's not your job to try to be your kid's best friend, and it's not your job to try to make your kid like you, and it's not your job not to intrude. Parenting is a very big job with lifelong consequences, and you have a relatively short window of opportunity in which to accomplish work that will shape future generations. Realize that if you mess up your kids, you increase the likelihood that they'll mess theirs up too, and so on and so on and so on. That's what the Bible means when it talks about the sins of the fathers being passed on to the third and fourth generations.

When we mess up with our kids, when we fail to take our responsibilities as their parents, their guardians, their caretakers seriously, we run the risk of damaging them so severely (or letting others do so) that it will take divine intervention for them to recover. In the meantime, they may be reproducing our same mistakes for future generations. Wouldn't it just be easier for everybody to just do the job right the first time?

WELL, those are the rules. No matter how you decide to proceed, trust yourself to do a good job. My dear friend Dr. Linda James Myers says, "Everyone is always doing the best they can at any moment in time. We're all in process." I don't totally believe that, but in this context I think I do. You have to trust yourself to do the best job you can at any moment. Trust in yourself is clearly an important factor. No matter which educational option you select for your child, you have to trust yourself as a parent to make an honest and objective analysis of it. The analysis needs to happen on an ongoing basis. Remember: God is in the details.

Finally, be a real American—value your independence. (Okay, I know this sounds kind of hokey, but I think this is an important and often-overlooked point.) Choosing your own path for your children and your family doesn't put you on the cutting edge of the lunatic fringe—or, at least, it doesn't have to, unless secretly that's where you've always wanted to live.

Seriously though, it's hard to step outside of the mainstream. Try to find a healthy balance between the wisdom to seek counsel and the courage to seek your own path. This balancing act is an important skill to pass on to your children, regardless of which educational option you select. After all, what's the point of freedom if you don't ever step out there and exercise it?

APPENDIX

Here is a list of websites that we found helpful during our home-schooling odyssey. We share them in the hope that you might find them helpful or interesting as well.

Basic Home-Schooling Information

American Homeschool Association http://www.americanhomeschoolassociation.org	This site covers national laws and regulations governing home schooling, as well as info for new home-schoolers
A to Z Home's Cool http://www.gomilpitas.com/homeschooling	This very informative site covers regional laws and regulations governing home schooling
Jon's Homeschool Resource Page http://www.midnightbeach.com/hs	Here you can find answers to most of your home-schooling questions
HSAdvisor.com http://www.hsadvisor.com	At this site, you can buy curricula, ask pros for help, and find support groups in your area, plus much more
LINK Homeschool News Online http://www.homeschoolnewslink.com	A national home-schooler newspaper online, with plenty of free information
Homeschool Central http://www.homeschoolcentral.com	A large site full of information ranging from the most basic to the very specific

National Home Education Network http://www.nhen.org	A support site designed to help facilitate the general workings of the home-schooling family
Homeschool Zone http://www.homeschoolzone.com	Site welcomes all educators and their students, with lots of activities, crafts, and recipes
The Ultimate Homeschool Directory and Search Engine http://www.rubyimage.com/cgi-bin/odp/index.cgi	A good place to begin searching online for home-schooling information
Homeschool Mag http://www.homeschoolmag.com/hsgl.htm	A guide and index for home-schooling materials, as well as for other home-school institutions
Oak Meadow http://www.oakmeadow.com	Home-schooling-related resources and instructional materials crafted for K–12
Homeschool Counsel Discussion Board http://www.homeschoolcounsel.com/ubb/ cgi-bin/ultimatebb.cgi	A home-school discussion board with many posted Q&A's
Homeschool/Educational Sites http://www.openmindopenheart.org/EdWeb/ History.html	A nice collection of educational and general interest links
Teach-nology http://www.teach-nology.com/teachers/ home_schooling	Index of other home-school sites, plus forums and more
Kaleidoscapes Homeschool Index http://www.kaleidoscapes.com/hs_link2.html	A rather large search engine for home-schooling info
HELM Online! (Home Education Learning Magazine) http://www.helmonline.com/pages/res/elists	E-mail listings for a number of home-schooling entities
The Caron Family's Homeschool http://www.megalink.net/~caronfam/	A great resource for home-schoolers of all ages, with many links and pertinent information
Sankofa: Look to Your Past http://www.nabrit.com/boyz	Web page with link to our free e-book about Rites of Passage for African-American male children

The Nabrit Family Adventure http://www.nabrit.com/homeschool	Webpage that chronicles our home-schooling experiences

Grade School Sites

Grade School at MommyLinks.com http://www.mommylinks.com/gradeschool	Good site for all educators, not just mommy, with articles on parenting, teaching, and more
Homeschool Resources http://www.nhsn.net/resources.htm	Many links for the new home-schooler
Windy Creek Homeschool http://www.windycreek.com	Site with attention to individual child's growth and development
Homeschool Teacher's Lounge http://www.geocities.com/Athens/Oracle/4336	Nice place for younger students, with an emphasis on math, history, and science skill development
The Teel Home Education Page http://www.teelfamily.com/education	An Alaskan perspective on home schooling, complete with cold-weather activities for restless kiddies
Links and Resources for HomeSchoolers http://home.dejazzd.com/brew/index.html	Detailed site with more than 400 links to points of interest
Kid's Online Resources http://www.kidsolr.com/earlychildhood/page2.html	Good place for younger home-schoolers, with many links to age-appropriate sites

Middle School Sites

Michael's Home Education Page http://www.geocities.com/Athens/8208/home_ed.html	General information for home-schoolers, with attention to curricular materials and their application
Homeschool Resources—Getting Started http://www.angelfire.com/in3/page1/School.htm	Overview of home-schooling laws, supplies, lesson plans, and more

Homeschooling On The Cheap http://www.bcpl.net/~owl/homeschool/ HomeschoolingOnTheCheap.html	Good place for inexpensive activity ideas, public libraries, television stations, and thrift stores
Middle School http://www.middleschool.net	Site full of information aimed directly at middle-school children
Northbrook School, Our School At Home http://www.geocities.com/Heartland/Hills/4921/ homedu.html	Lots of info for the new home-schooler
The Homeschool Mom http://www.thehomeschoolmom.com/ abouthomeschooling.html	Free information for all home-schoolers; guides on various methods of home schooling and resource books; and age-appropriate lessons and helpful hints

High School Sites

Cafi Cohen's Homeschool Teens & College http://www.homeschoolteenscollege.net	Find support and help for older home-schoolers here, with good college admissions and essay information
The Homeschool Digital Outpost http://homeschool.rimsnthings.com	High-school-oriented info
Peterson's Guide http://www.petersons.com	Begin the college search here
Educational Testing Service (ETS) http://www.ets.org	Central source for PSAT/SAT–related information
CampusTours http://www.campustours.com	Take virtual tours of many college/university campuses from the comfort of your desktop
Quadratic Equations http://www.mathgoodies.com/calculators/ quadratic_equations.htm	Get math help from Mrs. Glosser
FastWeb http://www.fastweb.com	Find scholarship sources and refine the college-search process

Black Excel http://www.blackexcel.org	College help network

General Interest [Eclectic] Internet Resources

Luminarium http://www.luminarium.org/lumina.htm	Multimedia anthology of English literature enhanced with music and period art
Project Gutenberg http://www.promo.net/pg	Archive of public-domain literary works that can be searched and downloaded
Washington Embassies http://www.embassy.org/embassies	Information about every foreign embassy in Washington, D.C.
Kidsource Online http://www.kidsource.com/kidsource/pages/ed.web.html	Online educational resources linked and rated
Don Mabry's Historical Text Archive http://www.historicaltextarchive.com	Source of historical articles, links, book references, diaries, etc., sorted by continent or subject
Kamusi Project http://www.yale.edu/swahili	Learn about East Africa and practice Swahili language skills
Worthless Word for the Day http://www.embers.aol.com/tsuwm/Frame1.html	Amaze everyone with your expanded vocabulary
The BlackMarket.com (Slavery: Frequently Asked Questions) http://www.theblackmarket.com/slavefaq.htm	Collection of well-known and obscure tidbits about the institution of slavery in the U.S.
Childstats.gov http://www.childstats.gov	Provides federal and state demographic reports on children and their families
History Place http://www.historyplace.com	A history site primarily focused on U.S. history
Languages for Travel http://www.travlang.com/languages	Site with a fun way to introduce the practicality of learning other languages

Nobel Prize Internet Archive http://www.almaz.com/nobel	Good information for the seriously goal-oriented student
National Public Radio http://www.npr.org	Convenient programming guide and archive for NPR broadcasts
PBS Online http://www.pbs.org	Convenient programming guide for PBS broadcasts
Library of Congress http://www.lcweb.loc.gov	The ultimate library card
U.S. Census Bureau http://www.census.gov	Link to the profilers of the human landscape of the U.S.
Purdue University's Online Writing Lab http://owl.english.purdue.edu	Broad-based resource for help with writing for all ages and skill levels
Quoteland http://www.quoteland.com	Searchable database of quotations for every occasion
Everything Black http://www.everythingblack.com	African-American portal
The Exploratorium http://www.exploratorium.edu	Link to San Francisco's Palace of Fine Arts' The Exploratorium, a collage of more than 650 science, art, and human perception exhibits
Science Guy http://www.billnye.com/billnye.html	Site of TV's Bill Nye, the Science Guy
Computer Demolition http://homepages.together.net/~tking/compdemo.htm	Learn how technology works from the inside out
Internet Public Library: POTUS http://www.ipl.org/ref/POTUS	Get the inside historical and biographical scoops on each U.S. president
Bartleby.com: Great Books On Line http://www.bartleby.com	Get electronic access to great literary treasures and reference works

Partnership for a Drug-Free America http://www.drugfreeamerica.org/drug_info.html	Get armed with facts to fight the war on drugs
Metropolitan Museum of Art http://www.metmuseum.org	Link to the Met
Art Institute of Chicago http://www.artic.edu	Link to the AIC

PAULA PENN-NABRIT received her undergraduate degree from Wellesley College and her law degree from The Ohio State University. Paula and her husband, Charles Nabrit, run Penn-Nabrit & Associates, an Ohio-based business management consulting firm. The Nabrits have three sons: twins Charles and Damon, and Evan. They live in Westerville, Ohio.